AMERICAN LIVES | *Series editor:* Tobias Wolff

WEEDS

A Farm Daughter's Lament

Evelyn I. Funda

UNIVERSITY OF NEBRASKA PRESS

LINCOLN AND LONDON

Library of Congress Cataloging-in-Publication Data
Funda, Evelyn I.
Weeds: a farm daughter's lament /
Evelyn I. Funda.
pages cm. — (American lives)
Includes bibliographical references.
ISBN 978-0-8032-4496-2 (pbk.: alk. paper)
1. Family farms—Idaho—Gem County—
History. 2. Funda, Evelyn I. 3. Czech
Americans—Idaho—Gem County. I. Title.
S451.I2F86 2013
636.08'40979627—dc23   2013008782

Set in Fanwood Text by Laura Wellington.
Designed by A. Shahan.

"What would the world be, once bereft
Of Wet and Wildness? . . .
Long live weeds and the wildness yet"

GERARD MANLEY HOPKINS
"Inversnaid"

———

"What is a farm but a mute gospel? The chaff
and the wheat, weeds and plants, blight, rain,
insects, sun—it is a sacred emblem from the
first furrow of spring to the last stack which the
snow of winter overtakes in the fields."

RALPH WALDO EMERSON
"Nature"

———

"I believe that the only good weed is a dead
weed, and that a clean farm is as important
as a clean conscience."

FOURTH PRINCIPLE OF "THE
PROGRESSIVE FARMERS' CREED,"
published by the *Illinois Educational
Bulletin* (found reprinted in the
June 6, 1912, issue of the *Buhl Herald*)

CONTENTS

LIST OF ILLUSTRATIONS

PREFACE: "In Dirt We Trust"

"To forget how to dig the earth and
tend the soil is to forget ourselves."

MAHATMA GANDHI
Mind of Mahatma Gandhi

In late 2001 my small family suffered what I think of as a triple
tragedy. On October 1, 2001, my father, Lumir Funda, age seventy-nine, was diagnosed with advanced lung cancer that, by the
time of the diagnosis, had metastasized to his brain, liver, spleen,
spine, and bones. The prognosis was two to four months to live;
he was briefly given radiation to relieve some of the pain and to
shrink the tumor that had compromised his speech and mobility
before he was sent home with my mother on October 23. On October 25, just two days later, my mother, Toni, age seventy-five,
suffered a heart attack. After nine days in a cardiac unit, where
she experienced additional complications of stroke, kidney failure, and internal bleeding, she died on November 3. My father's
death came shortly thereafter, on November 29.

These events were preceded by the sale of the family's farmland. Just a month to the day before my father's diagnosis, my
parents had signed the papers finalizing the sale of the last parcel
of farmland they had worked together since my father and my
Czech-immigrant mother had married in 1957. In fact, my father

had farmed this land for most of his life. His father, also a Czech immigrant, had originally purchased it for a small sum in 1919 when the parcel was nothing but a sheep-grazed, sagebrush terrain. Although the land was never hugely profitable, my family was always proud of how they had transformed that unlikely spot.

When people talk about the autumn of 2001, these are the losses I think about, not the Twin Towers. The news of 9/11 seemed like a blurry background to my own razor-sharp losses that fall. Some would say that the timing of these events in family history was merely coincidental; bodies fail, land deeds change hands, and people endure losses. Cutting through the hardpan of my family history, I could make out the repeated strata of losing home, family, and a sustaining belief in agricultural values. As I considered individual family stories, I found a series of literal and psychic displacements, a history of transience, obsession, and dispossession, and a hunger for permanence. Farmland came to represent a landscape of loss, and I recognized how my family stories were emblematic of a cross-section of American agricultural history, as it moved from the optimism of the immigrant homesteader, to the industrial illusion of control that characterized the postwar farm, to the economic and political pressures of the 1970s and 1980s that nearly erased the Jeffersonian ideal of one man—one farm, to the exodus of younger generations, like mine, who left because they felt the farm held no place for them.

Influenced by personal narrative, biography, and cultural studies, this cultural memoir traces how different factors (ethnic prejudice, an increasingly industrialized agricultural model, and prescribed gender expectations) lead inevitably to similar endings. The loss at the center of this farm story, therefore, is replayed and recast in ever-widening circles, first through my farm daughter story, then through the generations of my familial and ancestral history. Even though my father and grandfather trusted wholeheartedly that the Idaho farmland would sustain the family both economically and spiritually, instead displacement is the ever-present theme in the lives of three generations for whom farming became a ritualized enactment of the desire to set down roots in a land we could claim as our own.

Although the American farmer has been mocked as a "Reuben Hayseed" and an unsophisticated bumpkin, he remains iconic, an enduring symbol of strength, valor, and a distinctive connection with the land. The very word *human* derives from the same Latin root word as *humus*, meaning soil. No other work or occupation—with perhaps the exception of motherhood—is so profoundly invested with such symbolic weight or so fully spans the imaginative range of human experience in our culture. Read the agrarian novels of Willa Cather or the impassioned essays of Wendell Berry, consider the rhetoric of the Farm Aid organization (with its motto: "Family Farmers, Good Food, A Better America"), watch any number of films about farmers (from Jessica Lange's *Country* to the 2007 award-winning documentary *The Real Dirt on Farmer John*), study Victory Garden posters from World War II or farmers' market posters of today, and you will see agriculture cast in a wide array of starring roles. Farming is portrayed as a form of spiritual fulfillment, an act of artistry and divine creation, an expression of national commitment and patriotism, a means for proving heroism or manhood, a process of gaining personal empowerment, a foundation for community unity, a guarantee of personal independence and self-sufficiency, a chance to arrive at an authentic and wholesome life, a method for gaining dominion over and improving an imperfect landscape, a partnership with natural forces, and a battle against those same natural forces.

Farming is not just a job—it's a calling, and the farmer is ubiquitous in our lives. Take, for instance, the bumper sticker that reads, "If you've eaten today, give thanks to a farmer." Referenced in Senate hearings on the state of agriculture during the 1980s farm crisis, this sentiment's religious overtones are not, I think, by accident. Poised as he is between heaven and earth, the farmer is our mediator, a cultural idea emphasized by Michael Pollan, who writes in *The Botany of Desire*, "Wheat points [us] up, to the sun and civilization," because it is as "leavened with meaning as it [is] with air. . . . Wheat begins in nature, but it is then transformed by culture" through a "miracle of transubstantiation," in which wheat becomes "the doughy lump of formless matter [that] rises to become bread." This process, says Pollan, is one of "transcendence" that symbolizes "civilization's mastery of raw nature. A mere food thus became the substance of human and even spiritual communion, for there was also the old identification of bread with the body of Christ."

Pollan indicates the significant implications farming has for us as both spiritual and social beings; Thomas Jefferson, on the other hand, was most concerned with the farmer as the quintessential *national* figure. Identifying farming as the most important employment to our country, Jefferson called farmers "the chosen people of God, if ever he had a chosen people," and said they were "the most valuable citizens" because they were "the most vigorous, the most independent, the most virtuous," and "they are tied to their country and wedded to its liberty and interests by the most lasting bonds." This was Jefferson's farmer-citizen: a better farmer because he was a citizen; a better citizen because he was a farmer. And Jefferson's idea is one that has proven to have legs. For instance, homegrown.org (a website affiliated with the Farm Aid organization) recently tapped into Jefferson's national and religious rhetoric when it took as its motto "In Dirt We Trust." Whether you believe that such a motto means the organization has supplanted God with the farmer (a potential heresy) or that it is indicating a belief that God and nature are one, the line suggests the valorization of the farmer's work.

The point is that what the farmer does and what he produces are more than the sum of their parts. Take, for instance, the significant growth in the number of farmers' markets held around the country. We have an increasing interest in what I recently heard termed "SOLE food" (that is, sustainable, organic, local, and ethically grown food). The pun, of course, indicates that crowds don't gather on weekends in parks and parking lots just for the sake of a buff-colored organic egg with a low carbon footprint. The farmers' market has become a ritual where we get to experience a renewed commitment to long-held cultural values. It feeds our souls as well as our bodies. When we exchange greenbacks for green beans, we are buying emblems of the farmer's independence and self-sufficiency. As we chat with him or her about whether the warm weather is going to hold out—"Don't we always get a hard freeze in September?" we ask—we express how we feel a personal investment in the farm itself. As we move from booths of produce to booths where photographers sell prints featuring close-ups of heirloom tomatoes or local jewelry makers sell chili pepper earrings, we begin to link farmers to the company of artisans. Moreover, by bringing the farmer into the city centers, markets serve to integrate the farmer into the community at large. He isn't just the lone figure out in the fields. At the market tables, burgeoning with colorful chards, bushel baskets of corn, frilly stocks of dill, we bump into friends: "Gee, the only place I seem to see you is right here at Bill's stand!" After gossip and an exchange of recipes we say to each other and the farmer, too, "See you next week." Farmers' markets are, write Jennifer Meta Robinson and J. A. Hartenfeld, a "living performance" where we build community and play out a "desire . . . for a sense of authenticity and locality."

Such persistence of the farmer as a nationally significant icon is all the more remarkable, given the steady decline in our nation's farm population. In 1790, only a few years after the American Revolution, an estimated 90 percent of our citizens were involved in some aspect of farm-related economy. By the end of the twentieth century that number, according to the Agricultural Census, was down to just 1 percent, with each American farmer supplying food enough for an estimated one hundred people. In fact, in 1993 the Census Bureau stopped counting farmers as a separate occupational group (deciding to lump farmers together with fishermen and loggers) because their numbers were "statistically insignificant"—at least in terms of population figures.

Like people in hundreds of stories from western history and literature, my family was desperate to believe they could trust their connection to the land. My grandfather, for instance, was not that different from Per Hansa, in O. E. Rolvaag's *Giants in the Earth*, who envisioned his homestead becoming a "kingdom" where he and his progeny would thrive forever, emboldened and nurtured by their connections to the land. I think, too, of one of the most defining stories of Utah, where I now live: when Mormon leader Brigham Young and his party emerged from Emigration Canyon in 1847, he gazed out over the Salt Lake valley and proclaimed, "This is the place." Four unassuming words were a declaration of dependence on a specific place, the moment in which the displaced had found their Zion.

My grandfather may have felt that same certainty initially, reinforced by an old Bohemian myth that credits the very founding of Bohemia and of Prague as the capital city to the prophetess Libuše and her farmer husband, Přemysl, the Ploughman. Before their marriage Libuše had governed the Czechs alone since her father's death, but when she ruled in favor of a young farmer in a boundary dispute, the loser in the clash cursed Libuše and said his people ought to be ashamed to be ruled by a woman "with long hair but short wits." Calmly, the prophetess queen assented. She instructed her councilmen to ride three days, led only by her riderless horse, and at the end of those days, she said, they would find a farmer named Přemysl plowing in an uncultivated field surrounded by tilled fields. Following Libuše's instructions, the noblemen found Přemysl and summoned him to "take up the sovereignty ordained to you and to your heirs." Although Přemysl did not seem surprised to see the men, he dismissed his oxen, which vanished into a rock, and then said to the men, "If I could have finished ploughing this field there would have been abundance of bread for all time. But since you made such haste, and have interrupted me in my work, know that there will often be hunger in the land." Turning his plowshare on its side, he drew bread and cheese from his satchel, laid them on the plowshare shining in the sun, and invited the men to join him for breakfast at his iron table. After their breakfast Přemysl changed into the princely robes the men had brought from Libuše, but he placed his peasant shoes into a bag that he brought to her castle with him, "so that my descendants may know from what stock they are sprung, that they may go in awe."

Přemysl honored his duties as leader of the Czech people, and he and Libuše were devoted to each other. He was there when she looked out over the Vltava River and foresaw the founding of Prague, a city whose fame would touch the stars. Their children founded the Přemyslid Dynasty, which ruled the Czech Lands well through years of feast and famine, peace and war, until the early fourteenth century.

But Přemysl considered leaving behind his beloved fields a great personal sacrifice, one dictated by fate and necessity rather than his heart's desire. I imagine him years later, in the rare private moments a king can steal from managing wars and settling disputes. He pulls a rough burlap sack out of a trunk and removes the old sandals from the folds of cloth. He fingers the soil that still clings to the soles, and he tries to remember the smell of newly plowed soil. He imagines the glint of the sun on the plow that he left in that field of unbroken sod. He remembers how his fingers lingered on the smooth plow handle in the instant before he greeted the queen's emissaries, the moment he became not a monarch but a farmer in exile.

WEEDS

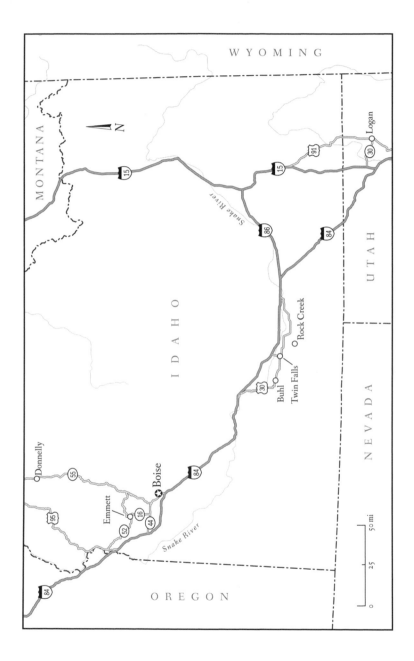

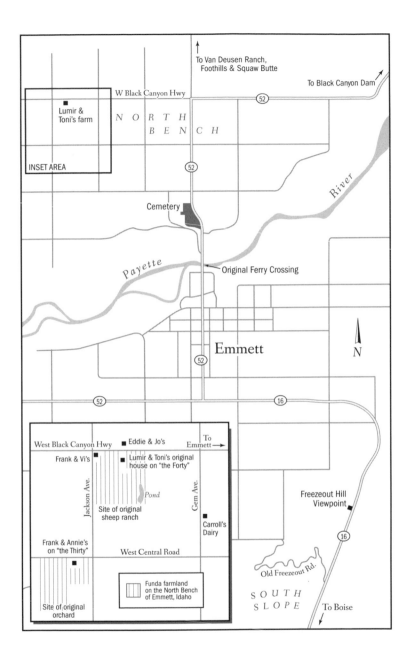

To Van Deusen Ranch,
Foothills & Squaw Butte

To Black Canyon Dam

W Black Canyon Hwy

52

NORTH
BENCH

Lumir &
Toni's farm

INSET AREA

52

Cemetery

River

Payette

Original Ferry Crossing

Emmett

52

N

52

16

West Black Canyon Hwy · Eddie & Jo's
To
Emmett →

Frank & Vi's

Lumir & Toni's original
house on "the Forty"

Jackson Ave.

Pond

Gem Ave.

Site of original
sheep ranch

Carroll's
Dairy

Freezeout Hill
Viewpoint

16

Frank & Annie's
on "the Thirty"

West Central Road

Funda farmland
on the North Bench
of Emmett, Idaho

Old Freezeout Rd.

Site of original
orchard

SOUTH
SLOPE

To Boise

1

Dodder

"O thou weed! . . .

Would thou hadst ne'er been born"

Shakespeare's Othello

Highway 16, the main route into my rural hometown of Emmett, Idaho, winds through a high desert country of sand and sagebrush before the road narrows and suddenly descends into the valley through a steep grade known as Freezeout Hill. Gouging straight through the terrain, the road drops more than five hundred feet in elevation within the span of a mile. Imposing, sheer banks on both sides of the road cast perpetual shadows over that portion of the highway, but only half a mile later and halfway down the hill, it emerges back into sunlight where I can pull off at the monument and viewpoint that overlooks verdant farmland alongside stretches of subdivisions.

Whenever I pull over at the Freezeout Hill viewpoint, I try to locate the acreage that my grandparents purchased in 1919. The land my family farmed for more than eighty years lies nearly ten miles across the valley from Freezeout, so I look for distinctive landmarks. I can make out the road that crosses the river, climbs the North Bench, and then skirts by the cemetery, but from there it's a visual guessing game where the distances seem to erase certainty. Squinting, I look for the blue dairy silo of "the Carrolls'

Place," which is what everyone used to call the dairy, even though the Carroll family moved away in the 1970s. When I can't tell if the silo I see is the Carrolls', I try to identify the bank of greenhouses south of our farmland, and I search for the house to the east of our place that was built right into the side of the foothills so that the windows seem to offer a glimpse into the depths of the earth. Like a dozen times before I'm never able to feel certain I've located the place where I grew up. Uncertainty is not a new feeling for me whenever I return to Emmett. Even when my parents were living, I felt tenuous about my connection to the farm. I used to think this out-of-place feeling was just me because I was a farmer's daughter instead of a farmer's son. And that made all the difference, I thought. It meant that from the moment of my birth I was destined to have to leave the farm.

I now live in northern Utah where I teach at a university, and I return to Emmett only as a visitor. Despite promises that originally brought my grandparents to this "Valley of Plenty," farming didn't make my family rich, or even solvent, and gradually, over the years, the farm has been sold off, acre by acre. The last twenty acres were sold in 2001, just months before both of my parents died—one of cancer, the other of a heart attack. Only two and a half acres and the house my parents built in 1972 on that original sheep ranch remain in my name. Strangers now irrigate the fields my father farmed, and I return to Emmett as an absentee landlord rather than a resident. I don't know what the locals call "the Carrolls' Place" anymore, and no one recognizes me in the grocery store where I stop to buy flowers for family graves.

Standing at the Freezeout Hill lookout, then, is like standing at the threshold between the ages, at some kind of boundary between past and present. The history of the road itself demonstrates the transition from a wild pioneer time to an age of modern, western agriculture that is now giving way to what some geographers call a "rurban" landscape. The paved highway I've just driven down is actually the cutoff route of Freezeout Road that was built in 1929, a decade after my grandparents Frank and Annie settled on seventy acres ten miles northwest of here. The narrow switchbacks of *Old* Freezeout—as the original road is known locally—still wind down the foothills just to the south of where I stand. The pass was so named in the late nineteenth century by a group of settlers who nearly froze to death just three miles from town while they waited out bad weather one winter's night at their camp near the windswept top. The original road was so treacherous that even on good days drivers had to lock their wagon wheels—or "freeze" them—and slide down the steep road, praying that they wouldn't plunge over the sandy cliffsides. Getting out of the valley proved no easier, and reports say that it sometimes took an entire day for a dozen team of horses to pull heavily loaded freight wagons up the hill.

Once the Payette River Valley was a place to travel through rather than a place to settle. Shoshone Indians often wintered there, but they maintained camps elsewhere during the rest of the year. Among the first white men in the valley was trapper François Payette, whose fur-trapping expedition came through in 1818, and although Payette's sons ran traps for years along the river named for their father, there was no permanent settlement in the valley until 1863, when a much-needed ferry was built at the present site of Emmett. Roadhouses and general stores catered both to the transient miners going northeast into the mountains and to those pioneers headed west to Oregon, but Martinsville, as it was originally known, didn't inspire as much permanence as it did hostility. A natural rock ravine at the base of Freezeout Hill named Pickett's Corral was refuge to an infamous gang of horse thieves, bandits, and swindlers who targeted those passing through, and hostilities between the outlaws and the men of the "Payette

Vigilantes" were a routine occurrence. According to a local history, confrontations with local Indians were common and violent, with one particular battle leaving Indian bodies "floating down the stream all summer" where they would "get lodged on a sandbar" until somebody "would take a cottonwood pole and drive them on down the river."

The monument references some of these harrowing stories of the valley and indicates points off to the left where you can still glimpse the sheer cliffs and hairpin turns of the original pioneer road as it winds down South Slope. But if you turn your back on that road, you can follow the route of the Payette River as it heads from east to west toward its confluence with the Snake River at the Idaho-Oregon border thirty miles away. Placid canals that thread through the valley have put the waters of the Payette to good use, creating a tidy vista of grain fields, orchards, barns, and houses that fans out below.

Originally, farming anywhere beyond the margins of the river seemed entirely improbable in this arid landscape, and agricultural settlement didn't really begin until the 1890s, when settlers united to form the "Last Chance" canal company, the first of several companies that tried to channel the waters of the Payette. For the next three decades these companies were plagued by lack of money and the difficulties of engineering canals in the sandy soil of the Black Canyon. The wooden flumes leaked, and the ditches often washed out, usually in the hottest days of summer when the farmers most needed the water. One year, desperate to fix a massive break in the canal, they shored up the banks with what was at hand—hundreds of loads of sagebrush that they had grubbed off adjacent lands.

But over time irrigation ditches reached from north to south. As a point of considerable state pride Idaho is one of the top five irrigated states in the country, and the state holds the record of most acres "reclaimed" by the projects of the Desert Land Act of 1894 (also known as the Carey Act). Saying that the Carey Act offered Idaho the promise of an "Industrial Eden," historian Mark Feige points to Emmett in particular as a "systemized and controlled landscape" evidencing "a progressive technological order" in which the engineer and the farmer triumphed over an unruly and flawed environment.

By the time Frank and Annie first drove down Old Freezeout, the area had been transformed by irrigation and the lumber industry into "the Garden of Idaho." Local boosters were keen on quantifying achievements. They bragged about twenty-five thousand acres that raised grain and potatoes and fruit, one hundred thousand sheep that were raised and shipped from Emmett yearly, and half a million board feet a day produced by the lumber mill. Boxcars of apples, Italian prunes, peaches, apricots, and sweet cherries from Emmett's famous orchards were shipped as far away as London, Australia, and the Orient. Eager to bill the community as simultaneously pastoral and cosmopolitan, a 1910 promotional pamphlet promised that the valley was "full of sunshine" and "genial the whole year through," calling Emmett a "radiant spot on the world's map."

The valley I grew up knowing, however, felt like neither a "wild west" nor a technological wonder intimately connected to the world's metropolitan centers. With one stoplight, a bowling alley, a farmer's co-op, two drugstores, and several bars, the town seemed like a cartoon version of provincial, small-town America. And during my teens the Old Freezeout Hill Road was less known for horse-and-wagons than it was for pot parties and the graffiti carved into the sandy cliffsides that proclaimed "77 Rules" or "Mike Loves Kristi." I'd heard the story that once it took a dozen team of horses to defy the gravity of that place, but—at a time when my friends and I "cruised" only as far as Roe-Ann's Drive-In, turned right at the stoplight, snaked around the city park block, and then circled back to start all over again—that story held more symbolic weight than historical relevance. It was a warning, emphasizing that ground under your wheels can crumble at any moment, that all ways, in or out, are treacherous.

Although I'm convinced I could still drive the backroads of this valley in my sleep, knowing a place and having a claim to it are two different things, and I realize that if Emmett has any message to offer me, it is that today's claimant is tomorrow's body, lodged precariously on a sandbar.

Thirty-five miles from the capital city of Boise, Emmett is considered a bedroom community, especially since the sawmill that once employed generations of residents closed in 2001. Only a seventh of the valley's thirty-five hundred acres that were once in fruit production still have trees. Just below the viewpoint asphalt streets named Plum Street, Cherry Lane, and Apple Drive meander through housing developments where orchard trees used to bloom. Although corn, wheat, and hay are still grown here, the patchwork of fields gets smaller every year.

Captivated by the idealistic cultural views of the farmer, my grandfather Frank Funda was undaunted by the fact that he knew nothing about farming when he first moved to Idaho. A plucky but poor Bohemian immigrant, he had no experience, tools, friends, or family when he arrived in 1910, but still he was certain, as the popular claims told him, that he could "Plant Dimes, Harvest Dollars." He bought his first acres of land in Buhl, Idaho—150 miles from Emmett—on a place he called Rock Creek Ranch because, as the family joked, all he could grow there were rocks. After he and fellow Czech immigrant Annie Martinek married in 1915, they sold the ranch and moved to the North Bench in Gem County, where they bought two parcels of land, one a young orchard where Frank raised Italian prunes and kept bees and another half a mile away that had been a poor sheep ranch near the base of the foothills. Over the years Frank and then his sons—my father, Lumir, and Uncle James Frank—transformed the undulating land from sagebrush to flat crop land. It was on this second parcel that I was raised in a drafty, converted sheepherder's shack that had been remodeled into a four-and-a-half-room house. With regularity the winter wind moved the curtains in my parents' bedroom. You had to be careful not to trip over the buckles and cracks in the gray linoleum. The toilet only worked some of the time, and we had an outhouse for the rest of the time. I bathed in an aluminum tub in the kitchen, and my mother washed our clothes with an old-time wringer washer out on the "porch," which was actually just a couple of plywood sheets laid over two-by-fours on the bare ground.

I imagine my father would want me to make clear: we were farmers, not ranchers. On such definitions he was unyielding. Even though we lived barely above the poverty line, he utterly believed farming was superior to ranching. While western mythology romanticizes ranching, for my father it was untamed chaos. Ranches were either remote, wild places like the Van Deusen Ranch, where he was hired to custom-farm on hilly land that was miles from the nearest phone and electricity, or they were like the Nevada ranch that he and his brother owned for a dozen years that had been nothing but sagebrush and didn't even have a well until two years after they'd bought the place. Those were "ranches" that aspired to be farms. At the bottom of Dad's agricultural hierarchy were ranches that had stock. These ranchers worked by brute force and were slaves to their animals—5 AM milking, for instance, or nights spent calving, the neighbor's phone call in the middle of the night to say your stock had breeched the fence and were wandering down the middle of the road. Farming, by contrast, was orderly and intellectual; the rows of crops or trees ran straight and true, and the farmer ruled with his machines.

I was a grown woman before I discovered that the word for *dodder*, the brightly colored, Medusa-headed weed my father righteously battled on our farm, was not spelled, as I had always assumed, d-a-u-g-h-t-e-r. Make no mistake, I knew the weed well enough. I had seen my father keep vigil for its burnished patches and heard him cuss "that goddamn dodder!" when it appeared in the clover and alfalfa fields of our small farm. I recognized how deeply he despised the choking tendrils of that plant vampire. But for some reason I had never actually *seen* the word as a child, had only heard a lax, Idaho pronunciation that did not differentiate the embedded consonants *t* and *d*.

I first saw the word months after my father's death as I cleaned out a drawer where he had kept years of farm-related publications, and an old illustrated pamphlet slipped from the pile and into the black trash bag at my feet. Even in the extension agency's fuzzy black-and-white picture on the cover, the weed's twining tendrils were unmistakable, but the title—where it spelled out in big capital letters D-O-D-D-E-R—was a revelation.

I now know, thanks to that pamphlet and the fine print of an *Oxford English Dictionary*, that the word for the weed and that for my relationship to my parents are only coincidentally related by sound and not sense, and they have, as far as I can tell, no common etymological history whatsoever. My concept of the word had been shaped by a non sequitur, a profound fallacy of homonyms: like hearing that the Book of *Acts* is about the ministry of Paul, the Apostle, and mistakenly picturing Paul Bunyan's *ax* carving out the Grand Canyon as his beloved blue ox Babe looks on from the rim. It wasn't even remotely the same thing.

Yet that essential misconception of equating dodder and daughter, however unfounded it was, had long ago engrained in me an analogy I found hard to shake, one where the boundaries between two things, weed and woman, are permeable and fluid.

Historically known by a number of other names such as love-vine, hellbind, strangle weed, tangle weed, devil's guts, devil's ringlets, maiden's hair, witches' shoelaces, and witch's hair, dodder is a pernicious and highly specialized plant with a malevolent character that has earned it a place on the Department of Agriculture's list of the ten most noxious weeds. Loathed by farmers, this many-tentacled, yellowish orange plant, which is found throughout the continent except in the most frozen reaches of northern Canada, has lost the capacity to synthesize chlorophyll and therefore has adapted to be one of the few truly parasitic plants. A botanical distant cousin to the ubiquitous morning glory and other members of the bindweed family that choke plants and compete for water and essential light, dodder—*cuscuta cephalanti*—is, writes naturalist David Attenborough in his book *The Private Lives of Plants*, "more sinister." It is a true parasite, a free-loader, "incapable," says another writer, "of any independent existence except as a seed." It has only tiny flowers and the barest hint of leaves, having bartered those flora essentials for specialized structures called "haustoria" that hold close a host plant while it anchors into the living stems and begins to suck off vital food stores that the host has manufactured for itself. Unchecked, the twining tentacles work their way under, over, and around crop plants like clover and alfalfa, creating bright orange cobwebs, masses of intertwined tresses that "envelope plants like an insidious veil." Crediting dodder with a calculating, cunning nature, Attenborough writes that the weed "not only actively hunts" its "prey" "but selects its victims with care." The plant has a "very sophisticated" capacity, say researchers at Penn State University, "almost animal-like," to differentiate a potentially good host from less succulent ones by detecting odors that help it "make a deci-sion" about which host to embrace. Scientist Colin Purrington has identified dodder as "one of the creepiest plants" he knows and added, "It's a horrible existence for the host plant. If plants could scream, they'd have the loudest screams when they had dodder attached."

I have a 1914 manual on weeds that advises that any dodder-infested patch must be burned, not once but twice, with kerosene and straw. But farm folklore warns that if the smoke from such fire swirls back down and touches the ground, however fleetingly, new patches of dodder will sprout and grow at that spot. If burn-ing is unfeasible, the manual advocates spraying with an arsenic-based treatment, and although this treatment will kill the alfalfa too, the manual insists that once "relieved from the strangler's grip," the crop will recover and come up from the roots. You can't pull dodder up by the roots either because even a small broken bit of stalk can seize onto a host and then start a new center, so farmers sought other methods of eradication. In the early twen-tieth century they tried sprinkling dodder patches with one of a variety of acids, such as the antiseptic crude carbolic acid (which was the same chemical injected into the veins of Nazi victims in the late days of World War II as a quick, effective means of exter-mination), or the extremely corrosive sulphuric acid (which at lower concentrations was used as battery acid but is now known as a main component of acid rain), or, finally, sodium nitrate (which had been used as a gunpowder in the late nineteenth century and was later used as rocket propellant). Dodder, it seems, is so dan-gerous it must be controlled by the most radical means.

With its brilliant curling tendrils of gold and auburn and straw-berry blond, dodder does have about it a fiendish, feminine beau-ty. But however bizarre or aberrant it is within the plant world, to my mind its most monstrous characteristic is that once fastened onto the host plant, dodder allows its own connection with the earth to simply wither away. Roots can entirely break off contact with the soil, and the parasite morphs in a weird, disconnected existence, well above the terra firma of its inception.

Because I was my parents' only child and, on my father's side, the only grandchild, people who met my parents for the first time would often drawl, "Bet *she's* spoiled rotten." The pronouncement required no retort; in fact, any reply to the contrary would only serve to verify the original conclusion. By acclamation I was considered lazy and useless, just by virtue of being an "only." Being a girl on a farm, however, removed any doubt.

The genre of "farmer's daughter" jokes demonstrates the pervasive cultural beliefs about those of my tribe. Portrayed as a wild, sex-crazed temptress—a pigtailed Barbie with ominous pitchfork—the farmer's daughter is simultaneously innocent and menacing. Happy for a romp in the hayloft with any passing stranger, she uses the farm (her *father's* farm, for she lacks a direct claim to it) as her sticky-sweet flypaper. But the trick does not leave her untouched. She is fenced in there on the farm, where she lacks the power of self-determination, and the isolation deepens her sexual hunger to a maniacal degree, erases all social niceties of courtship, robs her of the promises of unconditional love, and leaves her vulnerable to violence and rape.

They say that determining the gender of a fetus is work that falls to the sperm. I was a girl because of Lumir's seed, then, even though I'm pretty sure, if he'd had any real choice in the matter, he would have selected a boy as his only offspring. I take no offense at that. For my mother's part having only one child wasn't her choice either, but rather a cruel fact of her physiology. Before my birth she had suffered two miscarriages, and she would have another two after—results of her being Rh-negative in the years before widespread use of the drug Rhogam, which prevents a mother's body from spontaneously aborting the fetus whose blood is incompatible with her own. Unlike my unborn siblings I defied the insistence of my father's blood type and sided with my mother instead.

In late 1959 my mother was in the last weeks of her pregnancy, and everyone assumed my father would finally get the boy he wanted. The owner of the John Deere implement store where Dad sometimes worked as a mechanic in the winters gave him a little green metal-cast tractor. Likewise the local Ford dealer offered toy-sized samples of the latest models: a little sporty baby blue convertible and a dark red sedan. Later when I discovered these vehicles were too small for my Barbie doll to sit in and drive, I abandoned the Barbie—not the tractor or cars. Barbie, I thought, was useless, all frizzed hair and pointy breasts. She didn't go anywhere, didn't *do* anything, create anything, or inspire anything other than my contempt. The other toys, however, represented choices: to either set off for a place of your own choosing or change the character of the place you'd chosen to stay.

Whenever my father spoke of my birth, he never failed to begin the story with the words of his own father. With something strangely akin to pride, he used to say his father Frank had admonished my mother when she was pregnant with me, "If it's a girl, you send it back!" My father would then laugh and add, "But once you were here, he wouldn't have traded you for the world." The photos kept in old Brach's candy boxes and reels of 8mm film attest to the truth of my father's claim. One scene of the home movies shows my bespectacled grandfather settled on a stool next to a baby carriage placed out in dappled shade. As he coos over the carriage, cherubic hands reach up and try to clench at his gray moustache. He turns to the camera and laughs. I suspect he knew by then that I would be the only grandchild he would ever have.

The family women of that generation were all in their midthirties or early forties by then. His other daughter-in-law was "barren," as the family whispered; his own daughter had never seemed inclined to children, preferring to stay "Daddy's little girl" long into her adulthood. So maybe his delight was a matter of resignation. He was loyal, nonetheless. Even when the film shows my grandmother lose interest in the baby and wander over to the flowers or into the house, there my grandfather keeps his post by the baby carriage. And while this scene, composed by my father behind the camera, is supposed to convince me of my grandfather's devotion, it does make me wonder what magic I possessed to turn my grandfather's heart and why I had to redeem myself from my gender at all.

The memories I have of Granddad, who died when I was seven, include how willing he was to indulge me, how he used to be my main audience for frivolous dress-up dramas, enacted in front of a blanket thrown over the clothesline for a stage curtain. Photos show me in front of this curtain bedecked in my aunt's string of fake pearls that almost hang to my knees, one of the brightly flowered dresses she favored, her high heels, and a grotesquely large, white fur hat. In this peculiar exhibition of exaggerated femininity I would prance before him and bow to his applause and afterward slip a rose from his own garden into the buttonhole of his shirt pocket—confident in the fact that he doted on me and always had.

But my role on the farm was limited by clear albeit unspoken orders of the men of my family. As I grew up, I was expected to help my mother weed the garden, butcher the chickens, and feed any livestock we might have at the time. But I'd rather play with the pigs than feed them. With other farm chores I could delay and feign weariness or forgetfulness, or I could thin the radish sprouts right along with the weeds, doing the job so incompetently that my mother would ultimately think me unforgivably lazy or stupid and go out to gather eggs or weed the garden herself. The suspicion was that I didn't have much sense when it came to the farm. For years my family laughed about one of the many times I got shocked by the electric fence. Too lazy to take a big pan of wet and stinky chicken slop out to the backyard where the hens were scratching in the dirt, I just went out to the side yard next to the ditch and flung the contents of the pan out across an electric fenceline and into the ditch where it would, I thought, just float away, and no one would be the wiser. In one of those slow-motion, cartoon moments the stream of slop arced out toward the ditch and then settled across the hot fence wire, sending the electric shock down toward the ditch and right back up to the pan I was still holding. The jolt clenched every muscle into a blue hot spasm, and after a second, when the alternating current let me go, I screamed. My mother stuck her head out the back door and laughed. "That'll teach ya," she said, and by dinner that night the whole family knew about my foolishness.

I never seemed to learn some of the simplest farm lessons. Oblivious to where I was walking, I often stepped barefoot into green chicken shit that oozed up warm—or worse still, cold!—between my bare toes. I would whine and turn on the hose to wash the smell away. "Go put shoes on!" my mother would scold with impatience. She had little empathy for my dislike of confining shoes or for my need to directly feel the grass and dirt under my feet. By every summer's end my feet were so leathered that I could walk without pain into the stubble of a grain field—the Idaho version of walking on a bed of nails. I took some pride in that.

I dreaded the early mornings when my mother roused me to help with butchering the chickens. Incompetent or not, as soon as I was big enough to hold a flapping chicken by the legs, I was expected to help—and without "back talking," my mother would warn. My job was to grab the penned chickens by the legs, swing them upside down so they wouldn't fight, and bring them to my mother at the chopping block. I hated every minute of the dusty fury in the pen and the way they squawked and pecked at my fingers. I once saw my mother, while she was helping my grandmother butcher, hold eight fully grown chickens in her hands, but with me it was one at a time, and I was expected to be standing there with the next one when the headless chicken ran blindly from the stump, spurting blood from its mangled neck. Once they were beheaded, we put the chickens into huge tubs and poured boiling water over the feathers to loosen them up so we could pluck the birds clean. My mother would examine my efforts and often as not hand the bird back to me, saying: "You missed the pinfeathers around the tail and inside of the legs." By the time we were finished plucking, my fingers were scorched, and wet feathers stuck to my arms, face, and hair, but we were only half done. Inside the house now we inserted the tip of the sharpest paring knife near the anus, slit up to the bottom of the breastbone, reached into the bird and pulled out the innards, separated out the heart and liver, slit the gizzard and peeled away the inner sack filled with grain and sand, rinsed out the cavity, and then cut up the meat and dropped it in ice water to cool before we packed the meat into old bread bags and stacked packages in the used chest freezer we kept out in a shed. For days after we finished butchering, I could smell that lingering odor of scalded feathers and chicken guts on my hands and in my hair, no matter how my times I washed.

Barnyard animals and produce—destined for our own kitchen table rather than the open market—were women's domain on our farm. My identity as farm daughter, however, was shaped more by what I *didn't* do on the farm than what I did. When in my teens I aimed to get out of garden work by offering to learn to drive the tractor, my father told me that field work wasn't for a girl. Absolutely methodical and particular about setting his siphon tubes, he consistently shunned my efforts to help him irrigate. I was allowed to keep him company in his machine shop, where he would call me his "little grease monkey," because I knew which tools to get when he asked and I knew how to attach the grease gun to the nipples of the combine and then pump the handle until amber grease oozed from the crevices between the machine's joints. But if I admitted too much pleasure, Dad would frown, take the grease gun from my hands, and shoo me away to the garden where I was supposed to be picking tomatoes. Although I may have helped construct corn bins during harvest or shovel wheat toward the bottom of a thundering auger, these were duties that took place off the fields. On occasion, if I was bringing a Mason jar of cool water out to my father, I was allowed to ride on the combine and peer over the rim of the filling hopper behind his seat, but I was never allowed to touch the steering wheel or the levered controls, and after one trip, down the field and back, he expected me to hop off and leave him to concentrate on the straight lines of his work. My father did finally teach me to drive the John Deere 4020, but lessons took place in the farmyard, and I was forbidden out on the field unless we were picking up hay bales or gated pipe at the end of the season, in which case the harvest was done and I could do no harm.

For the most part, as a farm daughter, I felt peripheral, relegated to the edges of the fields, where the weeds had a grip on the soil, where to some extent their existence was watched with suspicion but was otherwise tolerated with benign contempt.

Sometimes I wonder what things would have been like if I had indeed been a boy. My parents used to tell me they had a name picked out if I was a boy: Ralph, after a cousin of my father's. I hated that name more than my old-fashioned, little-old-lady name, so on that count, at least, I was always glad I was a girl.

Call me Ralph. For the moment at least.

Even though I am my parents' only child, I was never once called spoiled. I was on a tractor before I could walk, and I spent my summers at my father's side, whether he was irrigating the fields or combining. I learned how to figure the yield on a field of grain before I went to school, and by the time I was a teenager, my father was asking me for advice on whether we should sell the grain or put it in the silo and hold out for a better price. We would consider whether next year we should plant wheat or corn in the fields around the house. And we used to laugh together when my mother complained that being surrounded by fields of corn made her feel claustrophobic. To us nothing could be finer than the weeks before harvest when every breeze brought the music of rustling corn stalks. It sounded like money. Last year I bought the farm next to Dad's, and now we call the place "the Funda and Son Farms."

I hate Ralph. That smarmy asshole. Golden boy of the family. I want to point out to him that "Funda and Son" is a twisted syllabic name about as poetic as a dirty mop—not that he'd probably listen to me, or any woman, anyway. Ralph would probably even marry a nice local girl named Ann or Jean, meek and obedient and as fertile as his crops. Though I do suppose, since he's a product of my own fantasy, I could make him anything I want.

Maybe, instead, he was a disappointment as a son: too selfish to care much about Dad's farm, more interested in smoking weed than killing weeds.

When I was sent out to irrigate, I'd go loaf at the edge of our pond, trying to imagine myself anyplace but on that damn farm. I left Idaho just as soon as I could and never looked back. I went east for a degree in astronomy, not accounting, like Dad wanted me to do. I liked how I could make endless sky—the great beyond—

comprehensible with mathematical certainty. Who gives a shit about the land? My father is proud of me, even if I'm not a farmer. Mother tells me she's lonely without me. Dad is too, I think. I ought to visit more, I suppose. But I send a check every couple of months. Lord knows, they need the money, poor things.

Condescending creep.

Maybe Ralph could be the farmer, after all, but one who fails because he's overextends himself, ambition being his downfall. Or he argues with Dad endlessly about using the organic methods he learned at the commune where he lived for a while (a scenario I've stolen straight from Jane Smiley's novel *A Thousand Acres*).

Is that what I wanted? A straw man, so easily knocked down, to make me, the daughter, look like their last, best hope?

Yes. Maybe.

Don't get me wrong: my kind and decent father never in any way voiced resentment of me. And like my grandfather, I think, he would not have "traded me for the world." When I was little, I ate breakfast with him every morning, stealing yolk-dripped toast straight from his plate. I flatly refused to eat fried eggs when my mother made me a plate of my own. "This tastes better," I'd say, and Dad would grin and indulge me. Whenever he was welding some broken piece of machinery, I was right there, wearing my own welding mask and watching the sparks fly like fireworks.

One year he designed a hammock out of rods and chains attached to the corners of an old iron bed frame and hung it between two poplar trees. We threw an old, thin mattress on it, and when the house was too hot in the evenings, he came out after dinner to push me for wild rides on the hammock. I clutched the mattress and screamed as I flew up and then back, but the ride was thrilling. After I lay there beside my father who, with one foot on the ground, rocked the hammock gently as we watched the stars came out. We didn't talk much. He was tired, and I was content. Sometimes one or both of us would fall asleep, to be awakened by my mother's whisper to come to bed.

As I grew up, he was proud of my accomplishments, and he made personal sacrifices so that I could achieve them. But his stories of the family's past, which demonstrated a real pride in the way he and his father and brother had shaped this land, always trailed off a bit at the end, as if his awareness of me as audience called into question his purpose for telling these tales in the first place. These weren't, after all, stories invoking a son to follow the row he'd chosen to hoe.

My family's expectation was that I would someday leave the farm, find a nice husband, sever my roots to that land entirely, and work, if I chose to work at all, outside of agriculture. I would let my father—sonless—be the last generation of my family to cultivate that land, as if I had chosen in the womb to forever cast the fate of family and farm. As a girl I did not possess the capacity to make a way for myself on the land, and there were few examples to suggest that a woman could have an independent existence on the farm. My family only knew one woman rancher, who bred horses and was tough and tanned, but when people mentioned her, it was always with certain veiled suggestions that were only silenced when she married a rodeo star and had a child of her own. So my models were few.

A high school English teacher once urged me not to limit myself according to the perspective of that valley. Miss Nutile was disdainful about the girls who went up the Old Freezeout Road to smoke pot and make out with their boyfriends. When one of my classmates, a bright but unmotivated girl named Sissy, got pregnant in our sophomore year and married her boyfriend weeks before her son's birth, Miss Nutile hardly disguised her censure. A feminist in a time when that was a dirty word in Idaho, she seemed decidedly exotic for Emmett. Unlike most of the teachers in the school Miss Nutile wasn't from our valley. She was young, wore miniskirts, had long, black, wavy hair that she wore in a loose ponytail, and she was the first person I knew who wore contact lenses. She rented a house that I could see from my family's living room window, and although the neighbors gossiped about her—noting especially the mornings when a man's car parked in her drive had frost on the windows—none of us ever dared visit her at her house. A teacher—especially a single female teacher—was of a completely different social order. At school, however, she was friendly to me, and I spent my lunch hours in her room, listening to the Simon and Garfunkel records that she would play on a small turntable. While the popular girls were out in the school parking lot, their arms wrapped around the warm torsos of their boyfriends and their hands anchored in the back pockets of jeans, I hovered at Miss Nutile's desk as she graded papers and ate spears of peppered cucumbers. She said she liked my poems and stories, and one day she suggested I major in English when I went to college. She said "*when,*" not "if"— as if a college education were a given. When I stuttered and mumbled a word of doubt, she lifted her eyebrows and said coolly, "Don't ever forget, there is a world out there beyond Freezeout Hill." It was a challenge. As far as she was concerned, to stay within the boundaries of that valley where I had been born and where my father had lived his entire life was to be paralyzed by small-town thinking. She made me feel it was my absolute duty to escape.

Her words evoked memories of a fantasy I had had as a child when we would take occasional drives out of the valley. As we would pick up speed on the highway that made a gradual curve at the bottom of Freezeout Hill before straightening out for the ascent, I used to pretend we were taking off in a plane. "Wing flaps?"

I'd say to an imaginary copilot. "Check." "Engines?" "Check." "Ready for takeoff?" "Check." We climbed the hill, and off to the right now the valley fell away like the view from a cockpit, and for a brief instant all we could see ahead of us were the carved hillside banks and nothing but open sky. For that brief moment our destination could have been Chicago or Hawaii or Paris.

The reality was that everyone I knew thought that a girl's relationship to that farmland had to be mediated by a wedding ring. When I was fifteen, one local farmer, who was much older than I was and smelled of dairy cows and silage, came for coffee one summer morning. This wasn't unusual, as neighbors often stopped by for a visit or on their way in or out of town. They knew the coffeepot was always on, and my mother often had baked goods that she could offer. My father was out in the field irrigating, so the neighbor and my mother sat drinking coffee at the table. I had been sent for the coffeepot, and when my back was turned to them, I heard him say, "Toni, don't you think it's about time you let me take Evelyn out on a date?" I was lifting the carafe off the burner when he spoke, and I remember I just stood there, paralyzed for a moment, dreading my mother's response.

"Hmpf!" she grunted indignantly. "Evelyn knows she isn't allowed to date until she's sixteen." I turned and went back to the table, giving him a weak smile as I refilled his cup. I hoped the expression struck the right balance between politeness and resignation—and that it revealed none of the horror I felt at the prospect of sitting next to him in the cab of his pickup on a Saturday night.

"And what is she now? Fifteen, isn't she? Isn't that close enough?" He drummed his finger on the table to make his point.

"Sixteen," my mother said. "She has to be sixteen." And before he could protest, she leveled her chilliest glare at him and added, "And *you're* too old for her anyway."

When I was seventeen, I did date a local boy closer to my age. Jack Shepherd was tall and lanky and ran with the "goat ropers"— that pejorative term applied to pretenders who reveled in rodeos and Willie Nelson, even though singing about Luckenbach, Texas, was as close as some of them ever came to a ranch. Jack's hat— and his entire wardrobe (or has my memory just colored it so?)— was black. He had black wavy hair that he credited to some long-ago Indian heritage, wispy scraggles of a black moustache, and even his eyes were so dark they seemed like small, black holes. But unlike the black-hatted, menacing figures in old westerns, Jack was open and gregarious, friendly to a fault in an age when to be cool meant to feign cynicism and indifference. A year older than I was, he had graduated from the local high school with nothing more than average grades. Now he was working as a mechanic and living in a small farmhouse he rented on the same side of the valley where my parents farmed.

For our date Jack took me to the "Cherry Bowl," where we bowled a miserable game and drank Cokes. Afterward we went back to his place, where he proudly gave me a tour of the farmyard. As if he were showing me a palace, he pointed to features like the small chicken coop he'd rigged up for a dozen chickens. For dinner he fried us eggs. "From my own chickens," he emphasized unnecessarily. I didn't bother to remind him that we had raised chickens and sold eggs to neighbors for as long as I could remember or that I had spent too many hours in our own chickens' filthy company to honor their productivity or appreciate them as the icons of his dream.

If I flinched from the idea of staying on the farm, Jack embraced it, told me plainly he wanted to own his own place and raise livestock and farm a few acres. When you're seventeen, you cannot help but look at the boy across the table and think, what if I married him? I have no doubt either that Jack was painting this picture of his ideal future in order to gauge my response. I could imagine us, ten years from that moment, with bawling calves and wailing kids, still sitting in that very same house at that same gray Formica table, where we would clink pennies into a Mason jar in hopes of saving enough for a mortgage on some little acreage down on the alkaline flats. At that moment the egg yolk on my plate was as cold as my heart.

Jack Shepherd isn't his real name (although his real name was nearly as evocative); it is, however, a name that perfectly sums up what he represented and I feared: a rural, cowed acquiescence, moving along in one direction because everyone else around you is moving in that direction, agreeing to someone else's idea of a future because you don't know how to make any other choice. I didn't want to be herded into being Jack's farm wife, and as kind and gentle as he was, I didn't need his shepherding. I'm sure that if I bumped into him today, more than thirty-five years later, I'd be happy to see him and ask him with genuine interest whether he had gotten that little farm of his. He was as nice of a fellow as I probably knew at the time, generous, even-tempered, always ready with a smile or a joke. But at that moment Jack the Ripper couldn't have scared me more.

It wasn't that Jack was getting in the way of my plans. Truth was, I had no plans. I just knew I didn't want what he might be offering. The farm felt like a hostile place to me, and behind it was a force that neither wanted me to stay nor would allow me to entirely escape.

Even though I always felt like the dumb farm girl from Emmett, I thought a college education would provide a way off the farm. I toyed with going to Cornell for a while when the university sent brochures and encouraging letters, after I'd placed in a national writing contest that Miss Nutile had compelled me to enter. New York State was about as far from Idaho as I could get. But the reality was there wasn't the money for a Cornell education. Worse, I knew that deep down I lacked the courage to move across the country. I moved instead just thirty-five miles south to Boise and enrolled at the university there—halfheartedly took classes, worked at a department store, and then dropped out after a year. Over the next half-dozen aimless years I was in and out of college and in and out of a series of rented apartments or houses where roommates came and went so quickly I can't even remember all of their names now. At one point in 1979 I started a job at a title company where I scanned microfilm and researched the histories of land records to find if homes and acreage were clear and unencumbered by unpaid liens and therefore free to be bought and sold by people whose claims to those pieces of land were "witnessed" and "notarized." It seemed like meaningful work for someone as homeless as I was at that moment. Although I had a researcher's mind and found the work interesting, my timing was lousy. Less than a year after I had started and just days after an exceptional performance review had my boss talking about promotion, the Idaho real estate market went into a swift and deep decline. Within a month I was jobless.

I spent the summer on meager unemployment checks, pretended on a weekly basis that I was actively looking for work so that the checks would keep coming, and then reenrolled at the university in August. College was a safe haven—a place where I didn't have to make decisions, other than pick a major. My father, who was perplexed by my choice of an English degree, never tired of suggesting I take a bookkeeping course. By his account bookkeeping, unlike literature, was practical and useful for a girl who might have to be out on her own for a while, until she married. "A fallback job," he said. I didn't bother to tell him that the university didn't offer "bookkeeping" courses anymore—that term having gone the way of poodle skirts. Neither did I tell him that the thought of accounting, or whatever you chose to call it, made me want to curl up and die. But because I couldn't mount a convincing argument to the contrary, I acquiesced and enrolled in an intro-level accounting course that was held in a cavernous lecture hall. The professor stood on a stage in front of a screen where we watched his disembodied hand—magnified to disconcerting proportions by the overhead projector—post numbers in their proper place in the debit or credit column, and at term's end a C was posted toward those three credits on my otherwise above-average transcript.

Whether my father liked it or not, I excelled at English. I drifted in with a group of English, history, and philosophy majors. All of them were what my childhood friends would have called "town kids," and I felt privileged to be accepted by them, so I never talked about the farm. We watched Woody Allen movies, which I pretended to like, spent hours after class (over amaretto-flavored coffees or cheap beers) arguing about the life-and-death decisions made by Madame Bovary, Daisy Miller, Jay Gatsby, Ivan Ilych, Gregor Samsa. It was the first time in my life when arguing—debating, we called it—was considered a virtue instead of the "backtalking" that had earned me more than my share of slaps across the face. I loved Emerson, and I thought that my Thoreau-loving, philosophy-majoring friend Randy had it all wrong. Thoreau was just cribbing Emerson's ideas, I argued. But Thoreau *lived* those ideas, he countered. It was intellectually stimulating in a way I'd never known before.

When a professor assigned Willa Cather's story "Neighbour Rosicky," the story of a Czech immigrant who farmed in Nebraska, I approached the story cautiously. After all, wasn't I at college to get away from the farm and my "Bohunk" background? For the main character, Anton Rosicky, however, the farm was a destination, not something to escape from. When I told Dr. Maguire that

I liked the story and recognized the culture because I was from a Czech farm family, he didn't seem to notice my discomfort at making the confession. Instead he laughed and pulled *My Ántonia* off his bookshelf. "It's kind of a prequel to 'Neighbour Rosicky,'" he said as he handed it to me. "My mother's name is Ántonia," I told him, with some surprise. "Toni, for short," I added. "All the more reason," he said, and I tried to gauge the sincerity of his nonchalance as he polished his coke-bottle glasses with a handkerchief. Was he rethinking the A he'd given me, now that he knew I was a farm girl from Emmett, a Bohunk at that? "Take it," he smiled, indicating the novel, before he put the glasses back on his face. "You'll like it."

And, of course, he was right. Much about the details of the fictional Ántonia's life was familiar, from gathering mushrooms right down to the fruit cellar just outside the back door. Cather, who had also grown up in a rural community, had seen beyond the parochialism of the country, and that meant maybe I could, too. Although Cather had feared the fate of "dying in a cornfield," two of her novels featured strong women farmers. In *O Pioneers!* it is Alexandra, not her brothers, who is successful because she understands the land and recognizes its inherent "genius." "For the first time," Cather writes, "perhaps, since that land emerged from the waters of geologic ages, a human face was set toward it with love and yearning. It seemed beautiful to her, rich and strong and glorious." And like a lover who recognizes his mate, the land responded to such comprehension and "bent lower than it ever bent to a human will before." Even if I had no ambition to become a farmer, it was liberating to see that it was possible for a woman to engender such a response from a rural landscape.

On the weekends I began dating another Emmett man who wanted to farm but who, like Jack, had no family farm of his own to claim. I thought I was in love with him, and one spring Sunday

morning, as I drove the rainy roads from Boise to Emmett to surprise him, I promised myself that life on the farm could work for
us. He answered the door of his tiny efficiency apartment in town,
and I could tell he was still groggy from a night with his friends.
Inside the only place to sit was next to each other on the pull-out
sofa, where the balled-up sheets were still warm from his body. I
expected him to reach out for me, but he sat, expressionless, on
the very edge of the unmade bed and looked out the window. I
don't remember how he began. The gist of it was he was calling
it off because he didn't love me. "I do *like* you," he reassured me.
This statement I remember vividly because of what followed: "I
even thought about us getting married. Your folks are going to
need somebody to farm the place someday, and that was definite-
ly an asset in all this." When I grimaced at the reference to the
farm, he rushed to add, "I'm just being honest with you here. I
think you deserve that." Yet in all the years I had known him, this
was the cruelest thing he had ever said to me, crueler even than
the night he had been wildly drunk and had pinned me to the
floor while he hissed in my ear, "I could force you, you know."
Over the course of our acquaintance he had carefully calculated
the cost-benefit ratio of wedding a farm daughter, and in looking
ahead to a time when my father was dead or disabled, he had giv-
en form to something I refused to imagine. Then in the end he
had decided I wasn't worth the price of those acres of land.

I did marry eventually—deliberately and perhaps defiantly
choosing a man who knew little about agriculture. Mark was a
city boy from Pennsylvania with degrees in history and anthropology, utterly useless knowledge on a farm. He read voraciously—one year he read every Pulitzer Prize–winning novel since
the prize's inception in 1918, another year he became fixated on
Nobel Prize winners in literature, and then it was all the works
of Herman Hesse. To me he represented the cerebral. This was

a man who *ironed* his blue jeans, for god's sake, and that seemed to me light years away from the men I'd known in Emmett.

When we moved to Nebraska so I could work on a PhD in literature, Mark worked in an agronomy lab where "farms" meant little more to him than murky water in test tubes or chemical compositions on a graph—so much nitrogen, so much alkali, cut and dried and followed by notations that listed suggested chemical applications to bring the soil into the optimal balance needed for fertility. Because the company was among the top agronomy labs in the country, he saw core samples of topsoil from Oregon to Arkansas—hundreds of them a week. And the chemical solutions he worked with made his hands dried and cracked, like my father's after a summer of farm work. But my husband felt no personal connection to that soil or those farmers, who were just names that appeared on the company's billing forms.

The deeper irony was that while my education provided a way off the farm, my chosen field of study took me back to it, intellectually at least. I focused on western American literature and history, and my dissertation was on Cather. After I began teaching in an agricultural valley in northern Utah, my research evolved to include women homesteaders at the turn of the century like Elinore Pruitt Stewart and contemporary women memoirists writing about their lives on farms and ranches, like Mary Blew, Judy Blunt, Teresa Jordan. I felt a sense of vindication when I read Jane Smiley's *A Thousand Acres*, where no good comes of a rural patriarchy and the obsession with the farmland poisons rather than sustains the characters. Quite by accident, I stumbled onto historical accounts and posters from the Women's Land Army, which was a unit of women who volunteered, à la Rosie the Riveter, to bring in the crops during the world wars, yet even my most well-read friends and colleagues had never heard of these "farmerettes."

It turns out, in ancient mythology, women were allowed complete agency within agriculture. For instance, several ancient civilizations, I learned, believed agriculture originated as the gift of goddesses—certainly not common knowledge in the western rural culture where I grew up. The Egyptians credited the blessings of agriculture to Isis, and the Greeks worshiped the yellow-tressed corn goddess Demeter. In Roman myth Demeter's name is Ceres, from which we get the word *cereal* to identify grain crops. The name derives from a word meaning literally "to grow," and Romans believed that crops grow, or do not grow, at Ceres's pleasure. Placed in charge of all of agriculture, the Ceres/Demeter figure reigned over a group of lesser gods—many of whom were women—who were each assigned to various aspects of farming: plowing, sowing, weeding, harvesting, and so on, and she was the first to teach a mortal how to plow and sow seeds and harvest grain. Then she gave him a winged chariot and told him to spread the knowledge throughout the world. Demeter's daughter Persephone was no parasite of the rural landscape either. Instead she was the very essence of her mother's agricultural impulse, the 'embodiment of her mother's power to make the landscape productive. Some have even said that where the daughter stepped, shoots of grain spontaneously sprang up from the ground.

The Demeter myth not only upended my whole understanding of gender on the farm. It challenged the western American myth that man transforms nature, brings it out of wilderness and into civilization, and from there the farm becomes eternal. According to that myth man compels the land to do his bidding by selecting what it will produce and improving upon nature with his ingenuity. He rids the land of the contamination of unproductive weeds, which are the emblems of nature's wild impulses, and because he has rightfully redeemed nature from its own wild inclination, the farmer justly assumes dominion over it. In turn the natural world expresses gratitude for that redemption by being productive and orderly under the command of his hand. The basic principles of the cult of Demeter, however, maintain that the gift of agriculture is what domesticated and civilized humans, not the other way around. Agriculture is the first cause, not the result. In these ancient myths Demeter is thought of as the "bringer of civilization," rescuing humans from lives as wanderers. Otherwise doomed to an antagonistic, fiercely tribal existence, pre-Demeter humans were driven by a desperate need to simply survive—not by a desire to claim or protect their rights to a plot of land. When given the ability to plant and harvest in one location, however, humans were transformed, able to form lasting connections to a place and to other people. Now that survival was less tenuous, they could turn their attention to establishing a culture that included the fine arts. According to this model of agricultural development a woman taught humans to have a "partnership" with nature; cultivation was not synonymous with male dominion. That idea was a radical shift for me.

Of course, recent historians like Deborah Fink have taken issue with the long-held notion that women took a back seat to the American icon of the lone, self-sufficient male farmer subduing the land. Fink has argued that the kind of work my mother did— selling eggs on the farm—often made the difference between a farm's failure and survival. And when selling garden produce, butter, or milk didn't provide enough of a cushion of survival, women often went to work off-farm, either supplementing the farm income or serving to transition the family to a non-agriculture-based living.

If it was my mother who helped the farm succeed, it was my aunts who led the way off the farm. Dad's sister Gladys left the farm at eighteen and never turned back. While she remained sentimental about the home place, her stories of leaving Idaho sug-

gested how much she felt handicapped by a provincial background
that trailed after her like a hungry wolf. Trained in bookkeeping
and secretarial skills, she eventually married a medical student
and moved to Portland, where she and her husband took up col-
lecting antiques, including French provincial furniture, Oriental
rugs, Russian lacquerware, and Japanese ivory. They traveled the
world, and she became fascinated by elephant figurines, always
posed with their trunks up, which are said to bring good luck. I
have a photo of her in India sitting on an elephant, his trunk up,
and when I look at it, I wonder if she felt India was far enough
away that she could stop running from the farm.

Gladys's escape coincided with that of her oldest brother, James
Frank, leaving for the Seattle shipyards. When he came back to
the farm after the war, he brought with him his new wife, Viola.
She had grown up dirt poor, daughter of a farm laborer, in a nearby town and had gone to Seattle to become a riveter in the shipyards. There she met and married my uncle before they returned
to Idaho and settled into a little house just across the field from
where we lived. Aside from driving the occasional grain truck to
the co-op when Dad and my uncle were busy with custom-combining all over the valley, she took no part whatsoever in the family farm. She wasn't even any good at growing a garden and would
often rely upon my mother's garden for her produce. My grandfather thought her lazy and hopelessly ineffectual as a daughter-
in-law, especially since she refused to learn to cook Czech food,
but Viola shrugged her shoulders and went her own way. I can't
help but think that, secretly, she liked being freed from expectations on our farm. She worked summers in a corn cannery and
autumns at Rolling Hills, the nearby apple-packing shed, and she
proudly, defiantly called her paycheck her own. I remember Viola stopping by our house on the way home from her shift to bring
us a bag or two of "seconds"—bruised or dimpled or unevenly

colored apples that the company couldn't ship. She sat on the fender of her car and lit a cigarette and freed her hair from the bandana that she had tied around her head, with the knot in front, the way women from that World War II era still did. Vi was a wage-earner, and that gave her an air of independence, defiance even, that compensated for her aching back and feet. One year she used that money to buy a huge roll of blue linoleum that she laid throughout her house, cutting and nailing down the edges of it herself. I can picture that floor yet, with its gaudy sprays of bizarre blue roses that were bigger than turkey platters, all set against a navy blue background. Even as it buckled over the years and the nail heads at the edges popped up and rusted from repeated moppings, that floor symbolized her unyielding independence.

Such symbolism was not lost on my mother. In 1971 my family was financially at the end of its rope. By this time Dad's brother had given up farm work for a steady job at the local sawmill, leaving my father to work long days on our farm and run the custom-farming business alone. My parents and I still lived in a four-and-half-room house that had once been a two-room sheepherder's shack. My mother had been ill the year before, and because we had no health insurance, we were still paying the doctor. Dad had planted wheat in a year when the demand for wheat exports dropped due to sanctions against the United States. In short, we weren't far from the old saying: "without a pot to piss in." The seriousness of the situation set in after the wheat harvest in late summer. Early that fall Mom made the bold suggestion that she should "go to work" at Rolling Hills. Vi had said she could get my mother a place on one of the sorting lines. To my mother it seemed like easy money. Certainly she was used to hard work. Every morning she rose before five and was usually on her feet until well after supper. She did the back-breaking work of gardening; the hot work of cooking and canning; the dirty work of caring for calves, pigs, and chickens. I'm sure she thought Rolling Hills would have been an easy eight hours.

To my father, however, it was the deepest of insults. "No wife of *mine*," he said through gritted teeth, "is going to work outside the home! You'd see me *dead* first!" My father was generally an even-tempered man. It was my mother who was typically more volatile, so when he reacted so strongly to her proposal, she was taken aback. She argued with the protests she imagined he was raising. "Evie's in school during the day. I can make your lunch before I leave for work in the morning. Besides, it will only be for a month or so."

"No. Wife. Of mine," he seethed and turned to walk to the machine shop. That was to be the end of it.

A month later, in spite of vowing that he would never work at the sawmill—"that slave yard," he called it—he took a job at Boise Cascade Lumber's power house, where he was a "fireman." He didn't put out fires; rather, being a "fireman" meant he tended the fires that heated the boilers that powered the entire mill. Those fires burned 24/7, whether the saws were running or not. "Stoking the fires of hell," he'd say bitterly. For him Boise Cascade represented the loss of his independence, and he hated the shift work as much as he despised working for a faceless corporation. Although he continued to farm the family's seventy acres, the farm work had to be done during his off hours. He still stubbornly refused my mother's help, either in the fields or with her persistent suggestions she take an outside job. Sometimes he would come home at six in the morning, have coffee and a quick breakfast, and then go out and irrigate until midmorning. If he was on the "relief shift," covering other crew members' shifts, he might have to turn right around and go back to the mill at two that same afternoon. He was tired for the next fifteen years. But the job served his purposes. Not only had our family made our way up from

"working poor" to blue-collar status, but going to work at the mill
had kept my mother from working off the farm. He resented the
mill so deeply, I think, because he would never allow himself to
resent the family that had made that work necessary.

I used to think of my parents' argument about my mother taking an off-farm job as an exertion of my father's power, an attempt
to control the details of her working life and restrict her access to
the economic resources that a more direct relation to the land
might offer. She could wash and cook and sew, but she would not
earn a paycheck any more than she would be an equal partner in
the job of farming the land. Her job was to be decorative, an ap-
preciative audience for the things my father achieved on the farm
like a level field and a good crop. But historian Mary Neth's study
of the family farm suggests that I had it all wrong. According to
Neth the golden age of agriculture (between 1900 and 1940, the
time during which my father was born and came of age) was characterized by reformers looking for ways to professionalize the farm
in the same way that "home economics" would legitimize work
in the home by renaming housekeeping "domestic science." It was
part of a class-conscious effort to empower farm culture as a whole.
Farm magazines, extension agents, farm bureaus, and granges were
all urging reform of the farm-family labor system and adoption of
the "new gender ideology" of a solidly middle-class agribusiness
model in which "farmers became businessmen who managed farms
with brains and technology rather than working their farms with
brawn." Chalking up my father's response to sexism, therefore,
had been an oversimplification on my part. It was not only a matter of masculinity but, argues Neth, a question of whether farmers were modern and progressive. For men "machinery, technology, and scientific methods changed farming from manual labor
to intellectual labor, giving it more middle class status." An essential part of this reform was reconceiving the role of the farmer's

family, relocating the children and especially the wife from the field to the home. By drawing upon traditional notions of separate spheres—an essentially middle-class notion—the woman on the farm went from field worker to domestic laborer because nothing was more telling about the class status of a farm than where a woman did her work. Women who were required to assist their husbands with the harvest in the fields were considered drudges, and by association their husbands were agricultural failures because they depended on the women's labor. Meanwhile, women who could turn their back on the fields served as evidence of their husband's success and superiority.

These ideas were widely promoted by the farm industry and adopted with special eagerness, says Neth, by immigrant farm families, like my own, who were freshly judging their success by American standards. In the same year that Frank Funda moved west, for instance, an Idaho paper ran a story about how in Russia horses and oxen were too expensive for some of the poorer farmers to work their fields, so teams of women were literally harnessed to the plows. This, then, was precisely the image of an Eastern European immigrant's farming practice that my grandfather and father were trying to escape. Allowing women to work in the fields in any capacity would have reflected poorly on Bohemian immigrants, suggesting farming methods that were backward, crude, and unsophisticated. According to Neth the "pin money" that came from women like my mother raising poultry and eggs "on the side" was considered a marker of improved social status because it could buy consumer goods that would improve the quality of family life.

For my father, then, his response to my mother working was a matter of social class, not pure sexism. It was easier to think of himself as a success if his wife stayed within her domestic sphere, no matter what the economic imperatives might be. From Dad's perspective keeping his wife and daughter out of the fields in fact liberated them from drudgery and ensured their status in a class he aspired to. However shortsighted I might think his declaration, my father saw this as progress, a purification of his claim to the land.

Our nation's agricultural system is profoundly hierarchical—and not just in terms of social class or gender politics. A class system even exists among the vegetation itself, a dictatorial order that pits the wild weed (typically cast in the role and rhetoric of "the enemy") against the autocratic king of the farm, the hybrid. Read about the science of plant breeding, and you will find repeated references to the principles of "pedigrees," "line of descent," and "pure-line mentality." The grain seeds that my father poured into the hopper of the seed drill could trace their ancestry back generation by generation. Modern American agriculture is so reliant on the blue bloods of the plant world that Charles E. Saunders was honored with a knighthood in the early part of the twentieth century for his development of a hybrid he called, significantly enough, Marquis wheat. Hybrid stock is meticulously, deliberately developed in environmentally controlled laboratories and then tested on pristine plots of farmland—like the university lots down the hill from my Utah home, where every stock of wheat is a genetic twin of the one next to him. Rows of grain are planted straight and true and come up in lines of handsome uniformity. The field is divided into test plots, just wide enough for one pass of a combine, and the grains in the plots show only subtle variations. In this plot the grain is just a bit taller; in that plot all the seed heads are near maturity earlier than the rest. Signs at the roadside are meant to distinguish these subtle variations with the mystifying gibberish of letters and numbers. But "DeKalb 486h" and the like—codes that indicate a grain's ancestry and sense of identity—have little meaning for me.

Hybridization is all about this toeing the line—this unforgiving conformity of results. Uniformity and predictability are demanded in this new order. Step out of line if you're a hybridized crop, or do something wild and unexpected, and like as not, that'll be the end of you. Your name, a foreign mix of numbers and letters, will be scratched off the clipboard, and you will be exterminated because in the farmer's field difference is contamination.

In general the aim of hybridization is to make a better plant, which can mean breeding out "unwanted" characteristics, and hybridization has resulted in a whole host of crop improvements that have changed the face of farming—most say for the better. Hybridization has been able to breed in higher yield or more resistance to disease and pests; or it has meant improving suitability for specific ecosystems that may face problems of drought, wind, flood, salinity, or high altitudes. In some cases breeders have enhanced the nutritional value or quality of flavor of a crop, or extended its storage time, made it hardier for mechanical harvest and shipping, ensured synchronous harvest and earlier maturity for short seasons and market demand, bred out the annoyances of seeds, pits, and thorns. The irony is that even while uniformity is the only thing tolerated in the field, in the scientist's lab difference is the very thing that hybridization exploits. Darwin called it "descent with modification." This principle, at the heart of plant breeding, recognizes the ubiquity of genetic variation in plants, and then by choosing the characteristics that fit their plans, the scientist uses that variation to human advantage. Too much variety in a field may be considered anarchy—a rebellion to be put down by herbicides—but too little diversity has its own dangers.

In *The Last Harvest: The Genetic Gamble That Threatens to Destroy American Agriculture* Paul Raeburn writes that of the half a million or more species of higher plants presently identified, humans cultivate only about 150. The other plant species may have the majority vote, but they have no conventional value in a commodity-oriented agricultural system. The result, argues Raeburn, is a global "genetic vulnerability," the likes of which once resulted in the disaster of the Irish potato famine. What plant breeders are increasingly finding, even as farmers work to eradicate weeds from their cultivated land, is that wild-crop germ plasm—that is, the genetic makeup of weeds—is a boon to hybridization. Recognizing that weeds have been made stronger by surviving the adverse conditions of their environment, scientists have been able to exploit some of those characteristics. Seed banks at the National Seed Storage Laboratory in Fort Collins and the National Small Grains Collection in my home state of Idaho (located just one hundred miles or so north of where I now live) attempt to preserve the genetic makeup of all plant species, even those that presently have no recognized, conventional value, so that perhaps in some dim future weeds will get their day, at last, in the sterility of the plant breeder's laboratory.

As I see it, my family's history in farming is entangled with the history of hybridization and has been thus colored by the hierarchical principles behind it that judge one plant "suitable" and another plant a "noxious weed." The father of hybridization, Austrian monk Gregor Mendel, who studied the variability of pea plants and published in 1866 *Mendel's Laws of Inheritance*, where he first proposed the idea of "filial" connections among plant descendants, was working out his theories while assigned to an abbey in Brno, Moravia, a town less than forty miles from where my mother's family farmed.

By the time scientists rediscovered Mendel's principles near the turn of the twentieth century and began to put them to practical use on an international level, my father's parents had emigrated to the United States and taken a homestead in southern Idaho, where farmers would discover some crops were not suitable for the Snake River region. Before my grandparents could "prove up" on that inhospitable land, they would buy and move to another farm in Gem County, 150 miles to the northwest, in 1919, just about the time scientists were experimenting with varieties of grains that might have made that first farm more productive.

The first successful hybrid was a corn variety introduced in 1929, when my grandfather was transitioning from raising beans and potatoes to grains (wheat, barley, and corn). Over the next years, as my father and his brother began farming with my grandfather and gradually took over the operation, hybrid varieties of corn and other grains were beginning to replace traditional varieties. Hybridization methods had been successfully applied to all of the other major crop species by the time my parents met and married in the late 1950s. In keeping with the sense in agricultural science that what could never be achieved before was now entirely possible, my farm family felt downright invincible as they increasingly adopted the use of hybrid varieties and all the postwar, chemically dependent methods of farming.

Just as hybridization meant that now each farmer could produce substantially more per acre, my family enlarged their vision of what they could accomplish as farmers. My father and his brother eventually farmed acreage (some leased, some purchased) in two states (Nevada and Idaho) and three Idaho counties (Gem, Ada, and Cascade), where dramatically differing conditions (arid desert near Tonopah, Nevada, and the mountainous high country of Cascade County) drew upon the remarkable variety of hybrids being developed by a science that had entered a brave new world of genetic modification, where plant varieties were manipulated artificially by chemicals, X-rays, radiation, or at the chromosomal level. Given the miraculous tools of modern agriculture, the Funda brothers were convinced that they could compel their land on the northern boundary of the Mojave Desert wilderness to become a viable farm.

By the time I survived the unfavorable conditions of my mother's physiology to be born at the dawn of the 1960s, hybridization had become the sacred cow of American agriculture, and my father was optimistic that the American farmer might actually get the respect he deserved. Scientists who cited the way hybrids could address world hunger were hailing the era as the "Green Revolution"; world agriculture had been transformed and directly affected the food supply of one quarter of the people of the world. As a result Norman Borlaug, who had developed a dwarf wheat variety in 1968 (a variety, by the way, that drew upon the genetic makeup of a variety of wild wheat), was awarded the Nobel Prize in 1970.

However, during the 1970s, while I was busy rebelling against the farm and its expectations for me as a daughter, the national tide was turning. That period would mark a decline—not only in the optimistic vision of what could be accomplished by American agriculture's reliance upon hybrids but in my family's vision of what was possible. For the family, clearly, the Nevada ranch proved a failure, and trying to farm in both Idaho and Nevada was overextending our family's financial and physical resources. It was time to go back to the basics, both for the family (who scaled back the operation to the Gem County property alone) and for some of the nation's agricultural seed companies, which began reaffirming the value of "heirloom" plants—those varieties grown from open-pollinated (nonhybrid) seeds that existed before the widespread proliferation of hybrids after World War II. In the early 1970s the corn-blight disasters forced some scientists to question the advisability of our nation's botanical reliance on such widespread use of a limited number of hybrids. Still, hybrids dominated in the fields, and a hybrid-centric attitude dictated the direction of mainstream agriculture. Farmers advocating less chemical dependency, the use of heirloom varieties, and agricultural biodiversity (including a reconsideration of how we deal with weeds) had now become the revolutionaries, while the hybrid-reliant methods of farmers like my father were now considered "traditional."

Even as my father resigned himself to an off-farm job with the corporate giant Boise Cascade, agribusiness began forcing small farmers out of business and dominating the methods of and philosophical approaches to farming. Since then conglomerate, multinational chemical and seed companies have come to rule with an iron fist. When my father retired from work at the mill, he aimed to return to the true independence of farming, to an existence where his days were guided by the notion that farming was a creative act. He entered instead a world where a farmer's independence had vanished. Seed varieties are now patented, and the companies demand that farmers buying them sign contracts in which they agree not to save the seeds and replant the patented varieties. Scientists have developed "terminator" hybrids, genetically engineered plants that produce only sterile seeds and thereby compel farmers to buy new seed annually from the seed companies. Incorporated into the very DNA ensuring the success of the hybrid seeds are the germs of their own demise. A morality play about my farmer father could not have scripted it more eloquently. Developed back in 1998, these "suicide seeds" have never been put into commercial use, thanks to a United Nations Convention on Biological Diversity in 2000 that questioned how Genetic Use Restriction Technology (or GURT, as it is commonly called) might compromise the rights of farmers around the world to collect and sow their own seeds and then recommended a moratorium on field testing and commercial sale of the technology. But that was only a recommendation. Standard operating procedure in genetic engineering, however, is the use of herbicide-tolerant crops (HTC), that is, varieties bred to resist the "knock-down" of chemicals applied to kill weeds. Playing it like a tease, these hybrids allow the weeds to emerge, even begin to thrive, until the well-timed application of herbicides leaves the hybrids to have the last laugh. Even though this technology is today little more than a decade old, most corn, soybean, canola, and cotton crops in the fields are already in this "Roundup-ready" class of hybrids, which were developed with funding from the very chemical companies who sell the herbicides. With hybrids it's become a case of the tail wagging the dog. Small wonder, then, that in the years since 2001, when my father faced the reality that he could no longer compete in the chemically driven vocation he had so faithfully championed and sold the last of the family's farmland, there has been increasing concern over what some see as agricultural fascism ending the farmers' rights to control what happens on their own farms.

Thomas Jefferson once advocated farming over industrial manufacturing as the proper foundation for American culture because he thought the farmer-citizen would impart an inherent goodness upon the nation. Citing Europe as his example, he argued that industry brought with it cultural decay. He called manufacturers "the class of artificers" and claimed they were "panderers of vice and the instruments by which the liberties of a country are generally overturned." He vehemently declared, "Corruption of morals in the mass of cultivators is a phenomenon of which no age nor nation has furnished an example." But Jefferson couldn't have foreseen the results of the industrialization of farming where profit, not virtue, was the bottom line.

Weeds compromise productivity—that is a given on the farm, an unquestioned assumption as fundamental as the $6 + 7 = 13$ my son worked so hard to master in first grade. However, among scientists devoted to the cause of weed eradication, there are quiet voices of dissent that resist believing weeds are botanical Eves, originators of vegetable sin, daughters of an agricultural fall from grace.

Back in 1964, when I believed that sitting on the tractor fender beside my father gave me a kind of ownership of the land, a little-known book was published by Joseph Cocannouer entitled *Weeds: Guardians of the Soil.* Claiming his as "the first book to be written in *praise* of weeds," Cocannouer dares to suggest that weeds may well be "of inestimable value to mankind." A perspective like this one, he acknowledges, is akin to heresy among most farmers, but, he argues, weeds perform a number of valuable services, for instance, transforming alkaline hardpan soil into tillable land and making important minerals and trace elements available in depleted topsoil. These services are so valuable that he advocates the perspective of looking at weeds benignly as companion plants, partners that can actually nurture healthy growth in crops. "Mother weeds," he calls them.

Hypocrite that I am, however, I write about the value of weeds but am inconsistent in my treatment of them in my own yard. I pry up dandelion roots and pull morning glory out of the vegetable garden. I rage at the puncture vine that, despite my best efforts, keeps coming back year after year by the compost pile, and as I go so far as to consider an herbicidal application, I curse the farmer who gave me the bale of straw that seeded the weed here in the first place. But each time I dig up common mallow, or what my family used to call buttonweed, I remember with great fondness how childhood friends and I used to hunt for and eat the plant's disklike seeds, which are enclosed like tiny little gifts in a soft, green wrapping. I leave alone the mats of purslane that spread under the tomatoes, and sometimes I even pinch off one of their rubbery leaves and chew the citrus-tasting flesh. I rather like the little patches of fragrant wild violets that dot my lawn in early spring, even though local master gardeners warn these weeds will take over my lawn, if I let them. The mint that I brought from Idaho and transplanted into a corner flower bed, on the other hand, has become so invasive that I consider it a weed, even though I like the tea it makes, which reminds me of my herbalist grandmother. I'm happy to give starts of the herb to friends who ask for some—but, fully knowing the plant's unruly nature, I always warn, "You'll cuss me someday!" And some of them have.

The bitterest argument my husband ever had with my father was over us planting staghorn sumac next to the south fence of our yard. We had admired the ornamental shrub's red fall foliage and the orange clusters of seeds that lasted the winter, but my father thought of it as a pernicious weed. "Je-sus Christ!" he bellowed. "I spend my whole life digging that shit out of my ditches, and you go and plant it in the yard cuz," he mocked, "ya think it's '*pretty*'!" Riled by the challenge, Mark told my father to mind his own business, and I actually feared the two were going to come to blows. Now, almost ten years later, I feel a bit sheepish about the whole thing when I annually pull out the volunteer suckers that come up from the sumac rhizomes all over the back flower bed. It's all a matter of your perspective, I guess.

According to my 1914 weed manual, most of the plants Mark and I chose for our drought-tolerant perennial bed were once classified as weeds: goldenrod, black-eyed Susan, purple coneflower (echinacea), sunflower, tickseed (coreopsis), blanket flower (gaillardia), yarrow, yellow chamomile, purple sage, bachelor's button, evening primrose. Plants once thought inelegant, they are now valued for their pluck and their ability to survive in adverse conditions. Their deep colors flourish in my yard, and even as I take pride in their masses, I wonder if I should confess this idolatry: "Bless me, father, for I have planted weeds."

I linger over the weed manual as if it were an enthralling story in which I can't help but sympathize with the misunderstood villain. The names listed in the manual certainly evoke compelling narratives of conflict and hope: stinking willie, stagger-bush, spreading dogbane, hogwort, sundrops, creeping bugleweed, deadly nightshade, apple of Peru, poverty weed, winged ironweed, gall-of-the-earth, sweet everlasting, and on and on. Hath not a weed beauty, affections, passions?

Consider, too, the plaintive name of dyer's woad, a plant that decorates empty lots and mountainsides alike near my northern Utah home with waist-high foliage and neon yellow sprays of cheerful flowers that sway in the canyon winds. Although its name suggests an unhappiness so dreadful that it took a redundancy to express it (I used to think it was dire's woe), the yellow-flowered plant's name actually comes from its use, dating back to medieval times, as a natural way to dye fabric, oddly enough, a beautiful violet-blue that we call French blue. With a distinguished history dyer's woad is considered an "elite" dye in Europe, where royalty were buried in woad-dyed cloth, laws were once written to protect the woad textile industry from being usurped by the indigo dyes from the East, and Queen Elizabeth I had to issue a proclamation against sowing woad—not because it was considered a weed but because farmers were cultivating the lucrative woad instead of cereal crops during a time of increasing food shortages. In the "Blue Triangle" region of the south of France it was said during the Middle Ages that those who cultivated woad could simply lie back in the sun and watch their money grow. Even today in France woad continues to have its own "Academy of Arts and Sciences," which promotes the rich historical and artistic heritage of the plant. Still cultivated throughout Europe, the plant has enjoyed a resurgence in popularity as people interested in natural dyeing techniques have become increasingly fascinated by how the dye works. After a complex extraction process the dye looks like diluted yellow water (think urine); however, when the textiles are taken from the dipping vats and exposed to oxygen in the air, in a matter of minutes the fabric miraculously turns from pale yellow to green and finally to the distinctive French blue. Textile artisans reverently call the transition "alchemy."

Yet in the Rocky Mountain region this very same plant is a villain with a price on its head. Cultivating it is illegal, and farming-related agencies consider it a dangerous, invasive weed that has caused millions of dollars' worth of damage to ecosystems abutting cropland. County extension agencies urge citizens to report it to a weed hotline when they see the plant spreading into new territories. A cooperative of Idaho and northern Utah weed management agencies has even set up a "bounty" system for the collection of woad plants pulled or dug up from rural areas, and they aim their "bag o' woad" programs at children by distributing colorful pamphlets punctuated with promises of riches (ten dollars per forty-pound bag) and a series of ominous puns about having "woad rage" and being "a woad warrior." The same plant that is revered in the south of France is thus vilified where I live.

For weeds success is a matter of location and timing. Consider, for instance, the reviled kudzu weed that is regarded as a pernicious, invasive pest in the Southeast, where locals joke that if you leave the house for a weekend vacation, kudzu will cover it over by the time you get back. Others warn that planting kudzu is grounds for "justifiable homicide" in some neighborhoods. That, however, is just the opinion of the day, according to Alan Burdick, who reminds us that "American gardeners of the late 1800s embraced its fragrant blossoms. In the 1920s it was promoted for its potential as livestock forage, and in the 1930s the Soil Conservation Service planted it widely for erosion control." It wasn't until 1972, Burdick writes, that the Department of Agriculture declared it a weed, thus placing kudzu among the ranks of species that have been "othered" and identified ominously as "aliens." Such species "do pose a threat," he admits. "But their real crime isn't against nature; it's against us and our self-serving ideas of what nature is supposed to be."

For most weeds, like dyer's woad, kudzu, or dodder, life is all about packing your bags and heading out for new territory. It's about counting on the promise that if not here, maybe the next place or the next time. A weed, by definition, is a plant that isn't valued where it grows, which, to my mind, always leaves open the possibility—that great dream of the transplanted, the pioneer— of finding a place where you're allowed to flourish.

My father understood the empirical end product: that which can be weighed at the end of a season in tons, its volume calculated in bushels, and its quality "graded"—that is, judged by impartial, definite standards of certification that are set by federal laws regulating interstate commerce (including the size of the seed head, its shape and density, weight per bushel, percentage of moisture content, and weed seed contamination calculated down to parts per million). What my father accomplished over the course of a year could be reaped by mammoth machines and then stored in granaries bigger than our house.

What I do, on the other hand, can be compactly contained on these, the insubstantial leaves of a few pages. What I do is cultivate the ephemeral, the evanescent, the contradictory. I produce no real product—not the kind of commodity my father could measure and value by any standards he knew. I remember a refrain from my childhood that my parents sang to me, one I still croon when I want to tease my now-teenage son—a sing-songy little tune that rocks back and forth like a scythe: "I love you / a bushel and a peck / a bushel and a peck and a hug around the neck." That's the way a farmer thinks: in terms of how things—even the abstract—can be weighed and measured. A peck is eight quarts, or more than 537 cubic inches, and a bushel is four pecks, or 2,150.42 cubic inches in US dry measure. More than 2,000 cubic inches of love. I should have felt lucky.

Instead, being a farm daughter made me feel like a weed, plucked and tossed aside before I could set my roots too deep. These days I teach literature at an "Aggie" school in Utah, one of those universities set up by the nineteenth-century Morrill land grant act with the expressed dual mission of making practical application of scientific principles to the real world of agriculture and educating first-generation college students in rural areas. In the year 2000, as a promise that the institution would remain true to those missions into the twenty-first century, the then-president of my university vowed to milk a cow in every county of the state—a gesture that should have reassured me. Instead I felt again that old panic, that need to distance myself from such quaint gestures before my red face betrays my real roots. Even at this Aggie school located in an agricultural valley, I worry that someone is going to recognize that I'm only a farm daughter, feigning my way into the field of academe, to be routed out by fire and acid.

At the end of Willa Cather's novel *O Pioneers!* as sweethearts Carl Linstrum and Alexandra Bergson discuss their intended marriage, Carl demonstrates a significant understanding and acceptance of Alexandra's devotion, first and foremost, to the land. He admits, "You belong to the land. . . . Now more than ever." The real love affair of Cather's novel is Alexandra's love of the prairie fields that she helped transform from a wild place into a productive homestead; however, Cather's heroine confesses that loving the land has come with costs that include family discord and loneliness. Complicating Carl's romanticized vision, Alexandra underscores that human claims to land are fleeting. Noting that fifty years hence many owners will likely be listed in the county records for that land, she concludes, "We come and go, but the land is always here. And the people who love it and understand it are the people who own it—for a little while."

Today I own the two acres where my parents' home sits, but my name never appeared on the deed of my family's Idaho farmland. It was my legacy but never my inheritance. Rather, it was sold to a wealthy couple from out of state who envisioned that ground as the perfect place for a sprawling home. They weren't attracted by the flat, tillable cropland that my father, his brother, and father had worked so hard to create during their tenure there. Instead the couple wanted the mountain view, the pond, and some vague notion of a rural lifestyle that they thought came with the land. They envisioned settling there for good, but I could have told them there's no such thing.

2

Loosestrife

"Exiles feed on hope."

AESCHYLUS

In January the fields of my family's farm lie colorless and bare. This is arid country, so any cover of snow to offer modesty is rare. Instead the land is exposed and raw, with the stubble of last year's crop looking as gray as a corpse.

I doubt my father ever saw it that way, though. For him January meant a time to begin envisioning the hope of the next year, and the fields were canvases that would paint themselves green and then gold. January was only a sigh before the faultless expanse of tawny wheat, the straight-backed dignity of corn, and the lush tumble of emerald clover dotted with amethyst blossoms.

Although an act of burial, planting a seed ironically obliges us to the future, and for my father there was always promise in that. I grew up fed on hope. Speculation about this year's crop was passed around at dinner along with the mashed potatoes. "If I can just get a decent yield this year," my father would begin as he pushed aside his dinner plate so he could scratch figures on a seed company notepad with a stubby pencil—bushels per acre multiplied by his vision. "If the price will just hold" was always his amen. This was my catechism.

Lumir Funda was born in 1922, just after the 1920 census had determined that more than half of the nation's population was, for the first time, living in urban areas rather than rural ones. The world he was born into, therefore, was a world transitioning away from farming. Lumir, however, spent his life bucking that trend. The year before he graduated from high school, the US Department of Agriculture (USDA) released its yearbook, ominously titled *Farmers in a Changing World*, yet the following year Lumir's own 1941 high school yearbook insisted he was "just a farmer at heart." No threat of change, no amount of peril, financial or physical, could change that. Still, he figured he had to adapt, so after his high school graduation he went off to enroll in a degree program at the University of Idaho, where he planned to study chemical or mechanical engineering—either a vocation that he thought would keep him at the forefront of modern farming. By the time he'd finished his first year of college, however, the nation was at war, and his father, Frank, was facing a long period of recovery from a serious farm accident that spring in which he had been thrown from a tractor and fractured his hip. So Lumir came home on an agricultural deferment to take over the farm, though I suspect he was secretly happy to return to the farm. After the war he started a custom-farming business—farming the family land in the hours between plowing and planting other people's farms. He was the hired man on the Van Deusen ranch in northern Gem County for a while after he and my mother first married. In addition to farming the homeplace, he and his brother leased land in nearby Cascade and Ada counties. When those efforts proved unprofitable by the late 1950s, they bought a ranch in remote Tonopah, Nevada, a place known less known for agriculture than it is for mining, legalized prostitution, development of the Stealth Bomber, and being the gateway to Death Valley and the Nevada Test Site at Yucca Flats, where mushroom clouds bloomed above Joshua tree deserts. At more than six thousand feet in elevation the arid desert around Tonopah is a hostile environment. My father and his brother were among the very first to try to farm anywhere in the desert that stretched the four hundred miles between Reno and Las Vegas, and even today, with drilled wells and significant technological advances in irrigation, the entire Tonopah Basin claims only a half dozen farms, and Nye County, the third-largest county in the entire nation, has fewer than fifty thousand people within its whole eighteen thousand square miles. But Dad didn't recognize the remoteness or the barrenness of the Tonopah Ranch, and he could never understand why he couldn't convince my mother to go live on the place. "Go there and find yourself *two* squaws," she would threaten him, "because I am *not* moving there!"

For my father the promise of the next year or the next field could erase the memory of the latest setback. Like any good cowboy, when Lumir was thrown, he got right back into the saddle— or, should I say, right back into the tractor seat.

I mean this quite literally. Sometime in the early 1960s I remember my father coming home one day bruised and battered from a custom-farming job on the Van Deusen Ranch, nearly twenty miles up into the isolated foothill country north of our farm. His face was all scratched up, and his wrist was swollen to twice its normal size—not just sprained but broken, we would realize before the night was over. As he iced the wrist, he told us about how he'd been bucked from the tractor while he was harrowing. He'd landed at the bottom of an old draw in the middle of the field where he lay, unconscious, as the tractor drove steadily on in wide circles, dragging behind it the spike harrow, a farm implement made of two low broad frames chained together that rake over the soil and break up any clods left from plowing and disking. As my father regained consciousness, he said, he saw the harrow bed sweep back over him and the tractor tires just miss his legs. He tried to shake off his daze and get up, but before he could, the tractor and harrow came back around. Again the tractor narrowly missed him, and the harrow bounced over the draw, where he flattened himself into the dirt. Just before the third pass he struggled to his feet and scrambled up out of the way.

His wrist was starting to throb, but at the moment he had a bigger problem: how to stop the tractor. There wasn't another soul to help him within miles, so he was on his own. He thought about just letting the tractor continue to circle until it ran out of fuel, but that could take hours, and he could see that the circle was getting just a bit bigger with each pass. The tractor was already coming dangerously close to a drop-off at the edge of the field. If he wanted to save it from dropping more than ten feet into a creek bed, he had no choice but to try to stop it before it went over that edge. He waited for the tractor and harrow to pass by him again, and then he darted into the circle, where he started to run alongside and then in front of the big rear tires. He couldn't possibly jump back onto the tractor. He knew that. But what he had decided to try was to reach up and hit the throttle lever up with his hand to kill the engine. He was still too dazed to realize how dangerous this plan was, dodging the tires, but after two failed attempts he succeeded in bringing the tractor to a standstill. Shaken and winded, he left it standing right where it was, walked back to his truck, and drove himself home. "If I'd a been disking instead of harrowing," he said matter-of-factly, referring to the steel-bladed implement farmers use to slice through soil after plowing, "I'd be dead." That night he splinted his wrist and took a handful of aspirin. The next day he went back to the Van Deusen to finish the job.

Another time up at the Van Deusen he'd been combining a field of grain when his old truck, parked at the field's edge, caught fire. By the time he saw the smoke and ran back through the stubble, the fire had engulfed the cab. He swatted at the flames with nothing more than the shirt off his back, desperate to put out the blaze before a spark could light the field of tinder-dry grain or the barrel of diesel fuel he'd been hauling in the bed of the truck. Afterward he always expressed more bewilderment about how the fire had started than concern about the danger he'd been facing, and whenever he told the story of that fire, he would puzzle it out again. His best guess was that a Mason jar of water in the cab had magnified the sun's rays onto gas-soaked rags that he'd thrown on the cab floor. For years he grieved the loss of that old truck, which he'd always joked was so noisy that the dog could hear him coming from a mile away and would set up barking to let us know that he was on his way home.

Dangers like these just came with the job, and they never stopped my father from loving what he did. He had a rough scar on his face from his lip to his chin where barbed wire had once snapped in the fencing stretcher and clawed his face. He'd been lucky, he'd say, that it hadn't been worse.

Shortly after Mark and I moved to northern Utah in the mid-1990s, my mother began begging my father to retire from farming their small piece of ground. He was well past retirement age and had begun to struggle for each breath. While his doctor called it asthma, Dad, who had smoked for forty years, was no doubt listening for the echo of emphysema that had already claimed his father and his older brother. Still he worked like one possessed, coming in from the fields wheezing and dripping with sweat. My mother had long expressed her fear: "I'm going to find you dead in a cornfield"—words that she spat out at him like a bitter gooseberries. It was about as self-revealing as she got, my stoic mother, and I couldn't help but picture it: Toni pacing in aggravation when he doesn't come in to eat on time, even after she honks the car horn—their usual signal—several times. Cursing in her native Czech and muttering, "He knows damn good and well that lunch is at noon, damn him!" Finding the pickup at the gate. Trudging the pipeline back and forth to see where he'd gone into the field and calling out into the thick stand of corn. Sensing a stab of panic at her heart (should she call for the neighbors?). And finally spotting out of the corner of her eye the telling glint of his sharpened shovel from deep in the field's darkness.

Until I imagined her fear in this way, I had resisted, like Dad himself, the idea of him retiring. "What's he going to do, Mom?" I would argue. "He has no hobbies, other than that once-a-year fishing trip. He'll sit around the house watching TV and hounding you to play cards with him all day. It'll drive you nuts. Farming is just what he does. Let him do it."

I knew that crop prices hadn't been good in recent years. In 1999 the crop had been clover seed, which had brought a good yield but no price. "The kind of price I used to get thirty or forty years ago," my father complained during one of our Sunday-afternoon phone calls. My mother's silence on the extension was ominous. Once you factored in the higher cost of spraying, property taxes, and harvesting, the bottom line was a loss. But I had willed myself to imagine that this loss was negligible—worth it, I reasoned, because farming still occupied his mind and body in the way nothing else could.

So when my parents came to Utah for Christmas in 2000 and announced that they had made the decision to sell the farmland, I wasn't entirely surprised. My mother expressed relief; my father was resigned, saying only that he would insist that the realtor make clear that no buyer could build directly east of their house, where a rising roofline would obstruct his view from the dining room table. I cringed and tried gently to suggest that it would be within the rights of whoever bought the land to do with it what they pleased. "If someone buys that land, they're going to want to build a house," I told him, but he wouldn't hear of it.

"No one is going to block my view," he answered flatly.

The metal sign was planted at the edge of his clover field near the highway in early January, like the flag of a New Year's resolution that, in your heart of hearts, you don't want to make. And my father haltingly confessed over the phone, "I kinda hate to see that thing out there in the field." Every morning, as he sat at the table drinking coffee and eating a sausage patty with two eggs over easy, that sign out to the east reminded him that not everything was routine. There was no escaping that the ground was for sale.

That part of the Emmett farm had been nothing more than a plot of sagebrush when my grandfather purchased it for next to nothing in 1919. Compared to Frank's original homestead more than a hundred miles to the south, this land held promise; in the early part of the century sagebrush was thought to indicate a rich soil that could be easily converted to farming. It was relatively flat and tillable land, and once the deed was Frank's, he set to helping engineer the bench canal system extension that would make this land that fronted the barren foothills flourish. Eventually water rushed down the ditches, a run-off pond was excavated in a slight draw, and when my father and his brother took over farming, they landplaned the ground to smooth out any final imperfections until it lay flat and beautiful, and the irrigation corrugates ran from one end of the field to the other, water moving straight and true like ribbons of silver among sprouting crops.

My parents always called this place "the ground"—not "our land" or "the property" or "the acreage" in the way most people refer to rural parcels they own. Rarely did they ever say "the farm" and never "the ranch." This place—with the barbed-wire fence framing the fields and the "No Hunting" signs nailed to the weathered posts and the gated pipe gleaming silver at the north end of each field—this place was just "the ground." Make no mistake: that was not a term of indifference, but rather the unquestioned premise of a syllogism. This is family homeplace, in the way the planet Earth—not named like the other planets for any flamboyant Greek god—is home to a species, in the way Indian tribal names, like Hopi, translate simply and literally as "the people," as if existence were a given and there were no other place or people imaginable.

Chuck, my parents' realtor, promised the acreage would go quickly. Within an hour's drive of Boise, Emmett had become a commuter town. The price of the land was right in a decent market, the run-off pond certainly was appealing, and they had done the impossible by securing a building permit from the county. That alone, Chuck assured my parents, added significant value. With the building permit Chuck envisioned luring an out-of-state buyer who would be attracted to the twenty-acre parcel, big enough for a horse pasture and a house, but not big enough to demand a full-time farmer or offer him a subsistence wage.

My homeland was in the midst of a land-use transition, a pattern played out throughout the West. Farmland was becoming "exurbia" or "ruralesque" (not burlesque, mind you). Houses are situated on large lots, and new residents draw upon a pastoral idyll to valorize and reenact a modern gentrification on what are variously called "lifestyle farms," "farmettes," "ranchettes," or "hobby farms" (this last term also being the name of a magazine catering to those people envisioning such lives). In this "rurban" world they seek to gain a more authentic relation to a country landscape and a natural environment. Calling these new residents "exurbanites," Kirsten Valentine Cadieux writes that they "fetishize agriculture" and make an agrarian lifestyle a commodity able to be purchased, right alongside the washer and dryer or

miniblinds listed on the real estate inclusions; however, exurbanites demand many of the amenities afforded by urban centers,
such as satellite television and high-speed internet and gyms within a five-minute drive. And exurbia is, writes Cadieux, the fastest-
growing land-use segment in the United States. Therefore the
land of my childhood can now be categorized as "the rural-urban
fringe" in which "neo-agrarians" are involved in "co-optation of
'real' farmer identities and plights." The phenomenon is fraught
with contradictions: "subdivisions with farm related names but
covenants and restrictions against vegetable gardens and livestock,"
acre-large lawns that have replaced agricultural-use lands, and
sites where the "symbols of production" (Cadieux cites the pe-
rennially favored wagon wheels that decorate these farms) are
privileged while the real and messy productive processes of a farm
and farm yard are kept out of sight.

The development of Idaho land, from volcanoes and glaciers
to development of the soil to the time that the sagebrush emerged,
had all taken millennia. In the span of my grandfather's lifetime
that land had gone from sagebrush to productive farm, and in the
span of my father's lifetime that newly emerged farmland saw its
heyday and then just as quickly began to be devoured by people
who demanded other things of that land: a view, privacy, a rural
retreat, rustic without roughing it, symbols of an agrarian past.

Aware of this dilemma and reluctant to let productive farmland
outside of town be eaten up by hungry housing developers, the
Gem County government long maintained a policy that disallows
farmers parceling out their land for new homes. Owners battled
to get permits, but road by road from the outskirts of town, the
commissioners relented over the years. Just south of our farm there
used to be a quiet expanse of wheat. By January of 2001 it had
been split up into an odd mix of manufactured homes next to
grand, custom-built "McMansions" with their huge, two-story,

glassed-in entryways, or their faux Alpine architecture, or their three-car garages with attached boat bay. As the land became increasingly carved up into parcels too small for farming, the county commissioners had been forced to sanction such building. Legislation followed reality.

Hoping, I think, that Dad would look infirm, Chuck took him to a Monday-night county commissioners' meeting, so that he could argue, with Dad as obvious evidence, that my father was too old to farm the land, which was his only financial investment, and that my parents should not be financially forced to sell the home they had built on what was originally part of property owned by my grandfather, a recognized figure in the history of farming on the North Bench. Chuck had told my father he would be expected to make a personal plea at the meeting, a fact that made my typically loquacious father nervous. He loved to "visit" for hours with the neighbors or old friends or even just the Schwan man who came by once a month to deliver his two gallons of strawberry ice cream, but the thought of giving a "speech" in front of elected officials petrified him. Months after his death I would find the pad of lined paper where he had outlined his remarks in preparation: that his lung doctor had advised he stop farming and had "threatened," as my father wrote in shaky script, to put him on oxygen; that the small acreage wasn't doing anything to supplement his small pension from the sawmill; that he and my mother wanted only to stay in the modest house they had built in 1972 and retain less than three acres of "non-farmable ground" where he had his shop and farm machinery. The speech was apparently persuasive; the county commissioners granted the building permit.

With the planting of the sign on the edge of Dad's clover field that read "For Sale, Emmett Realty," my parents' twenty acres joined the league of other small lots—some with, some without attendant building permits—that were for sale in the area. When Mark, four-year-old Jake, and I came up to visit in late spring, I was struck by how many "For Sale" signs were posted at the margins of fields—ten acres here, twenty there. We couldn't help but compare. The people across the road were moving out of state: twenty acres for sale (with house, outbuildings, and recently added pool—and a quarter-of-a-million-dollar price tag that would dissuade most). The land that abutted Dad's to the east had been posted after the farmer, someone I went to school with, committed suicide last winter over an impending divorce (twenty acres of ground that needed leveling, no building permit). Another place up by the irrigation canal where friends and I used to swim had been listed by the family after their widowed mother died the previous winter (twenty weedy neglected acres, poor soil, no building permit, no pond, but asking the same price as my parents, Chuck pointed out confidently). And there were a dozen others within a ten-mile radius. Mark and I counted as we drove the highways that loop around the valley. Ten acres over on Mesa Road (but the view of the Squaw Butte to the north and Bogus Basin ski resort way off to the east wasn't as good as Dad's view from the dining room). Half a dozen twenty-acre lots were scattered down in the salt flats southwest of town (unproductive, mosquito-ridden land that wouldn't be much competition). These were all little patches of land broken up by family dramas, some no doubt similar to ours, parcels now too small for subsistence farming. Change had taken root in this place and spread like some unstoppable weed. And I felt torn between the hope that my parents would find buyers willing to release my father from his obsession with this ground and an unaccountable dread.

Back in Utah I confessed my concern to a friend that the land wouldn't sell, but she was surprised by my worry and asked if *I* didn't want that land. "It's your heritage. You could build a house there someday," she argued. But I could only reply feebly that my parents needed the money—leaving unsaid how bereft the sale would indeed make me, both for losing the land itself, that plotted-out piece of ground marked by survey coordinates, and for losing some place that claimed me.

After that conversation I spent more than an hour at the computer trying to track down the realtor's web listing for the place. Dad had told me he'd given Chuck pictures of the clover field, the pond, and the view of Squaw Butte to post on his website. But all I could find in this surreal cyber landscape were the words, the flat, generalized description of what I thought was my parents' land but what sounded much like a handful of others listed on the same website: "Twenty acres available in Emmett, Idaho. Level. Mountain views, pond." Less than a dozen words meant to entice a buyer, but they couldn't communicate what it meant for my father to be giving up the ground where he had annually buried seed in certainty of harvest.

Farming and financial hardship go hand in hand—every farmer knows that. My father collected irreverent caps over the years that made light of the certainty of poverty in farming; one read, "My heart is in farming but my ass is in debt!" and another joked, "If Dolly Parton were a farmer, she'd be flat-busted too!" When some other farmer he knew came to the back door, he would don the newest of these caps, grin, and calculate how long before they noticed. Of course, these were inside jokes, meant only for those who knew firsthand the gallows humor of being "flat-busted" on the farm.

My parents' ground had been posted "for sale" for months without any response when the midyear property taxes and the irrigation bill for the farm came due in June. Property values had steadily risen with the popularity of the town, and what had always been a financial burden was impossible to pay during the summer of 2001. I didn't know this, however, until our late June visit when my mother whispered to me, "We need to talk."

"We borrowed the money from Jo," she told me after we'd cleared the supper dishes from the table. JoLynn and her husband, Eddie, had lived across the road from my parents for years, during the period when Eddie farmed a few acres and worked in the valley as a heavy equipment operator. Nearly every Sunday for a decade they ate Sunday dinner at our table and lingered over coffee for hours after. I babysat their kids, we helped each other with the chickens at butchering time, and after Sunday supper Jo didn't have to be told where the clean dishes belonged. They were, in other words, as good as family. "Your dad didn't want to," my mother continued, "but Jo kept offering, and finally he said yes. I was so relieved."

"But you never said a word to *me* about needing money for the property taxes," I protested. Even as I said it, I felt petty, but I persisted, "Why didn't you ask us?"

"Because we knew you'd have a hard time coming up with the money."

"We could have done it, though," I argued, knowing even as I said it how much Mark would have complained about a cash advance on the credit card for the farm's tax bill.

"Yes, but it would have been hard for you," my mother said. "And I told your dad that we sure as hell weren't going to borrow it from Gladys, no matter what!" My mother often complained that Dad's sister would "lord it over us" if she sent them money or bought them gifts. One year she had given him a little, beat-up Toyota "farm truck" that she had spray-painted baby blue. The color inspired several jokes among my father's friends, who all drove big black or white Chevy or Dodge pickups, and Dad was always fiddling with the engine to keep it running, but my aunt always talked about how cute that little truck was. "Don't you like it?" she would say with a whine if she didn't feel he expressed sufficient gratitude. So I understood my mother's dictum: borrowing money from Gladys was not an option.

"Jo kept saying that the money was just sitting in their account," my mother continued. "We might as well use it. They refused to even charge us interest. Evie, I want you to know this. We owe Jo and Eddie fifteen hundred dollars. If anything happens to us, make sure they get paid."

"I know, Mom." I squirmed with discomfort.

"Just as soon as that land gets sold, we'll pay them back. Your dad made up a note that says we owe them."

"You'll pay it back soon," I assured her with false cheer.

But I was nursing an old resentment. Even though Jo had been like another daughter to my mother after her own mother died years before, I knew it must have pained my father to admit that their crops didn't even bring in enough to pay the taxes, most especially to Eddie. For years after I moved away from Emmett, my father had cited to me on a regular basis how much money Jo and Eddie were making. Whether Eddie was working in Emmett as a backhoe operator or had taken a construction job in Alaska and then later in Las Vegas, my father kept me up to date on how much per month Eddie was bringing in. When Eddie and Jo returned to Emmett valley to retire in their early fifties, my father bragged about how they had managed such a feat of finance. If their names came up in any of our Sunday phone conversations, the latest news on their economic status was sure to follow. I didn't resent their success, but I certainly resented my father's constant reference to it. "Is money all you ever talk about with them?" I snapped at him once when he told me how much Eddie was making per hour in Vegas. Certainly, when I talked to Eddie or Jo, money was never the main topic, and I couldn't help but feel that my father cited these figures to me in order to communicate how meager was my own salary as a teacher.

But now I wondered if, frankly, it wasn't a matter of Dad being envious himself of Eddie's financial success. Like Eddie he had been good with heavy equipment, had operated plenty of machinery in his day. Was he was regretting choices he'd made, perhaps thinking that, had things been different, he might now be "sitting on Easy Street," as he said of Eddie and Jo, instead of borrowing money from them to pay the taxes?

In July, after seven months on the market, my parents had potential buyers, a couple from Alaska, looking to build in Emmett, where they planned to enjoy their early retirement. Their retirement at fifty-something, we all realized, would allow my father to spend his eightieth year getting used to the idea himself.

The couple came twice to slog through irrigated fields and check the perimeter of an L-shaped section of land that cupped the small ground where my parents would continue to live. Dad and Mom, characteristically as generous as they were curious, offered them unending cups of coffee and buckets of this year's plums and last year's abundant walnut crop from the orchard. In return they got snippets of a story and, they hoped, the beginnings of a neighborly friendship. The woman told my parents they wanted to build a ranch home—"nothing fancy," she assured—back by the pond. My father was relieved that his view would be spared. The buyers said the pond was the clincher, and they planned to dig out the silt that had built up over years and restore it to its glory. They envisioned fishing with their toddler granddaughter and hosting winter skating parties. They were also planning to build a corral for horses and fence in the remainder as an alfalfa field for hay.

"Horses!" my mother snorted after they left. "I'll be *surrounded* by them!" And she was right. What had once been land devoted to a crop—wheat, barley, corn, alfalfa, and clover seed—had been invaded by a flashy foreigner: the hobby farmer who makes his living outside of agriculture, like the neighbor who commuted to a job as a business manager forty miles away and who had five horses that were never ridden—as my mother *tsked* indignantly— except for once a year in the Cherry Festival Parade. People for whom farming was not a living income were transforming the look of the landscape, and rural life had become a decorating choice that meant stripped cow skulls and old pitchforks hung on new red barns.

When the Alaskan couple first began to seriously look at the twenty acres, I asked my mother if she had told Jo the news that someone was interested in the property. "Absolutely not!" my mother answered. "We owe them money. I'm not going to jinx it." The loan for the taxes, I realized, was getting in the way of what had always been an easy relationship.

"But Mom," I argued, "she'd be happy for you. She'd want to know." But my mother shook her head.

Even when my parents received an offer to buy the land and entered into the period of negotiation, they stayed mum when Eddie and Jo drove out weekly for their visits. When they accepted an offer and began discussing a settlement date with the buyers, my mother still refused to say a word to Jo. When we came up again in July, just after the acceptance, she swore me to secrecy. "I want to have the money in my hand," she explained in hushed tones one day as we saw Eddie and Jo's pickup pull into the drive.

Mark, Jake, and I were in Idaho to witness the "perk test," one of the final conditions of the sale to the Alaskan buyers. Necessary for all new building permits in the county, the test determines a site's suitability for installing a new sewage drainfield by gauging the soil's ability to percolate water. Too much hardpan clay or a hardpan layer that comes too close to the water table means land that won't drain properly. If that happened, the Alaskan couple would never be able to get their building permit, and very likely the whole sale would be called off.

The soil was still damp from a recent irrigating when the back-hoe operator drove out into the middle of my father's clover field. My father, concerned about the heavy equipment tearing up his corrugates, planned to follow Chuck and the geologist out to the site the geologist had selected, but when Dad complained he was too "winded" to walk very far, Jake and I rode in the truck with him to the middle of the field, bouncing over corrugates in the back of the truck bed. Almost immediately, mosquitoes, which had taken refuge in the damp field of clover, were biting us, even in the bright sun of midmorning. Jake, however, was focused on the backhoe. "Dad's missing this," he wailed as he glanced across the field toward the house, where, at my mother's request, Mark was sawing down dead tree limbs on an elm tree in front of the house. It wasn't just that Jake loved heavy equipment or "erf mov-ers," as he called them. He seemed to sense how this was an im-portant event in the life of our family, and he wanted his dad there. Bucket by bucket the backhoe skimmed off the topsoil, and as the machine went deeper than anything my father's plow had ever turned over, I could hardly believe this land would no longer be ours. It felt like we were unearthing secrets, private intimacies that no one else should see. As the backhoe hit the clay soil of Idaho hardpan just two and a half feet below the damp surface of my father's irrigated field, Chuck and the geologist began mak-ing bets on how deep the hardpan layer would go.

Dad didn't join into the banter, however. He was leaning heav-ily against the open door of the truck and rubbing his forehead. When he looked up and saw me watching him, he said only, "Headache." He'd been complaining about headaches for a few weeks now, something the rest of us chalked up to the stress of the sale. "He'll be better," my mother said, "when he's got the check." My father, on the other hand, had become unwilling to talk about what this sale meant to him at all. He was as resistant as the heavy clay soil itself that now slowed the progress of the test hole. The backhoe groaned and struggled to scrape up buckets full of the sticky clay earth. "I'm going to go take an aspirin," my father said at last and climbed back into the pickup just as Mark casually walked up to join us. Chuck's cell phone rang. Mentally, he was already moving on to the next big deal. Half an hour later and at six and a half feet below the surface, the backhoe broke through the hardpan to the sandy layer of soil below. The geologist, who had predicted they'd hit sand before seven feet, looked self-satisfied and grinned over at Chuck, who shrugged a good-natured defeat. The geologist poured several gallons of water into the hole and then timed how long it took for the pool of water to disappear and percolate through the soil. When the results satisfied him, he nodded in Chuck's direction. The sale was going to move forward.

After the successful perk test my mother suggested we celebrate with a nice dinner at a favorite restaurant over the state line in Ontario, Oregon. As we drove along the lower valley roads, we could see masses of brilliant purple flowers wherever there was the trickle of a stream or ditch. Purple loosestrife, an aggressive, fast-spreading weed, had invaded the valley, transforming ponds and riverways completely.

As we drove from Emmett through Payette, along the backroads through the lower salt flats, and on across the river to Ontario, we indicated to each other, with guilty expressions of delight, particularly impressive stands of purple loosestrife in ditches and along marshes, where with broad strokes of color the invasive weed had revised the still-life painting of the valley. I wondered how such glorious masses of flowers can bear such a disconsolate name. The notion of strife, with its tendrils of discord, chaos, and sorrow, seemed so incongruent with this showy plant.

My botanical books note no utilitarian, no medicinal or nutritional values for the opportunistic plant. But there is no arguing that this temptress has about it a purple vitality, an energy that is admirable in its sheer force of glory and productivity. With its deep green foliage and soft, swaying wands of bright lavender flowers, it is, quite frankly, a beautiful, vigorous perennial—one Mark and I had actually seen for sale at our local nursery, and we had wondered whether or not such a marshland plant could thrive in the drought-tolerant flower beds we had been trying to develop in our Utah yard. But in many states it is illegal to plant loosestrife. While we were visiting in Idaho that July, we heard story after story on the local news about this menace. In interviews the head of the Idaho Weed Board urged farmers to guard against this "noxious" weed, offering tips on how to identify the young plants along irrigation ditches so they could be cut out or sprayed before they got a foothold, choked the essential waterways, and evicted long-standing native plants that attracted wildlife. Idaho farmers were preparing for battle.

"Well, at least it's not up on North Bench yet," Dad remarked from the front seat. "So far, at least," he added. None of us pointed out that his concern for the future of that farmland was a denial of the impending closing date. Soon loosestrife wouldn't be my father's concern. But then everything else on the farm looked pretty much as it always had. The original cattails still lined our pond, where red- and yellow-winged blackbirds screeched and trilled nightly. Although the clover field had some stands of the weed burley dock in it, the bloom had been acceptable, and the crop was nearing harvest. For now I could still think of it as "our farm." We, the long-standing residents, hadn't been evicted by the newcomers yet.

An immigrant from Eurasia, loosestrife refuses to be mindful of old ways or prior claims to landscape. Almost unstoppable, it is so vigorous that if you kill one plant, another will simply step up and sign the deed. Whether we were willing or not, change had taken root. I envy the loosestrife's ability to settle into a place with a flourish of color, so certain of itself and its right of domain. I identify more, I'm afraid, with one of those displaced species—with the mousy brown cattails that used to line the ponds around the county. But we all knew there was no going back to that innocent world of cattails. Pandora's box had been opened.

Sometimes I wonder what Pandora thought awaited her in the darkness of her hope chest. When given her dowry, with the ominous caution never to open it, Pandora must have protested. What is a dowry if it doesn't help you settle into your new homeland? After all, a gift that can't be opened is just an empty promise. So with anticipation she raised that lid, and the screeching fury began, with all the ills of humanity letting loose strife for body and soul, like angry black starlings with a clamor of cries and flapping wings. Panicked, she slammed the lid down and succeeded in trapping inside only one of the tiny, squawking creatures. Hope. And now there was no going back. Did she wonder, as scholars have, what hope was doing in the bottom of that bejeweled chest along with the countless sorrows of humanity? Does it, as one critic asks, "enable man to survive the terrors of this life and inspire him with lofty ambition," or is it by nature "delusive and blind, luring him on to prolong his misery"?

A month after our family's celebratory dinner my parents signed the final papers to sell the last twenty acres of land my father and his father had farmed. I was back in Utah, but I called my parents the next day to see how it had gone. "You okay, Dad?" I asked and heard only a terse, "I'm fine." My mother took up the conversation instead, telling me how after the closing she had called Jo to ask if they would be home. "I told her we had something to bring them," she said happily, adding that she had wanted the sale of the land and the repayment of the loan for the taxes to be a pleasant surprise. She was banking on the fact that it wasn't unusual for them to stop by to deliver a loaf of bread or drop off one of her fruit cobblers.

"Were they surprised?" I asked.

"Of course!" she said. My parents had kept the secret well. And as my mother talked about how they'd spent the evening talking about what my parents could now look forward to—a new dishwasher to replace the one Mother had had since the mid-1970s, for instance—my father even conceded that now they could afford to have hopes for an easier future.

Over the next month my father continued to be plagued by headaches. He wouldn't eat, and he was rapidly losing weight. He was morose and quiet. He claimed that the only thing that gave him any relief from the pain was Jack Daniels, and he was drinking that by the tumbler-full. He began slurring his words, but we thought that was the whiskey. Then when he developed a limp, we all feared a stroke and begged him to see a doctor.

My father was finally admitted to a hospital in Boise just a month after the sale of the farm. The physical symptoms were not stroke-related but instead caused by a tumor pressing on the spinal cord at the base of his skull and another in his brain. These tumors led the doctors to discover the first cause: the advanced lung cancer that was, by then, metastasizing throughout his body. When I broke away from a new semester at the university and drove up to Boise to see him, my father's oncologist told me grimly, "I can treat brain cancer with success. I can treat lung cancer with success. But I can't do anything when he's got both." Six months at the outside, he said. All they could do was treat him with radiation to shrink the spinal and brain tumors that had caused the limp, the headaches, and the slurred speech. He'd be more comfortable, they said, and he'd be able to walk out of the hospital.

Dad was moved from the hospital to the Boise tumor institute, where he received two weeks' worth of treatment in an oncology "transition unit." Transition to *what*? I kept thinking. As far as the hospitals were concerned, however, his future was a ticking time bomb that they kept passing on. "Home to die," which to them meant "not on our watch."

But even as anxious as they were to be rid of him, they kept an eagle eye on him while he was there. I had sent my exhausted mother home to rest. I sat alone by his bed in his ninth-floor hospital room. Through the window beside me I could see trees reluctantly turning gold, but the ground seemed a long way away. My father seemed unaware of the view, however, which was, according to my mother, a much better one than the last room, where all he could see were the walls of another hospital wing. A nurse bustled in, looking officious as she handed him his meds and held a straw to his mouth. She barely looked at him. "You know he's been trying to escape, don't you?" she announced. She said it as though he were a naughty child who deserved a scolding. She nodded in answer to my disbelief. "He doesn't get very far," she went on. "Usually we catch him at the elevator. But it's a very serious security issue." She narrowed her eyes at me as though I were a conspirator in my father's break-out attempts.

Still suffering from aphasia because one of the multiple tumors was located near his speech center, my father mounted no protest or explanation, even after the nurse left. I kept looking at how the skin on his face sagged, making more prominent than ever the rough scar where barbed wire had once clawed him. The effort to fence the land had actually inscribed his body.

Finally, I broke the silence. "Dad, were you really trying to leave? Were you really trying to escape?" I couldn't imagine my father mounting any cogent plan to elude capture.

He didn't respond right away, and my question hung in the air. He just stared at some point beyond the foot of his bed. "I guess," he confessed at long last. That is all he would say; even this he admitted only reluctantly, as if it were the behavior of someone else, as if he were detached from the desperate hope that had driven him toward the elevators, without a plan formed, without a cab waiting downstairs to take him out to some open vista or a field that was no longer his.

In the closing days of that autumn I kept thinking about the shrinking parameters of the world my family could rightfully claim, especially when the surveyor came, in anticipation of the new owners building a split rail fence, to mark off the boundaries between theirs and ours with mathematical certainty. Surveying is a science based on a notion of relative position, and now my family's relative position in that agricultural valley felt so insignificant, down to just two and a half acres of what my father called "waste ground," marked off with little yellow flags the surveyor planted in the soil only a few days after my father was released from the hospital.

I went back to Utah, still trying to pretend I could salvage the semester by driving back and forth between Emmett and Logan. My father had been home for two days when my mother collapsed in the bathroom. I wasn't there the evening she fell. Jo and Eddie had been at my parents' home earlier in the day, and they had noted how tired Mom looked. "I'm fine," she'd insisted. We all knew she wouldn't be able to take care of Dad by herself long-term, but the hope had been to give him a few days back on the farm before we made any other decisions. But that night she put on her nightgown and, as always, neatly laid out on a dresser in the bathroom the pants and shirt she would wear the next day. And then she collapsed. My father, who could still barely walk or talk, heard the fall, tried to rouse her, and then stumbled to the phone, where he called 911.

Pandora's hope must have been such a small thing in the big empty of her trunk. You never realize how small you are until you face the considerable blankness around you after all the others have left. Pandora's hope—so diminutive and thus so beguiling— was what I thought about that October, as I shuttled my way between my dying parents, my father at home until we could arrange for a care facility where they could better manage his pain, and my mother in yet another hospital in Boise, where she lay dying of heart failure.

"You don't have to worry about where to put us," my father said. These were my father's first words in the hour since I had told him that Mother had died, alone, in a Boise hospital, late the previous night, while I took care of him here at home, less than a month after the oncologist discharged him with the grim prognosis "weeks . . . maybe months, if he's lucky." The news of my mother's death had not been unexpected; she had been in heart failure for ten days since suffering a heart attack brought on, we knew, by her distress at my father's cancer. But nevertheless, my father seemed stunned by the news, still too wrapped up in the horror of his own terminal diagnosis to fully comprehend a grief like this one that demanded he see beyond the circumference of his own betraying body.

"What?" I asked. With my mind on the funeral service and the pending arrangements for my father's hospice care, I was unable to immediately assign meaning to his phrase "where to put us." Dad's radiation had brought back some of his mobility, but I knew that communication, especially when he was emotional, remained a struggle.

"You don't have to worry about where to put us," he repeated. Nothing more. He set his jaw. I'd get no elaboration.

"Oh, the grave!" I said, comprehending at last. He flinched. "I know. I know, Dad. Mom told me a long time ago." He sank back into his recliner when he knew he wouldn't be expected to offer more detail.

Years before my mother had awkwardly but very purposefully worked the subject into our conversation. It is a strange moment to hear your mother tell you that your parents have picked out their gravesite. "It's near the rest of the family," she had said, "closer to the road, but near Dad and Mother Funda." She had nagged and badgered and pouted until my father agreed to take care of these details and purchased this last piece of ground, the smallest and perhaps most significant of them all. Once when she and I were at the cemetery setting coffee cans full of peonies on my grandparents' flat headstone, she pointed off vaguely in the direction of the road. "It's over there," she said, and as if to clarify her pronoun, she added, "where we will be buried." I nodded, not able to speak but knowing that if I didn't respond in some way, she would press until I acknowledged this reality. "The paperwork you'll need is in the safety deposit box," she continued. I nodded again and was relieved when she changed the subject to how pretty the peonies were that year.

But my father had never before spoken to me of this grave or his own death. "Where to put us" was his only concession—couched in a phrase that was mundane and ordinary, as if we had been trying to decide where to put an old dresser in a new house or where to seat relatives at the Thanksgiving table. The phrase, however, did express the manner in which he thought: first and foremost in terms of a piece of land. Bought and paid for. Even in death, it would seem, we need land and deeds. They had chosen, with care and forethought, the ground in which their bones would forever lie.

And yet, I thought, wasn't that assumption of eternity itself a lie, a falsehood, given what I remembered from a story I was told in my childhood? I had heard that in the pioneering days of the valley, the bones of an Indian were found by gravediggers working near the bluff edge of the town's cemetery. It was a lone grave where an Indian, probably a Shoshoni, had once been laid to rest in a lovely spot overlooking the valley and the tree-lined river below. And although that part of the cemetery now offers bucolic views of cows grazing in a pasture by the river and the highway winding out of the valley to the south of town, people of Emmett were superstitious for many decades about laying their loved ones in the bluff-side section of the cemetery, as if the fact that Indian bones had been unearthed there made the place inhospitable. Maybe the wind whirled dust devils up from the bluff and then whistled in some eerie way that raised the hair on the back of some gravedigger's neck. Or maybe it was a more general worry that revoking that Indian's final claim to land would subject the early citizens of my town to some imagined curse, some retribution upon the souls of their loved ones laid in that part of the cemetery.

No stone marks the spot where the Indian bones were unearthed. They were not reburied or, as far as I know, claimed by any tribe. Those were the days before Native communities would push for repatriation of relics and bones, before there was a political voice to say, "Those, there, are mine." The university in Boise wasn't even established until the 1930s and had no anthropology department until much later, so it is doubtful those bones were claimed by a museum. I do know, however, that even as late as the 1970s Indian relics such as arrowheads and beads were thought of by locals merely as curiosities to be tossed in a shoebox or the back of a junk drawer. So what happened to those bones that had once been housed in flesh and sinew and later in Idaho hardpan? I picture them being brought up from the earth and scattered across the ill-kept grass before they disappeared forever, existing only in the valley legends, having no secure claim to any piece of ground.

Truth be told, I cannot remember who told me about the discovery of that Indian grave. My father, I believe, though I'm not certain. Or maybe it is a ghost story I heard as a child—a complete fiction—that haunts my imagination and threatens the quiet of my grief with these questions. It could be that I've made this story up entirely on my own and along the way have become so enamored of it that I simply believe it wholeheartedly, especially now that I understand how sad the loss of land is.

I never have found reference to the Indian grave, either in the detailed chapter entitled "The Anthropology of Idaho Indians" in the 1937 WPA Idaho guide book or in a green-bound history book I have that was written about Emmett in the late 1970s. The Emmett history details that the cemetery was first used by white settlers around 1882, that a decade later families moved their deceased from a cemetery across the river to this cemetery on the bluff. It says that the North Bench cemetery was a desolate place of cheatgrass, sagebrush, and ill-kept graves until 1918, when a father began a beautification project to ensure that the body of his war-hero son would lie in a worthy place. Yet there is absolutely no mention of an Indian grave. Of course, there is no discussion of Indian settlement of the area before white settlers at all. In the history Indians, what few are mentioned, are portrayed as either unaccountably savage or foolishly childlike. So what's to keep me from wondering if that historian failed to see the story as important, just as the gravediggers failed to see the Indian's claim on the site of his grave as inviolable?

Regarding the burial practices of Indians, Idaho historian Leonard Arrington's book, written nearly twenty years after the history of Emmett and more willing to concede to a long-held Indian presence in the state, confirms that both northern and southern

Idaho tribes would bury a tribal leader in a grave that was marked by a plain wooden stake and located on a high-point overlook. *That would account, then, for the location. And a leader, well, of course that makes sense, though I don't remember that detail used in the story.* Sometimes, if his horse were a particular favorite, says Arrington, it would be killed and left near the site, while his precious possessions were buried with him. *No, no relics or horses in the story I heard.* And the burial ceremony included rituals conducted by the tribal shaman to prevent the ghost of the dead from bothering the living. *So it would seem that the superstitious avoidance of that area was borne of white guilt rather than any Indian haunting—that is, if you believe the story in the first place.* All of which says to me that the story I remember but cannot confirm is, at least, plausible.

I know that believing that story—so vivid among the narratives of my mind—would explain why that part of the cemetery remained sparsely occupied for years. Only in recent years have families new to the valley begun to take advantage of the open vista offered only there. The gravesite my parents chose, however, is on the other side of the cemetery, almost as far from the bluff as one can get.

Before my father died, I watched from his chair at the dining room table as workmen erected the split rail fence between the house and the clover field. As handsome as the fence was—sturdy construction, beautiful wood, more picturesque than the barbed-wire fences I'd grown up with—I was glad at that moment that my father was in the nursing home, protected from that imposing emblem that so effectively cut off his claim to that ground. Even I, who hadn't spent seventy-nine years living on that land as my father had, felt "unearthed"—like Dorothy caught up in the tornado winds, ripped from her tether to the ground before being flung into a bizarre neon landscape where witches own the four corners of the world and she has a claim to nothing but her loneliness.

All I was sure of was that in this strange world that I now inhabited, "blooming" was the word the hospice nurse used to describe the darkening under my father's fingernails—a sign that his death was imminent.

The last crop my father grew on his land was clover seed, which he grew under contract with a seed company in Ontario, Oregon, that he had worked with for forty years. Producing a high-quality feed for cattle, clover is used to plant pastures for forage or hay and has the added benefit of increasing the soil's nitrogen, organic matter, and friability. No wonder then that clover, like its cousin alfalfa, was once called the "queen of crops." Certainly it was the queen of my father's heart, his favorite crop to grow. Growing clover seed, however, isn't easy. Modern varieties require significant care, even watering, and costly amounts of herbicides and pesticides. Still, if the crop is good, the profits can be considerable, and clover seed had been profitable for Dad in the past. It is fitting that it was the last crop he grew.

Dad's clover had been combined in August, just days before his diagnosis and very shortly after he and my mother accepted the offer to sell the land. By the first of the following year I still hadn't heard from the seed company about when I would receive the final check from the crop. I knew, however, that unlike other crops where a farmer can be paid right away, with clover seed you have to be patient. Even after it is harvested, clover seed has to go through a complicated process to be cleaned of all contaminants (dirt, weed seed, imperfect clover seeds) before it can be certified and sold. When I called Dad's friends at Andrews Seed Company in January, John Andrews hemmed and hawed and reluctantly told me that Dad's seed still hadn't gone through the gleaners. He'd get back to me, he said, just as soon as he could. "I miss Lumir, you know," he said with genuine emotion. I'd known John all my life, and I knew this hadn't been easy for him to say.

Among all the matters of my parents' estate the sale of the seed was of minor importance. I knew the check wasn't going to be much anyway once we figured in all the costs, so I didn't think much more about it until I was preparing to file my parents' taxes, and I needed specifics about the previous year's income. In March I called John Andrews again, leaving messages for him to get back to me. Two weeks went by, and no answer. I called yet again, and when I got through, I could hear the tension in John's baritone voice. "I'm really sorry to tell you this," he said at last, "but you won't be getting a check. The seed contamination was much worse than we thought. Any number of things could have caused the problems," he rushed on apologetically. "Maybe it was uneven irrigation. I know Lumir was having a hard time of keeping up with the watering. And you know he'd been worried about the spraying, telling me that bringing out the crop duster cost too much. But the problem with clover is if you try to scrimp on that, if you don't hit the field at just the right time . . . well . . . " he said, and let the rest of the sentence hang. The upshot was that John couldn't possibly sell the crop as certified seed, as he had sold my father's crops for years, and there just wasn't any market for such poor clover seed. By the time he figured in the spraying costs that the seed company had been carrying since the previous spring and the cost of gleaning, Dad's account was actually running in the red. I owed them money. "Now don't worry," John rushed on. "It was less than two hundred, and your dad was such a good customer all those years, well, we're just going to call it even."

All told, when the accountant figured up the expenses of seed, chemicals, hired labor, trucking, combining, water assessment, taxes on the land, and so on, that last crop actually resulted in a net loss of four thousand dollars. I was stunned. Dad would have been better off renting the land out or even just letting it lay fallow. The reality was that after more than sixty years of farming, my father had failed, not because of an act of God. No drought or hail or locusts had ruined his crop. He had failed because he had outlived his physical and financial ability to do it well. He had lost his touch.

Before he died of lung cancer that choked and strangled him and then made its insidious way into his liver, brain, spine, and bone, my father passed on to me the old 8mm film projector and two grocery bags full of small reels of home movies. He had bought the camera when I was born, having planned to record momentous first steps and the like. As he gave them to me, he again told the story about me watching these films when I was a toddler and crying because I saw on the wavery screen my mother holding some "other" baby—which was, in fact, the infant version of me. But now as I sort through the images, I find there are as many reels in those bags that feature farming as they do me toddling about in a Red Riding Hood corduroy coat that my mother had made. Dozens of them show grain flowing like liquid gold from an auger, or they linger over the slow progress of a combine at harvest, or they record the dusty furor of a landplane that levels the imperfections of the ground.

In one scene among the reels dated from the late 1950s, my father stands on the ditchbank at the end of a field, training the camera on the flight of a crop duster spraying an emerging field of clover. The plane lines up with the green rows, and at the south boundary it begins to release a mist of gray. The crop duster heads straight for my father, and then, at the last moment, it climbs over the north ditch, directly over where he stands, and quickly cuts off the sprayer. Before the scene ends, the cloud of herbicide begins to settle toward the eye of the camera—and then blackness.

I know my father well enough that I can imagine the rest of the scene: he would hunch his shoulders and adjust his cap as the mist settled over him and he sprinted down the ditchbank toward the edge of the field. He would be grinning as if he had gotten away with some delightful practical joke. And then, once clear of the settling spray, he would look back to catch the plane circling around and lining up for another pass. My father was always fascinated by those aerial shows. He used to marvel at how the skilled pilots could bank precipitously at the ends of the fields to avoid hitting the powerlines on the margins. "Jesus, that's dangerous," he used to say with admiration, each and every time.

People have asked me what I think caused Dad's cancer, as if that certainty could change anything. Perhaps it was the decades he spent smoking, or maybe he was right when he suspected that asbestos lined the boiler room where he worked at the sawmill. Perhaps it was the fact that we were downwinders from the nuclear testing that went on in Nevada from 1951 to 1962. I learned after his death that Gem County was once considered one of the top five counties in the United States to have absorbed the most radiation from the clouds that drifted north on prevailing winds from the Yucca Flat and Frenchman Flat test sites near Las Vegas. Or his cancer may have been a result of the way he handled herbicides and pesticides on the farm. My father used to brag that DDT "never bothered" him, and I saw him stroll through clouds of the stuff, before it was banned in the 1970s. "Helluva pesticide," he would sigh. I doubt that my father would have been surprised to learn that the man who discovered DDT was awarded a Nobel Prize for science in 1948.

Spring seemed insistent that year, petulantly demanding that I look to beginnings. At the farm that April the fields still looked bare, but as Jo and I walked down the lane, we noted that the forsythia was in bloom, as were both the apricot and the Italian prune trees. The wild plum, we could tell, would also open its pink blossoms within the week. Jo reminded me of the previous spring when Dad had babied the plum trees one cold night, lighting smudge pots in our little orchard when the forecast had threatened a killing frost. "Just so your folks would have more fruit to give away," she added.

"At least Mom didn't can it! " I replied, and we looked at each other and giggled. In March we had spent days cleaning out my mother's storeroom, where she kept decades' worth of canned goods—peaches that had browned in their jars, rows of jams for a family that rarely eats jam, pint and quart jars with my mother's angular scrawl noting the dates on the lid: Cherries 1987, Plum Jelly 1993. This hoarding of food was my mother's defense against poverty, just as giving away fruit cobblers and garden tomatoes was her denial of it. Mark, Jo, and I had hauled load after load of home-canned fruit and cases of long-expired groceries Mother bought on some irresistible sale up the basement steps and tossed them over the sides of a huge dumpster. By the time we'd gotten rid of everything that couldn't be sold at the auction or wasn't claimed by one of us, that dumpster weighed nearly two tons.

Now everything that remained in the house had been cataloged by the auctioneer and readied for the sale that would take place in a week's time. The sum of my parents' lives was inventoried on an 8.5-X-11-inch sheet of paper, from tractors to cookware, with the only nod to them as people being the line: "Estate of long-time residents of Emmett, Lumir and Toni Funda." After the auction the plan was that the house would become a rental. My name would appear on the deed, but others would roam those acres. Mark argued that I should cut ties entirely, put an end to grief by selling the whole place. "Move on," he insisted—but that option seemed akin to casually cutting off an arm.

The next afternoon I wandered alone through the farmyard, mentally taking my own inventory of things that would stay or go or change. The "little house" where we'd lived until 1972 was going to stay as a storage shed, but Dad's old machine shop—which leaned and had a sagging roof and missing shingles—was slated to be torn down after the sale. All the machinery behind the shop would also be sold off at the auction, including several farm antiques that dated back to my grandfather's time—a planter, a plow, a wooden threshing machine, a Farmall H tractor. Some of these things hadn't been used since long before I was born. Tall grass grew up between the hoppers of a four-row planter, and lichen was creeping over the wooden hub of an old iron wheel that leaned against an antique corn grinder. The rusted metal and splintered gray wood of these weathered implements were quite a contrast to the new split rail fence that marked the yard's boundaries. Barbed-wire or electric fences might have been just as effective when it came to keeping animals in or out, but this handsome fence wasn't just about utility. It was a statement.

On an impulse I climbed over the new fence and headed out across the field toward the pond. I picked my way carefully across the irrigation corrugates and the undulating rows, careful not to twist an ankle. I was aware that I was trespassing, of course, walking across land that used to be my father's, and before that his father's, to a pond that had always been a private refuge for me. As a teen I had spent countless hours there brooding over this boy or that as I thumbed a cigarlike cattail and released the soft down of seeds to make their own claims on a new place.

The pond had its own history. My father used to joke that the most lucrative crop ever grown on the farm was grown right there along the banks of our pond and wasn't even a crop he'd planted. One summer the teenaged sons of our neighbors, whose property line abutted the east edge of the pond, thought the place could work beautifully for a little homegrown weed. In pierced-bottom black garbage bags, filled with potting soil and set out on the edge of the water, they grew their crop in the camouflage of cattails. This was not ditchweed, mind you—that poor cousin of marijuana sometimes found growing wild along roadsides—but first-class, smoke-it, toke-it marijuana. No one would ever be suspicious to see young men walking along the edge of the pond because neighbor kids were known to go down and try to fish the murky waters, or someone could easily be down at that end of the neighbor's field checking on whether a head of water were coming through the field adequately. But one day the sheriff, having been tipped off by someone, pulled into the driveway. "We hear you've got a special crop growing this year," he chuckled, and my father, who was always willing to show you an outstanding stand of wheat or corn, was mystified why the sheriff would make a special stop in their yard to remark on the corn.

"Not that crop," he continued to bait my father with a grin. "Someone told me you've got an *extra* special crop growing out here." He winked.

"You mean the poppy seed?" my father asked incredulously. Every year my parents raised a row of bread poppy seed for use in various Czech dishes that my mother made, such as fruit dumplings, a seeded cake called a *babovka*, and *kolaches*. But the seed we grew wasn't the same species as those cultivated for opium, which was extracted from the tender, green plant—not the dried seedpods. "Hell, you've eaten Toni's kolaches many times."

The sheriff chuckled again and told my father what he had heard. My father, who loved a good joke, even one in which he was the target, grinned and laughingly said, "You're shitting me" and "Hell, you say," when the sheriff revealed all. "Guess I just don't have a head for picking the right crop," he said with a smile before they headed out across the field together to confiscate the crop.

Although the pond had been dug originally as a run-off pond for irrigation water, it was the one place on the farm that my father didn't seem to begrudge as "waste ground" and therefore ancillary to the real work of the farm. We were all sentimental about the pond. During my father's childhood he and his siblings hosted ice-skating parties there in winter. Bonfires burned on the bank at the south end, where my grandparents would bake potatoes in the coals while teenagers twirled and flirted. One summer my uncle stocked the pond with trout, perch, and catfish, although the perch and catfish took over. When my grandparents hosted their Czech lodge parties in the summer, those who lingered after the picnic often pulled pole and tackle box out of their trunks and then wound their way up the ditchbank to the pond. Everyone had their favorite spot: the women clustered on the west bank, where they could gossip, while the men, standing on the south bank, puffed on pipes and shushed the children. Whether they caught catfish or trout didn't really matter, except that one person always came away with bragging rights—until next time. Even on ordinary weekdays grandmother had a habit of sneaking off to the pond to fish alone, too, sometimes at the hottest part of the day, still with her apron on over her baggy dress because she hadn't bothered to cast it off after the lunch dishes were finished. I suspect now that the fishing was a ruse, a way of securing private moments of her own, perhaps to think about other ponds in her Czech homeland.

I've often heard stories of how when my father and his siblings were children, the entire family used to walk down to the pond on hot summer evenings. There was a little green boat, just big enough for two people, that was kept tied up to a scrubby locust tree at the south end, and my grandparents would row it out to the middle of the pond to watch the sunset. Dad and his brother sometimes challenged each other to swimming contests, to see who could swim across the pond faster, while my aunt chased tadpoles and gathered cattail bouquets at the margins. Among the screeches and trills of the red-winged and yellow-winged black-birds settling in to their nests, Frank and Annie began to serenade each other with old Czech songs about love and homeland. Annie's voice was a little unsure, but Frank's was true and strong, and it urged her along through the familiar melodies of songs like the plaintive "Kde Domov Můj?"—that poignant national song that begs "where is my homeland" with its gardens so "glorious with spring blossom" that the land is a "paradise on earth." Frank and Annie's voices carried across the fields in the breeze that came up with the twilight. Undoubtedly, they recognized that for Czechs the song's central question is one without sufficient answer, expressing a yearning rather than a fulfillment.

One by one my father, aunt, and uncle, aware they were intruding on something sacred and private, made their way back across this field to the farmyard, leaving Frank and Annie, accompanied by the croaks of frogs, to sing to each other and the emerging stars.

On that April day of my trespassing, however, the pond was empty. Years of drought meant that it had completely dried up over the winter. The new owners had taken advantage of the drought by hiring a backhoe operator to excavate the pond—recreating the deep places where my father and uncle used to challenge each other to see who could dive down and touch the bottom. The backhoe had dug deep, especially down at the south end, and it had mounded up the clay-filled dirt to create two small islands. These, in particular, bothered me as being . . . well . . . kitschy, some Disney version of islands. They were wholly inauthentic rather than a real restoration of the fishing hole Frank Funda had first excavated with a team of horses in the 1920s.

The new owners were hopeful that when the canal system opened back up for the irrigating season, the pond would refill and become a place of beauty. But at the moment it just looked like a ragged scar in the earth. The inlet at the north where I walked directly into the pond bed was still shallow, and some cattails looked as if they might have survived the savagery of the excavation process. And then the earth sloped off until the center was deep and the clay dirt dark and damp. My footing was unsure as I made my way over large clods of dirt to the pond's center, where the bottom was more than eight feet below the lip of the pond. Here, below the pond's rim, I couldn't see out over a vista of landscape. I was closed off from the world, with just the dome of sky above me and this hole of scarred earth around me. I felt a momentary claustrophobic panic until I turned and saw the tip of Squaw Butte—that geographic touchstone for my sense of the land. But when I sat down on the pond floor, even the butte disappeared from view. I steadied my breathing, and then, on an impulse, I stretched out my legs, laid my head down, and crossed my hands over my chest. I felt foolish—glad no one could see me—as I looked up at the sky and imagined this hole in the ground as my grave, like the graves of my parents just two miles to the southeast. But it also felt important to play out thinking of the pond bed as my final bed. I closed my eyes, but it was too bright out to get the full effect of the ground closing in over me, of being buried in the hardpan of Idaho soil. The cold of the spring ground seeped into me, and the unyielding clumps of earth made it difficult to lie still and give myself over to the image of my own dead body enveloped by land my family owned. I hoped my parents, in their silk-lined coffins, were lying more comfortably.

When picturing the hole as my own grave failed, I tried to imagine what the pond would be like in a year or two from this perspective. Beneath me the silt would make for a cushioned pond bed. I could look up through greenish water at the arc of sky. I could watch the moving silhouettes of catfish and perch above me. At the fringes of the pond the cattails, once again making a home in our pond, would create dancing shadows, like so many fingers caressing the pond's surface.

Either way, I thought, this was no place for me any longer. The blood hadn't stilled in my body, and I never did like to open my eyes underwater.

As I rose, I tried to brush all the dirt off my jeans and back as best as I could. I could imagine Mark asking me just how I got so dirty, his eyebrows drawn together in an expression of mild annoyance as he tried to brush me off. I could think of no adequate lie to silence questions. But I couldn't imagine telling him the truth either, without sounding sentimental or melodramatic. Would a shrug and a change of subject be sufficient? I couldn't begin to convey to him this desire to let my bones become part of this place, to imagine my blood and muscle crossing the boundaries of flesh and mingling with the soil.

As I walked up to the bank, I gathered snail shells—remnants of other deaths and burials in clay—and I thought about leaving some of them—salty and musty smelling though they were—on the new gravestone just erected on my parents' cemetery plot, between my father's side, where a chaff of wheat is engraved in the granite, and my mother's side, where a rose arches above her name.

Folklore abounds with rituals for settling into a new place. New residents lay out the welcome mat and hold a housewarming to honor the promise of what might be. In some cultures a priest or elder is invited to purify the boundaries of a new place by walking the perimeter with sage incense smudge sticks, which are also meant to cleanse the house of bad luck. Offering gifts for the new home is almost universal. Friends bring bread baskets and tea towels embroidered with designs that say "Home Sweet Home,"

"Bless This House," "Home Is Where the Heart Is," "My Home Is My Castle," or embellished with pineapples, a symbol of hospitality and good welcome, or sheaves of wheat, meant to attract household prosperity. The broom is a typical housewarming gift, both as a practical cleaning implement and as a symbolic way of sweeping away any sickness, lingering evil spirits, or unwanted troubles. Other cultures offer horseshoes for luck, houseplants to represent a long life, olive oil for good health, candles for light and enlightenment, honey for sweetness. In the film *It's a Wonderful Life* Mary and George Bailey offer the Martinis three gifts for their new house: "Bread . . . that this house may never know hunger. Salt . . . that life may always have flavor. And wine . . . that joy and prosperity may reign forever." That particular blessing, which draws directly upon Eastern European traditions, is often replicated in today's housewarmings, where food is a sacrament that says we offer our community's best wishes to this home and family.

And after the housewarming new residents continue to ritually underscore their claim to a place. They attach the front door keys to a highly personalized keychain decorated with their astrological sign or their initials. They send "We've moved!" announcements to far-flung friends. They stamp their names on the mailbox, put up new house numbers, paint the front door red, according to the teachings of feng shui. By the same principle their grandparents may have painted good luck hex signs on barns or over doors to petition God for fortune and fertility or hung wind chimes to keep evil spirits away. In the tradition of perceiving a threshold as a symbolic place of transition, brides are carried over the threshold so that bad luck cannot follow the couple into their new home. The occasion of bringing a new child into the home is commemorated with the planting of a tree. Sometimes when residents remodel, they leave time capsules behind a wall or in the footings of a new addition, as a way of saying this was who we were when this was ours. They gauge commitment to their neighborhoods by how many lights the neighbors hang at Christmas or how well the front yards are tended in the summer. And although increasingly rare in our mobile society, they throw a "mortgage burning" party when the last payment to the bank is made and they can *truly* call the place their own.

Our culture, however, has no counterpart rituals for the leaving of a place. Because we are so anxious to see what the new holds, we give no offering of thanks to honor a home that has already witnessed so much of our lives. We just casually pack our bags and go, usually without even looking back. When Mark and I moved from southern Arizona after three years living there, he bought a cap that said, "Happiness is Yuma in the rearview mirror." That cap was as close as we ever came to a formal goodbye. Glad to be done with the place, we packed the U-Haul, hitched the car to the back, and were on the road by the same nightfall.

Being unable to so easily say goodbye to a place is considered unnatural, a notion embodied by our cultural ideas about ghosts haunting a site. Ghosts are thought to have unresolved issues associated with the locale they haunt. They are trapped at the threshold between life and death, between here and there. Something so tragic or so profound holds their spirit there so fully that not even death can end the connection; only exorcism can release the soul's obsession and at last send them peacefully on their way. But while we believe we can exorcise a soul from a place, we have no way to exorcise a place from the heart of a living person.

The transition my family's Idaho farm underwent was, I concede, merely a part of a natural process. Microbial plants had once given way to the first embryonic seeds of sagebrush. With the help of my grandfather Frank, Idaho sagebrush gave way to wheat, corn, clover, and a run-off irrigation pond where cattails thrived. Today the farmers must guard against the encroachment of loosestrife and other invader species, just as now the Gem County planning and zoning officials struggle to balance the needs of agriculture and urban growth. Ponds evolve and vanish as silt builds up and shorelines shrink. And purple loosestrife replaces cattails.

Botanists have a word for this change: succession. One of the most important principles of botany, succession is the concept that ecological communities are ever dynamic, that there is no certainty as great as the certainty of change. The principle of succession teaches that the success of any one species—lichen, sage, wheat, even humankind—is fleeting. Barren rock gives way to the centuries of lichen's alchemy, eventually transforming stone to fertile soil. Then comes what botanists call a "pioneer" period dominated by "opportunistic" and fast-growing "fugitive" species before these "colonizing" species give way to secondary communities of successive plants. At the turn of the last century scientists believed that botanical communities were ever moving through a relatively predictable sequence of change toward some stable, penultimate community that, once achieved, would remain relatively static—what botanist Frederic Clements termed a "climax community"; however, more recently, even that theory has undergone change. Botanists have recognized that invariably the penultimate communities undergo subtle, and sometimes not so subtle, changes, too.

At the core of succession is a notion called "facilitation," which says that organisms progressively modify their environment until it can support the successive species. In other words, we change our world, so as to better fit our own needs, and in so doing, we change our world to make it more fit for our conquerors. They displace us and exploit the ecological disturbances we have made.

Succession within the plant world, therefore, means that the success of any one species' takeover is, at best, temporary. Today's joyous victory is inevitably tomorrow's loss. Our claim to a place begins slipping away as soon as we sign the deed. By this token farming is just one more ecological disturbance, the artificial creation of a plant community that is certain to change and be changed. The canals of the irrigating West made the takeover of loosestrife a sure thing, just as my family's shaping of that land in Emmett made it all the more desirable to the people who have now displaced us.

The drama of my family's leaving that land is a microcosm of what has been happening for years in my home state. Adopted from the National Grange (the oldest farm organization in the country), Idaho's state motto is "Esto Perpetua"—"Let It Be Eternal," but that sentiment is a hope, not a promise, made in a place where change is as sure as the sunrise. For most of the twentieth century agriculture was Idaho's main industry, a fact on display in the state's seal (originally adopted in 1891), which features cornucopias, a sheaf of wheat, and in the center a farmer plowing the land. But in recent years agriculture has been replaced as the heart of Idaho's economy and culture. Science and technology are now the largest employment sectors, and farming doesn't even come close, with, according to the most recent census, less than 3 percent of this "rural" state's population employed as "principal operators" of a farm.

For me the change on what was once my father's farm was drastic, though to those unfamiliar with the place the transition might seem more subtle. Shortly after my last visit to the pond, the Alaskan couple broke ground on a sprawling 3,200-square-foot, one-story home, with vaulted ceilings and custom European tilework throughout. On display in the middle of their circular drive among the perennials of a flower bed is an old antique plow that once belonged to Frank. They had offered to buy the plow from me

before the auction, where strangers took away my mother's household goods or drove away my father's farm machinery, but I had
just given it to them—because I know that's what my too-generous
father would have done and because it was right and necessary
that some emblem of my family should stay there on land that remains ours—mine even—in every way but in deed.

I don't know if the plow is still there, however. I rarely go to
Idaho anymore since my parents' house has become a rental, and
when I do go, it's difficult to get a good look at the new house or
the renovated pond, so set back as it is from the road, where the
traffic speeds past at fifty miles per hour. If I want to see my own
parents' house, I am expected to call Chuck, the realtor, who is
now acting as the property manager, and he in turn will inform
the renters that they can expect me—all of which feels too odd.
Can a landlord expect a cup of coffee? Must I really knock on the
backdoor that my mother always kept unlocked so that friends
could walk right in?

I do keep up, however, with what's going on out on the North
Bench, through several sources. Friends told me that for a while
the Alaskans farmed some of Dad's ground themselves, but when
they found irrigating to be much harder than it looked, they rented out most of the land to a local farmer looking for a place to pasture a few head of cattle. As I am the owner of record of those last
2.5 acres of Funda land, the county sends me notices when the
commissioners have before them a new proposal to subdivide land
adjacent to mine. They are obligated by state law to discuss these
petitions in open hearings like the one where my father spoke
years ago. So far there have been efforts to subdivide land to the
west, to the northwest, and to the east of my parents' home. I am
informed as one of the neighbors, not as a member of the family
that once owned one of these parcels under question. Just last
year the Alaskan couple decided to put the home they had built

on the market. Restless, they were off to a new place. Because they knew they could see a huge profit from their twenty acres, they petitioned the county commissioners to allow them to subdivide that land into three additional five-acre lots, each with a building permit. As far as I know, none of these petitions were ever denied. On the Emmett bench change—they call it "development"—is inevitable, and the main thing that will now grow here on my family's farm is the number of houses.

3

Wild Oats

"Fondness for the ground comes back to a man after he has run
the round of pleasure and business, eaten dirt, and sown wild
oats, drifted about the world, and taken the wind of all its moods."

CHARLES DUDLEY WARNER
My Summer in a Garden, 1870

When my mother—a Czech immigrant born and raised in a small
rural town in southern Moravia—first came to Emmett valley in
the late summer of 1956, Freezeout Hill was a dramatic introduction to the valley. Ántonia, or "Toni" as she preferred, had been
living in Munich from 1951 to 1955 and then in New York City
since she immigrated to the United States. Over the previous six
months she had been corresponding with my father, son of Czech
immigrants, and he had invited her to come to Idaho. She arrived
from New York City late one night, when darkness had just fall-
en, and so it was too dark to see the agricultural town that lay before her. All she saw from the backseat of my grandparents' Ford
were the glow of farmyard lights, house lights, car lights. Apparently stunned by the number of lights, she exclaimed, "My God,
I've gone from one big city to another!" The comment made my
father's parents laugh, and my mother's misunderstanding became a long-standing family joke, for Emmett has never been
what you might call a city. When I was growing up in the 1960s,

the population sign at the town's edge read three thousand, a number that many locals thought was a downright exaggeration.

When I was a teenager, I was sure that I would never leave that valley. I envisioned the next seven or eight decades there canning string beans and feeding chickens. My life would take on the pattern of my mother's, who, after a brief courtship, had married my father and settled down to being a good farm wife—a rural June Cleaver with plates full of Czech kolaches rather than snickerdoodles. Occasionally, I would try that fantasy on, like a tagged suit of clothes at Woolworth's. Could I be happy married to a farmer, spending my days hanging sheets from a line and unearthing the beets that I'd serve at supper that night? Could that life fit me as well as it seemed to fit my mother?

But then, of course, I knew that my mother led a remarkable life before her arrival here. She had escaped her homeland of Moravia in 1951, during the postwar Communist regime, after having worked for several years to help dissident countrymen flee. Her work in the Resistance began when she was hired to be a companion and nurse for the ailing wife of a newspaper editor working in Znojmo, a town twenty kilometers south of my mother's home village and twenty kilometers north of the Austrian border. Josef Pejskar and his wife, Frances, quickly came to love my mother, and soon they confessed to her that Josef was also the leader of a dissident group in Moravia that helped refugees escape into nearby Austria and then on to safety either elsewhere in Europe or in the United States. It was profoundly dangerous work, but, with a fearless gesture of trust and determination, my mother offered to help. While most of her subsequent assignments included jobs like passing messages between other operatives— relatively tame stuff for dissidents—on at least one occasion the job was more risky.

She was scheduled to meet a woman trying to flee the country in a church one afternoon. The two women, similar in build, exchanged clothes—coat, boots, scarf over the hair—and my mother, now a decoy, left the church, followed by the unsuspecting secret police who had been tracking the woman, now wearing my mother's clothes. The officials trailed Toni as she pretended to be out for a walk along the streets of Znojmo. After a time she entered a busy bakery where numerous people came and went; there, in a back room she changed again into a set of her own clothes that had been previously stashed there, allowing her to slip out of the building unnoticed and return to the house where she lived with the Pejskars.

After several members of his dissident group were arrested, Pejskar himself had to escape in late 1948, but Frances and my mother were left behind in Znojmo. Josef lived in Austria for a while and then joined the staff of the newly established Radio Free Europe in Munich, where he was a regular commentator who became famous broadcasting under the pseudonym "Jozka Pen." He attempted to arrange for Frances and Toni's escape for three years, and finally, in 1951, he was able to exert his growing influence at Radio Free Europe when he learned that the arrests of his wife and my mother were imminent. The region of southern Moravia has a temperate climate and is famous in Eastern Europe for its vineyards, which provided their means of escape. Hidden under the false bottom of barrels used to transport grapes to area wineries, my mother and Frances crossed into Austria, a border that was heavily guarded by the Communists, who established broad, fortified "frontiers" where armed guards patrolled the border. In December 1951 Pejskar wrote a letter to a fellow Czech then living in New York, saying, "I have been able to arrange for my wife and nurse to join me in Munich. . . . In only three days, they illegally crossed the Czechoslovak-Austrian frontier, passed through the Russian and American zones in Austria, and crossed the Austrian-German frontier. This was a passage in record time during which they were accompanied by armed persons."

My mother was just twenty-five when she escaped that December, and until she left, her family had no idea that she had been working in the Resistance. After her escape she couldn't directly contact her family. Only through coded messages broadcast on Radio Free Europe did Pejskar get word to them that she was alive and safe. Nothing more. For years they had no idea about what country she was in or whether she was still even on the same continent.

After Toni immigrated to New York in 1955 and before she came west to Idaho, she spotted a man in the subway whose escape she had directly aided during those years in Znojmo working with the Pejskars. He failed to recognize her as he went about reading his paper, but she knew exactly who he was, and she used to say that seeing him—during what was apparently a period of loneliness and disconnection—offered a small compensation for leaving family and community behind.

What little I knew of Toni's past was full of this kind of daring and boldness of spirit. Her life—although you would never know it from the way she swiftly took a hatchet to a chicken destined for the dinner table—had not been confined to or by our Idaho farm. Before coming to Idaho, she had lived in cities, and she had traveled through Austria and Italy. In addition to Czech and English she could speak German and knew a smattering of Russian, Polish, and Italian. Although she grew up in a tiny Czech village, she had become a cosmopolitan, in the truest sense of the word—belonging to the world, not merely local, but having developed the ability to construct home anyplace, including Moravia, Munich, New York, even Idaho. She had chosen to settle in Emmett, and now she hated the thought of all travel. She refused even to drive by herself the thirty-five miles to shop at the new mall in the next county or at a bigger grocery store in Boise. She made excuses not to go on vacations, dragged her feet in those rare years when a few extra dollars meant a drive to Portland, Oregon, where Dad's sister would put us up for a week ("Who will feed the chickens or water the garden?" she would protest). She flatly refused to go on family camping trips to a cabin Dad's brother owned in Donnelly, Idaho, less than one hundred miles away. She disliked even going on a picnic in the mountains unless we timed it with mushroom season, and she could gather the fragrant, earthy-tasting morels that reminded her of her Czech homeland. Even then she wanted to be home before dark. She wasn't reclusive, but she was a homebody, and I, for one, couldn't understand the attachment to our little plot of land. Didn't she *ever* want to get away from that damn farm? But her answer was simple. "Why should I travel?" she used to say. "I did my traveling when I was young. Now I want to stay in my own home."

But when I thought of my mother's pre-Idaho life, I saw a model for the soaring female courage I doubted I had in me. I wanted to leave that farm behind at the same time that I feared doing just that. Unlike my mother I felt timid in the world, certain that I had no valid claim on anything but the circle of our pond. I was bright, but not exceptionally so. I had no overriding ambitions, such as astronomy or the French horn or marine biology, that might offer a direction—this in an era when bra burning and Gloria Steinem were icons for a woman's certainty of purpose. In that era of sex, drugs, and rock and roll, I was horribly prudish, though more out of cowardice than any sense of moral outrage. I was "mousy"— doomed, I thought, by dishwater-blond hair, gangly legs, and, worst of all, extreme nearsightedness that meant I wore thick, wire-rimmed glasses and looked at the world with a perpetual squint. With my myopic perspective how could I envision my life beyond the mighty fact of the "here"—the place that, with the exception of my mother, only kept those who lacked the courage to go elsewhere?

We were so poor we often depended on my mother's "egg money" for necessities, which is, perhaps, why I remember so vividly the summer afternoon when our chickens were attacked by a pack of half-wild dogs that would sometimes roam the farms and foothills in the bench area of the valley. I was out in the barn when I heard the chickens' panicked, screeching cacophony of fear. By the time I emerged from the barn, my mother was already slamming open the gate between our weedy lawn and the farmyard and rushing out to see the damage. We knew what it was. Sometimes a stray cat would rouse a single chicken into a loud but brief protest, but this kind of clamor from so many chickens was clearly more serious.

When we reached the well house at the back corner of the yard, there were feathers everywhere. Chickens cowered under pieces of farm equipment they thought provided safety. And lying in limp piles of dust and broken feathers were several chickens whose necks had been snapped. With wings and legs and necks akimbo, they were posed in bizarre death postures that belied their typical stiff, priggish appearance. And out through the clover field we could see several of the dogs skulking away, one with a chicken still in its mouth.

My mother and I stood in the middle of the chaos, trying for a moment to still our hearts. She swore in Czech and then stooped to pull a chicken out from under the tangled grapevines that covered the well house. "God damn dogs!" She looked at me, standing there stunned and mute, and ordered, "Help me with these chickens!"

And so we spent the next hour looking under machinery, reaching into weeds and shadows to gather the birds. Worse than the dead bodies left by the savage and reckless attack, though, were the living chickens we pulled by their feet out from under the combine or from between the disk blades or from under the grapevines that died of fright in our hands before we could walk the fifty yards to the barn.

I felt physically ill, not at the sight of bloody feathers or limp fowl, mind you—I had seen that often enough at butchering time—but sickened by the cowardice of the birds that had survived the initial attack but had succumbed to their fears while suspended in our rescuing hands. It was a refusal to prevail, a lack of the defiant will that seemed an imperative on the farm.

My parents met face to face in late 1956 after they spent six months corresponding. While my father had been farming his parents' acreage in Idaho and doing custom-farming on the side (plowing and planting in spring, combining in the fall), my mother had been working for over a year as a nurse's aid at New York Hospital—making less than $150 a week, according to her tax return from that year, and living on Seventy-second Street, in the bustling Czech neighborhood near Yorkville, not far from Central Park, Midtown, Times Square, and the Theater District. She shared a small apartment with another Czech couple, the Valentas, who subscribed to a widely read Czech American newspaper published out of Chicago, which occasionally printed short immigrant stories or vignettes, including some my father's father wrote about homesteading in Idaho. Charmed by these stories, the Valentas had begun a correspondence with Frank; then my mother began corresponding with Frank and Annie, and at last she began her correspondence with my father. Some time during the summer of 1956 my father invited my mother to come to Idaho, where she stayed with his parents until they were married the following January.

I knew the details of this love story well enough—the storybook meeting of two people, their correspondence, my mother leaving behind everything she had established in New York to come to Idaho. The farmer, rugged and honorable, takes a refugee bride, and in the process they rescue each other from a life of loneliness. When my parents eloped to Nevada, the story even made the local paper, with the headline "Lumir Funda Takes European Bride in Winnemucca Ceremony." It was, as far as I know, the only time my parents' lives together were significant enough to make news. The write-up, with references to my mother's escape from Czechoslovakia and the claim that their marriage "culminated a romance which began through correspondence," makes it all sound so exotic and wonderful, like something out of one of those romance novels Toni loved to read in later life and stashed away by the hundreds in the closets where she thought my father wouldn't find them.

The reality wasn't quite so romantic. They had eloped during a bitterly cold January, driving with Dad's brother, James Frank, and sister-in-law, Viola, who would act as witnesses, more than two hundred miles south to Winnemucca, a Nevada cow town where you could get a quick, no-fuss wedding. They drove down and back in the same day because Dad's brother had to be at work the next morning. On the trip home that night the heater in my uncle's car went out somewhere near Jordan Valley, and the only thing that kept their feet from freezing, they used to say, was Vi's little terrier, Blackie, who huddled on the floorboards in the backseat with them.

Toni and Lumir's black-and-white wedding photo, taken on the steps of the Humboldt County courthouse, evidences little more than affection. They lean slightly toward each other, but they do not embrace. My mother grips her white gloves, not my father's hand. Her hair is tightly permed; her lacy white collar peeks out of the dark suit and seems too tight around her neck, but her smile looks genuine. Dad's hands are in his pockets. He looks dapper in his Frank Sinatra pinstripe suit—his shoulders are broad, his hips are narrow, and he wears a nice tie, something I only knew him to wear for solemn occasions like funerals. But despite his dashing look there are signs that he is moving into middle age: his hair is thinning, and his dimples have deepened into creases.

I wonder sometimes if my parents both simply thought, in those opening days of a new year, that it was time. Romance aside, it was time. My mother was less than a month away from thirty-one when they married, and my father would be thirty-five that same winter—this in an era when most all of their contemporaries were married by their middle twenties.

But when the newlyweds came home from Nevada, married friends of my father made sure that some of the customs were observed. These were people who had all wondered whether Lumir would ever "take the plunge," and now they couldn't let the event slip by uncelebrated. Women my mother had only met weeks before threw her a bridal shower, duly noted in the newspaper account. The shower was complete with silly games—this I know because my mother saved a pink slip of paper from the "It's a Party Game FUN Book!" where the instructions ask participants to answer questions with responses beginning with A. F.—my mother's new initials:

What do you expect from a husband? *"absolute fidelity"* or *"admitting faults"*

What is your greatest hope? *"acres of farmland"* or *"an affluent future"*

Where would you most like to spend your honeymoon? *"the Alps of France"*

What type of man attracts you? *"an amorous Frenchman"*

I make these answers up, of course, because mother didn't save her own responses. I imagine that the task was probably difficult for her. She could probably only think of Czech answers, and she would have felt the added pressure of the instructions' admonition, "Don't get serious; the funnier the better." But still, I would love to know what she thought when she read these questions and the others: What are you afraid of? What is your greatest virtue? Are you romantic? Are you superstitious?

On the back of the slip, in my aunt Vi's precise handwriting, is a record of who gave what:

Mrs. Robert Canfield: green sheet set

Mrs. Bob Stanley: embroidered dish towels

Mrs. Frank Veselka: blanket

Mrs. Jim Stover: frying pan

Mrs. Don Garmon: bread basket

And on and on. Twenty-seven women, almost all noted by their husband's names, came and offered my mother flowered tablecloths, Melmac mixing bowls, a red rooster canister set, the beginnings of friendships, and a sense of belonging that would last for decades. The gifts themselves were unremarkable—I cannot remember a single canister set in my mother's house, though the list claims she received three. However, the names are familiar. Most of these people, like my mother, are now dead, but that slip of paper attests to what was a thriving community, one that my mother would adjust herself to and be an intimate part of for nearly forty-five years.

Shortly after my parents' marriage some of the couples represented on the shower gift list came in the dark of one night to shivaree Toni and Lumir. I imagine it was as much a test of my mother's good nature as it was a payback for the couple eloping without a word. Friends of my father arrived at the house in the middle of an unseasonably warm March night two months after the Winnemucca ceremony. The wives banged pots and rang cowbells outside the windows of the bedroom while their husbands, slightly tipsy from the whiskey that had warmed them on the drive out to the farm, pounded on the door until a groggy Lumir pulled on a pair of pants and met them just as they burst into the kitchen. At some point during the din he hurriedly explained to Toni just what they were in for. My mother had just enough time to throw Dad's heavy coat over her nightgown before the two were marched out to a pickup and instructed to join some of the others in the truck bed. They were driven through the night the four miles to the center of town, where Lumir pushed Toni in a wobbly wheelbarrow down Main Street, from Ron's Barber Shop past Rexall Drug and all the way down to the small city park. There were pauses for laughter and cigars and flasks of more whiskey to take off the chill, and just before dawn the group drove back to the farm, where everyone would have breakfast. In what was now my mother's kitchen the other wives made themselves at home by frying eggs and bacon and pouring coffee. Toni, meanwhile, pulled out a loaf of homemade rye bread and, as she always did, first blessed the bread, the family, and the home with three crosses scratched into the bottom crust with a knife, and then she sliced into the bread that would make her fame among these people she could now call friends. That ceremonial initiation of shivaree and breakfast welcomed my mother into Lumir's circle, and I've heard the story of that night a dozen times from the various participants who marked that as the beginning of their friendship with Toni. Over the years theirs became a community of pinochle parties and impromptu potlucks. They traded gossip and recipes and, one year, the brandied fruit starter of an Amish Friendship Cake I remember so well that I think I can even smell the memory itself. These same people could be certain that Toni's kitchen door was always unlocked and that she always had hot coffee brewed and a loaf of bread waiting.

My mother loved the idea of romance. Her favorite movie was the tragic love story *Dr. Zhivago*, which she watched faithfully each time it reran on TV. She arranged her daily chores around the romantic twists and turns of her soap operas, first *The Edge of Night* and then some years later *The Guiding Light*, which she watched every day after lunch for decades. She used to play stacks of Al Martino records all day long, singing the love songs along with his sultry voice, which she thought was the best voice she had ever heard. She had a ritual of getting up extra early in the morning just so she could enjoy in peace one of the romance novels she'd bought with her "mad money." Although she used to claim that she only kept the novels she liked best and traded the rest at the little local bookstore, after her death Jo and I found nearly two thousand paperbacks secreted away in closets and cardboard boxes and doubled up on bookshelves draped behind heavy curtains. She never tired of their predictability, never wanted to know what transpired after the happily-ever-after, never cared that, if statistics were any gauge, half of all such romances would end in divorce. My father indulged her novel reading by turning a blind eye to it all.

In reality Lumir hardly fit the pattern of the romance novel's hero: he wasn't wealthy or sophisticated; instead he swore casually ("*sun*uvabitch"—with emphasis on the first syllable and the phrase slurred together like it was one word), and he never managed to get out all the machine oil from under his fingernails, despite the gritty Lava soap my mother kept in a dish next to the sink. I remember how as my father would pass my mother in the kitchen on the way to refill his coffee cup, he would sometimes tenderly pat her behind while she was basting a fresh dumpling with bacon fat. But typically my mother would frown and impatiently swat him away.

This impatience with his teasing began early in their married life. Certainly, I see it evident in the 8mm home movies Dad used to take. My father often had to resort to sneaking up on her in these pictures because increasingly she hated to have her picture taken. He captured her as she waves her hand at him in that dismissive way of hers, glares at him, and mouths curses. In another scene she sticks out her tongue as if to say, "There! How's *that* for your picture!" There is a whole reel—taken around my first birthday—where she holds me in her arms as I mug and laugh. But she plainly refuses to turn her head to the camera. Even with her head turned away, her anger at my father is palpable in the line of her neck and the stubborn turn of her head. She stares out at some distance across the field, refusing to respond to my flailing hands.

And when I find a rare moment of ease in these reels—as when she realizes that my father has caught her admiring a spray of her climbing roses and she cocks her head, hikes up her skirt, throws her shoulder forward like a vamp, and breaks out in laughter—I run the scene forward and reverse, again and again, trying to make it last. I want to find some solid, indisputable evidence that she was happy in our little life together, that in her way she loved the man behind the whirring camera. I'd like to believe that she cultivated no deep resentments at the way Dad and I bound her to that place. I can only hope that the sharp lines of her turned head on that one day were only evidence of a passing spat, perhaps about muddy boots on a newly mopped floor, or money spent extravagantly on a new vise or drill when they needed groceries. I cannot bear to think that she was staring out across that field that day, while I bounced in her arms, and felt anew her own foreignness in that landscape.

The love story of my parents' courtship and impulsive wedding had for so many years seemed like a fairy tale that belonged to someone else. I had never actually seen any letters between Toni and Lumir, and so the story of the correspondence, with all its overtones of a "mail-order bride," seemed like a nice fiction but too far-fetched to be anything but just legend. And in and among the dropping price of wheat, the nauseating smell of butchered chickens, and the endless, steamy summer days of canning tomatoes, their romance had been an anomaly that didn't fit empirical evidence.

After my mother's death a friend of mine said to me, "If it weren't for all the doctors and the hospital and the IV tubes, it would almost be romantic. Your mother couldn't live without your father. She died of a broken heart." It's hard not to think of such conclusions as just more of the same old fable. Even so, the last thing my mother was able to say to me in the hospital was in reference to her wedding ring, which she hadn't worn for months because it needed repair. "Look!" she croaked out through a ventilator as she waved her hand at me. And there, newly restored to her ring finger, was the gold band and the little diamond ring my father had bought her on their twenty-fifth wedding anniversary. The last time my father saw her, a week later, after she had suffered a stroke and lay unresponsive in the hospital bed, he hated to leave her side, and when I insisted it was time I took him home, he struggled up from his wheelchair, precariously balanced himself against the bed railing, and tried to bend down to kiss her. Too weak to balance himself on his unsteady legs, he kissed his fingers and tentatively touched them to her cheek. He never saw her alive again. Call it a romance or not, my mother had formed an attachment to a man and a place that ran so deep she couldn't survive their loss.

And as if scripted by one of my mother's favorite soap operas,

I found the first three letters of their romance just an hour before my father's funeral, which was exactly one month after my mother's death. Moments before we were due at the chapel, I pinned on an amethyst birthstone pin from my mother's jewelry box and decided that also bringing one of her many old-fashioned floral hankies would sufficiently represent her presence at the service for Dad. I opened the top drawer of her dresser and saw undies and bras—bleached glaringly white and folded into achingly tidy packages by my mother. I felt guilty scavenging the privacy of that drawer, but still, I reached in the back where I knew she kept the hankies. Rather than lace or cotton, however, my fingers touched paper. I opened the drawer wider and pulled out three yellowed envelopes slipped into the back corner. I recognized my father's handwriting. "Tonie Kratochvil" was written on the address line of the first envelope, and I saw the New York address. The date stamped next to the three-cent stamp commemorating "a century of Great Lakes Transportation" was February 10, 1956, less than eleven months before their wedding.

That I should find these letters at all was surprise enough, but that I should find them at that very moment makes it hard to remain entirely cynical about love. I glanced over them, recognized them for what they were, and quietly tucked them into my purse before joining Mark and Jake in the car. I considered having the minister read them at my father's service, but quite selfishly I decided against it because I knew I'd never manage to maintain any sense of control if I heard them read out loud. Later that day, after the service, I pulled the first letter, a single sheet folded in quarters, out of the oversized envelope. As if he had worried that his words would slip out of the envelope before they reached my mother, he had made sure to secure that envelope's seal with two strips of stamps bearing the double-cross insignia of the American Lung Association. I unfolded the letter and read:

Dear Tonie,

I received your letter today and am sending it to Dad. Him and Mom went to Portland on a vacation to visit Sis.

I stayed at home to look after things. I can't say that I like this batching. I'm not to crazy about cooking and cleaning house.

I hope that you can read this scribbling. I'll bet that it has been lonesome for you; coming over here and not knowing the language or anyone. I'll bet I'd be lost in the same kind of predicament. It sure has been cold around here lately.

Well not much of anything new around and I am not much of a writer so I'll close.

Bye now,
Lumir

P.S. Excuse the envelope but I can't find another one.

They had begun writing, not because they had been "set up"—by some postal blind date arranged by friends or family, as I had thought—but by the accident of my mother writing my grandparents while they happened to be out of town.

Despite his disclaimer about his "scribbling" and one or two cross-outs, the letters are neatly written, and I remember my father always being proud of his penmanship, even if he wasn't as adept with what he had to say. I am, however, touched by his somewhat awkwardly expressed sentiment about my mother's lonely "predicament," but the next sentence about the cold weather, without so much as a paragraph break, suggests his characteristic discomfort when talking about emotions.

The next letter is postmarked February 28, 1956:

Dear Tonie,

I received your letter the other day and am finally getting

around to answering it. I am sorry that I didn't write sooner, but I'm not much of one for writing. I can never think of anything to write.

Are you going to a night school and taking English or did you learn it in Europe. I can't get used to your letter t, although I have seen it used the way you use it (t) many times. I thought that you done very well. Did you know the English language before you came over here? I'll bet that it was a lonely life for you when you first came over.

I'm still batching but I don't like it. I'm getting old maid knees and dishpan hands. My cooking don't even agree with the dog anymore.

Well if the weather here ever breaks maybe I can get to farming. It keeps raining, snowing, and freezing. I sure wish that it would. I am getting tired of not being able to get started farming.

Well it is one in the morning so I guess I better close. I have a big day ahead of me today and I have to get some sleep.

As ever,
Lumir

My father doesn't even mention that February 27 was his thirty-fourth birthday or that the next day—when the letter would be mailed—was the day his family traditionally celebrated both his birthday and his leap-year-born older brother's birthday. Did the late hour he referenced mean that he had been out with friends, toasting another year passed, before he came home to write that letter? My father's second reference to "batching" makes me wonder if my mother, who had just turned thirty herself two weeks before, bristled at the reference to "old maid knees." I certainly would have. Was his remark that the dog wouldn't eat his cooking anymore a line he had practiced on his friends that night—gauging its success by their laughter—before he wrote it in his letter? Had he said anything to them about his new pen pal?

He had probably wondered what she was like, as he sat in the house those rainy weeks, drinking coffee and waiting out the weather. That loneliness like hers should be so closely associated in his mind with language, with the ability to communicate and be understood, strikes me as ironic, for my father was, in so many ways, a man who loved to talk—even if he found it difficult to write—and yet, within the borders of our family, meaningful communication was lacking. Like these letters we always talked around what troubled or inspired us.

For instance, although farming is a constant in his letters, he doesn't reveal what it meant to his heart and mentions nothing about being forced home from college on an agricultural deferment in the early days of the war. He doesn't reveal why he had put off marriage for so long and doesn't speak about the failed engagement I later learned had been ended by the girl's Mormon parents, who didn't approve of my family's freethinker ways. I'll never know if Toni appealed to Lumir because of something she confessed in those letters, with her efficient letter *t* that he complained of (swing up, straight down, and then over to the next letter without ever having to pick up the pen for the crossbar). Of course my father may have begun to think of marriage to a refugee bride only when he realized my grandparents might approve of him finding a nice Czech girl. One of his greatest faults was always trying to placate his parents, and I know that both his brother's and his sister's marriages to non-Czechs had already been disappointing. James Frank's wife, Vi, had been married and divorced before she met my uncle, and she was childless and disagreeable, and Gladys's husband, while charming, only learned two Czech phrases: the imperative "Dej mi hubičku," meaning

"Give me a little kiss," and the "good night" salutation "dobrou noc," which he intentionally mispronounced as "double roll of nuts." So was my father imagining the pleasure on his parents' faces when he married a Czech bride?

In my father's third and last existing letter, postmarked April 2, 1956, he writes:

Dear Tonie:

I'm sorry that I didn't answer your letter sooner, but I'm not much of a one to write. I've been pretty busy lately farming. I've got all the ground plowed and now I'm waiting for the right time of year to plant corn and beans. I have my grain planted and it is coming up. I have been doing plowing for the neighbors around here.

We have had some nice weather but it has been threatening to rain for two weeks. All that it does is the wind blows. We had a couple of cold mornings and it froze most of the cherries.

Well tommorrow is Easter. What are you going to do? I want to go for a ride to the hills, to a small town where a person can have a lot of fun. I don't know whether my plans will work out or not. Well there isn't much of anything else new to write about so I'll close.

Bye now,
Lumir

Three letters, and only those written by my father, are all that remains of their correspondence. As if they were deeply intimate, my mother kept them for forty-five years in the privacy of her undies drawer, but they seem rather inauspicious to me. Surely there were others, ones where my father must have invited my mother to come to Idaho. But I don't know if he proposed marriage in one of these letters or saved that question for when he met her face to face later that summer. He could have told her that Idaho was more like her rural homeland than New York was, or he might have cited the small but active Czech lodge community my grandparents belonged to, which held monthly meetings and dances and potluck dinners noisy with Czech music and casual gossip and the sound of her native language. But I doubt he ever "sold" the place in quite that fashion. His other letters were too cautious to have been followed by anything that might have tempted her with attractive details. So I'll never know what served to convince her to come to a state, and a man, she knew next to nothing about.

It was sometime in those months before she left New York when I presume she bought a luxurious black silk robe, imprinted with pink, blue, and yellow flowers, similar in size and shape to carnations. The profoundly impractical dressing gown offered no warmth from the Idaho winters, and it's not the kind of thing she might have found available in our local stores. With such useless features as the small, flimsy triangular pockets sewn on the front, it's stylish, if not sensible. I never saw my mother wear it, but when I was little, I used to crawl into the deep, dark closet where it hung on a hook in the back. I'd huddle in the darkness and let the folds of the fabric whisper against my fingers, and if the door was ajar, the silk shimmered, and the flowers glowed in the dim light. In the midst of my Idaho childhood that dressing gown represented for me the possibility of glamour in the world. I couldn't help but be a little jealous that my mother had once traveled in the world that this elegant dressing gown represented for me; moreover, I was puzzled about why she had chosen to leave it for Idaho.

More recently, when I rediscovered the gown packed away and tried it on, I realized that it was the 1950s version of a fashionable but sexy negligee, undoubtedly designed for passion rather than modesty. Three cloth-covered buttons that easily slip through the buttonholes decorate the bodice; material gathers just below the breast line, accentuating the curves of the bust. From there the ample skirt gracefully flounces down to midcalf, but no ties, snaps, or buttons allow you to modestly close the front of the robe, and with every movement the front seductively swings open.

This chic gown that my mother had chosen in the weeks before her marriage was therefore a tease. Although it must have been a financial extravagance for a nurse's aide who was too poor to rent her own apartment, it suggests an awareness of her own sensuality and a belief that every young bride needs a pretty dressing gown. Even though I can't find evidence in the letters that my father had already proposed, this robe tells me that she expected marriage, or at the very least seduction, when she came to Idaho.

For my father's part their marriage wasn't always easy, but I don't think he ever failed to love my mother. Moments of crisis attested to that. One afternoon my father and I returned home from my grandparents' house to find the kitchen door left wide open and pools of blood trickled and smeared across my mother's usually spotless floor. My father frantically called out for my mother, but no answer. He sent me out to call for her in the yard, but I couldn't find her anywhere. Meanwhile he began calling James Frank and Vi on the phone—no answer—and then the Stovers and the Stanleys and the Garmons, neighbors nearby who might know something. But no, they hadn't seen Toni. By the time my uncle's car pulled into the driveway, my father was shaking, certain that my mother was dead or dying. Everyone was laughing as they got out of the car. My mother climbed out of the backseat, her hair uncombed, her apron still on with spots of blood on it, but she was smiling and looked all in one piece. My father approached the car, his jaw set.

"The kitchen door's open. Blood everywhere. You nowhere. Where the hell have you been?" my father demanded.

"Hell, Lumir," my uncle chimed in. "Relax. We took Toni out to the bluff to see the flood. The Payette's so high that it's covered the highway. It's like a lake down there."

My mother, no longer smiling, said only, "They didn't even let me take off my apron."

"Where's the blood from?"

"I'd just butchered a goose. I was letting the blood drain when they showed up." My father didn't move, and my mother, now defensive, added, "It's hanging in the corner of the bathroom! If you'd a just looked, you'd have seen it!"

A similar event happened another summer, when once again Dad and I were at my grandparents' house visiting. It was getting late, and the sun was starting to set. As Dad and I got into the pickup, Dad looked over toward our house, which was about half a mile northeast, as the crow flies. "Christ!" he yelled. "The shop's on fire! Toni's alone!" My grandfather, who had walked us out to the drive, turned to look in the direction of the house, where the west side of the shop glowed orange. My father slammed his door and threw the truck in gear, backing out of the drive and onto the highway without even checking for traffic. I looked behind, and my grandfather was hustling my grandmother into their car to follow. I looked toward the house again and saw what looked like a red blaze. The shop was just feet away from the side door of the house, where we knew my mother was busy canning. She couldn't possibly fight a fire alone, and any spark could set the dry shingles on the roof of the house aflame. I know both my father and I were thinking that she might get caught inside a burning building. As my father tore down the highway west of our place, he slowed for a moment. "What the hell?" I looked again. The shop glowed red, but the closer we got, we realized the flames weren't leaping up, and there was no smoke. "Are you shitting me?" he exclaimed as we pulled into our drive and stopped the pickup between the shop and the house. My mother was standing outside, leaning against the screen door and calmly smoking a cigarette as she swept back her sweaty hair. She was fine, and there was no fire. The red glow we'd seen from a distance had just been the setting sun shining on the west side of the shop, where my grandfather years before had planted a reddish-orange climbing rose. The rose was especially profuse that year, and my mother was standing there admiring it as the evening cooled. My grandparents pulled up behind Dad's truck, and as the sun went behind the house and the shadow climbed up the shop wall, we all laughed about the "fire."

I don't remember in either of these cases what happened next between my parents. I don't remember hugs of relief or even an admission that my father had been worried about my mother. My parents didn't work that way. But his concern proved something to her, and sometimes when we'd bring up these stories, and laugh about them, my mother would be especially solicitous to my father over the next few days.

My mother had had romances before she married my father. She used to keep dozens of photos from her days in Germany in an old Brach's candy box that was stored high on top of a dresser, and on summer days of my youth, when my father was out irrigating the fields, I used to thumb through them at the kitchen table, while she worked nearby. My favorite photo was one that I think of as "The Kiss." My mother is lying back on a blanket, laughing heartily, her arms in front of her in a mock defense position. It appears that she is trying to fend off the passionate kiss of a male admirer who wears nothing but swim trunks and on his head a wreath of flowers that makes him look like some arrogant

Roman emperor. He appears cocksure of himself, certain that she welcomes his embrace, that she will, eventually, welcome his kiss, too.

I used to ask my mother about this provocative photo, and she would laugh, "Oh, an old boyfriend," and dismiss the question with a wave of her floured hand. Pressed further, she would reveal that she knew him from the years that she worked under Pejskar's direction at Radio Free Europe. "Did you love him?" I would probe. "That was a long time ago," she would say and shrug her shoulders, effectively ending my questioning.

Yet I am drawn to that picture not for who her "lover" was so much as for who she was. If the photos from that time are to be believed, the years balanced between her escape and her marriage to my father must have been relatively happy times. She appears quick to smile at the camera, even to flirt with whomever stands behind the lens. She is poised and carefree. Even her picture for an identification card, issued by the International Refugee Organization (IRO) in Munich that December, just days after the armed guards and her terrifying escape with Frances, belies the gravity of her situation. She wears lipstick and earrings, her hair is curled, her clothes are pressed neatly, and her face is relaxed and smiling.

The card identifies her as one of the millions of European refugees ousted from their home countries by the aftermath of the war. The IRO was the United Nations' humanitarian agency charged with feeding, clothing, sheltering, employing, retraining, and finding home countries for the refugees. As long as Toni was living in Munich under the safeguard of the IRO, she would be legally known as a "DP" or "displaced person"—someone who, according to the IRO's definition, was in a state of "statelessness." It was the IRO's mission to see that she was either repatriated (her work in the Resistance clearly meant that was not an option), reestablished (which meant finding her permanent work in Germany, a country overrun with so many refugees, more than a million, that the United States and its allies worried that the unsettled refugees threatened Germany's economic and political stability), or resettled (find one of the twenty countries working with the IRO, from Palestine to Paraguay, that was willing to take her in, provide her with housing and job opportunities, and consider her application for citizenship). My mother was lucky, I suppose. Because of Pejskar's patronage and his position at Radio Free Europe, she continued to live with him and Frances in Munich for nearly four years and didn't have to join more than half a million refugees housed in camps in Germany, Austria, or Italy. Each year, however, she had to renew her German certificate of residence, and if she moved, she was required to immediately notify the authorities of the change of address. As for her potential for permanent resettlement, she was fortunate not to be a specialist, like a doctor, lawyer, journalist, teacher, because the "embargo against brains" philosophy—which treated such immigrants as competition for jobs rather than as potentially contributing members of society—meant few countries would have seriously considered admitting her, and when she did receive a visa for the United States in the spring of 1954, she was only one of thirty-three hundred refugees to gain visas under the Refugee Relief Act of 1953.

The application process, however, took months. Visa applicants attempting to enter the United States had to find an individual or organization (refugee organizations could offer "blanket assurances") to vouch that they would not become a public charge, that they would find adequate housing and employment that would not displace an American worker. Even though the Eisenhower administration was particularly sympathetic to escapees from Communist countries because they thought that their anti-Communist positions would make them good citizens, Senator Mc-

Carthy and the Red Scare of the mid-1950s meant Ántonia would have to undergo rigorous investigation that one congressman of the time called a "mystic maze of enforcement." In addition to carefully assessing an applicant's political sympathies, immigration and naturalization officials would investigate her character, reputation, and mental and physical health, and they would expect her to be able to document her work and residential history for the previous two years.

Meanwhile, as the IRO helped her make these decisions about emigration and helped her through the paperwork, she had a German passport that identified her as a *Haushälterin* (a domestic) but forbade her from finding paid employment in Germany (her work at Radio Free Europe was on a volunteer basis). The passport also gave her a certain freedom to travel in Europe, and Toni and her friends visited numerous tourist spots in western Germany, Austria, and western Italy. She had left her home without any belongings, and now no one and nothing tied her to any one location.

To look at the personal photos from that time, however, you'd never know Toni had a care about where she would settle. Certainly, after the confinement of the oppressive Communist regime and the enormous responsibilities of her work in the Resistance, such a life must have held a profound appeal for my mother. It must have felt good to fully inhabit her own clothes and her own thoughts and to function in a world where future concerns only went so far as the next picnic or rowboat excursion. In picture after picture her life appears to be a perpetual bacchanalian celebration of laughing companions. In and among these places, most of which I cannot identify—mountains that look surreal compared to our tame Idaho buttes and foothills—my mother's confidence shines through. The photos include images of a young Toni posing in front of the lion statue that guards the harbor of the Bavarian town of Lindau, relaxing on sunny picnics with friends, playing cards on a blanket tossed out into the sun, boating on a forested lake, pausing on a dirt road with alpine mountains rising in the background, lounging on her stomach in a meadow with her bare feet crossed in the air, showing off a new stylish dress, dabbling her toes into a stream, toasting life with a wine glass. These pictures give the impression of a perpetual summer, an endless summer vacation. Even the winter photos that show my mother standing in a dark fur coat seem bathed in a warmth that belies the need for the hat and gloves she wears. In the years after her escape my mother seems to be relishing the life of a vagabond, enjoying the freedom of belonging no place.

I am struck by the ambiguity of the word *escape*. Even with the same root as the rock-solid *landscape*, *escape* can mean "get away" (a relief and release), or it can mean "run off" and "run away" (in other words, the pejorative notion of avoidance, shirking responsibility to place or family). Is escape an effort to "break free" (which means claiming your human right to liberty) or to "break out" (with its images of criminals and prisons and blood-sniffing hounds)? *Escape* suggests ending a connection to a landscape because of a political or personal necessity or desire, but it fails to explain the spiritual reality that precipitated the leaving. You can escape a political regime, but can you ever escape the loss you feel when you quit the place and people of your upbringing?

Likewise, a border is both a real and an elusive thing, a thin, invisible line on the landscape that nevertheless is negotiated by complicated treaties and hefty legal documents and boldly drawn in black or red on large-scale maps. As subtle as the single letter that differentiates *refuge* and *refugee*, a border is so insubstantial you can cross one without knowing it, in that tiny pause between inhalation and exhalation. And yet, as with my mother, crossing a border can throw into question everything you believe about your citizenship in the world.

However happy my mother's post-escape photos might seem, this leaving was a thing against her will. She had been too afraid to even tell her mother goodbye, and without such rites of passage, how can you emerge from the darkness of a wine cask into the darkness of a forest and believe that you've left at all? When my mother first escaped, she only traveled as far as the liminal space between the home she had lost and the safe haven that she hoped to find.

In fortifying the borders around such Iron Curtain countries as Czechoslovakia, the Communists made a correlative for that liminal experience of escape. Depending on where you crossed, the "death strip," as the buffer zone along the border was called, could measure as little as thirty yards wide or as much as twelve kilometers, and it might have concrete walls, earthen berms, bunkers, guard towers, razor wire, and high-voltage fences. The spring after my mother escaped, this "no-man's land" was even further fortified with mines, booby traps, motion sensors, and anti-vehicle ditches. The upheaval along this border represented the breathless fear of that long and difficult transition, that inexorable change. Somewhere in that landscape a single step across an unseen line meant there was no turning back.

The hedonism of my mother's time in Germany, then, was a matter of thumbing her nose at all the terror that went before. The boyfriends and picnics and wine and vacations were all a denial of the power of loss. The riotous, pleasure-seeking decadence meant that, by damn, she was going to live. Engaged as she was in the frivolity of her twenties, Toni was, one might say, out "sowing wild oats." The engendered and sexual implications of that metaphor aside, the message of the phrase is apt. Its motto is *Carpe diem!* Its objective is to throw caution to the wind, to recklessly indulge in the luxury of doing things without thought of future consequences, without attachment, responsibility, or commitment, to anyone or anyplace: living carelessly and carefree.

Nevertheless, characterizing wild oats—the plant itself, that is—as reckless and carefree is a significant misnomer. In fact, wild oats is uniquely equipped to make strong attachments to the place it lands. My father, who had an uncharacteristic respect for this particular weed, once urged me to examine it closely and see that each individual hull in a head of grain has a long, needlelike hair (identified by botanists as an "awn") that shoots off from the seed at a slight angle; together in the head of grain these hairs make up the grain's "beard." While individual awns appear to be stiff and straight, my father pointed out how each is a mesh of tiny fibers, twisted tightly like the coils of a hemp rope. He put a single blond grain in his mouth, wetting both hull and hair with his spittle, and laid it down in the palm of his hand.

"Watch," he said.

"For what?" I asked.

"You'll see."

Slowly the small twists began to unfurl and move the seed in his palm. "Any water, like rain, makes that little rope uncoil," he explained. "It's like an auger. This seed will drill itself right into the ground." With slow but certain movements, the seed in my father's palm deliberately arched and circled and tried ineffectually to corkscrew itself into his skin. Here, in the palm of his hand, was the vegetable world animated, in an instant taking action, determined to implant itself into a new home, unconcerned about the suitability of environment (in the way some finicky hybrids could be), well suited to anyplace. The twirling plant was sentient, conscious, acting on a will to affect its destined relation to the land. Unlike the parasite dodder, which cuts off its ties to the land, wild oats waits with faith and certainty for the opportunity to make itself a home. To quite literally sow wild oats, then, suggests a resolute will to take root in the community of vegetable sisters, wherever the wind blows you.

When you've lost your past and you have no family, work, or citizenship to connect you to your present life in a new place, imagining the future may be all there is that still makes you human. That, I think, is what attracted my mother to seek the council of a fortune-teller during her time in Germany. At first, she told me, going to the gypsy was purely a lark, and I imagine Toni and her friends, all as rootless as she was, laughing as they drew Deutschmarks out of their purses and wallets and handed them over. After all, what did they have to fear from the future when they had all braved great difficulties and survived? The palmist gazed at Toni's hand and then apologized for bad news she was about to give. She was not destined for a long life, the gypsy said; she would only live to be forty-nine. Given that Toni had already spent most of her life fearing first the threat of violent Nazis and then the authoritarian Communists, a guarantee of more than twenty years ahead of her was good fortune. Essentially, the gypsy had freed her to imagine a life beyond this rootless refugee period. That palm reading marked a shift in Toni's life. Shortly afterward the American Consulate General in Munich granted her a US immigrant visa, and in July of 1955 she boarded a boat for New York. She had to leave the Pejskars behind in Munich because Frances's health was still precarious (she would die the following year), but Toni didn't have a choice in that matter. Once again she was leaving behind loved ones. She couldn't stay in Munich any longer, and she couldn't return to Czechoslovakia. According to her immigration records Toni also left behind what belongings she had managed to gather in her four years in Germany— perhaps this time by choice, as a way of welcoming the future the gypsy had promised her. Unlike her fellow boat mates on the *General Langfitt* who had checked bales, suitcases, and trunks full of belongings, Toni was traveling light; she entered the United States only with what she could easily carry, a small overnight case and a purse.

For the first time in a very long time my mother could imagine having a new life. It didn't matter that she believed her future was limited in years or that she didn't know what it would hold. After all, as Doris Day would sing the following year, "The future's not ours to see." "Que Sera Sera" climbed to the second spot on the *Billboard* charts just as Toni was celebrating the first anniversary of her arrival in the United States and preparing to move to Idaho, and throughout her life she kept a typed copy of the lyrics in her dresser drawer. Even though the song emphasized an acceptance of the unpredictable nature of the future, it also promised the certainties of things my mother had lost: family and love. Whenever she heard the opening's mandolin tremolo on the radio, she would turn it up and sing or hum along.

The summer after my mother turned forty-nine, in 1975, her doctor advised her to undergo surgery for her varicose veins. Even though he assured her that the procedure was routine and he expected nothing less than a full recovery and alleviation from the pain she had long suffered, she fatalistically saw it as the fulfillment of the gypsy's prediction. In the weeks beforehand she cooked extraordinary amounts of food and labeled and packed away in the freezer months' worth of casseroles for my father and me. She packed her bag for the hospital stay with a grim resignation, and then, looking shaky and gray, she drove away to the hospital with my father, staring straight ahead as he pulled out onto the highway.

To no one's surprise but her own, she came through the surgery without complications, and two days later, with her legs wrapped in bandages and wearing support hose, she returned to the farm and never again said a word about the gypsy's prediction. Months later, healed and less self-conscious about the appearance of her legs, she marked her fiftieth birthday and the end of that dreaded year. Death still lay ahead of her—that she accepted, but she had joined the ranks of the rest of us blessed with the Doris Day luxury of an unknown future.

My mother had moved from New York City to Emmett, Idaho, in late summer of 1956. According to shipping receipts dated August 14 of that year, she put everything she owned in two boxes weighing a combined seventy-nine pounds with a declared value of $500, and for $16.21 she shipped her belongings via the railroad to Idaho, posted in care of Frank Funda. Two days later, at 8:15 a.m., she boarded a United flight at LaGuardia that took her to Chicago and, that same afternoon, on to Boise.

Apparently, however, my father was not there at the airport to greet her. This I infer from dates in one of his pocket ledgers where he kept records of custom-farm work he did—the wages owed to the hired men, the cost of barrels of grease, the parts he needed, the gallons of gas used, the names of farmers he worked for—who owed what, who paid in cash, and who still owed money ("check with Dad on this," he would write, or "Mom has the money from this"). When I found the ledger in a drawer after their deaths, I set it aside in a "keep" pile only because it contained my father's handwriting and because the names of the farmers in the ledger reminded me of the faces of people I'd once known: Whitsell, Fulghum, the Blaser Brothers, Tolmie, Stover.

It was much later, however, when I took note of the title he had penciled on the worn cover: "Combining, '56." This ledger, then, documented the custom-farm work he did the summer my mother came to live in Idaho, and I'd like to believe that he had kept this particular log book, not others from the year before or after, to remind him of the summer days that had brought Toni to Idaho.

According to his ledger, by the end of July he was logging eleven-, twelve-, and thirteen-hour days on the combine, moving from farm to farm. Every day during the first three weeks of August, save one, the log shows twelve hours or more of work. August 16, the day of my mother's arrival, shows only eleven hours, but the next day he worked thirteen hours, and twelve hours the day after that. With grain in the fields there was little time for romance.

Only August 19, the Sunday after Toni's arrival, is blank, presumably because he uncharacteristically took a day off during harvest to get to know this woman with whom he'd only exchanged a few letters. I've heard they took a drive north along the twisting riverside road up to Cascade Lake, so he could show her the place he had referenced in his Easter letter. With my grandparents and the new couple in one car and Dad's brother and his wife in another, they all drove up the canyon for a picnic in Donnelly, where the family leased farmland next to the lake. My aunt from Portland tells me that she heard from her parents that the couple was tense and silent during the drive. Every one watched and presumed an argument—but on the way home, she reports, they were talking again, and everyone was relieved they had made up. But this information comes to me third-hand, a story half remembered and told more than forty years after the fact.

My father's log does not reveal any such emotional complexities. It shows only that once again on the following Monday, the 20th, he logged twelve hours on the combine.

It must have been inconsolably lonely for her—but by then, I suppose, Toni, the refugee, was accustomed to loneliness, practically saw it as a companion in itself. When my grandparents brought out lunches to Dad and the hired man, she might have ridden in the back of the old Ford, bouncing in the backseat over rough fields next to a hamper full of salami sandwiches, a thermos of black coffee, a supply of fresh water in a canteen made of a wet burlap bag, and a warm slice of a fruit kolach that she had baked herself. She might have delighted in the warm, sensual smell of the grain harvest, recognizing the aroma as one from her childhood. She may have lingered at the edge of the field as my father climbed back on the combine and coaxed the engine and combine header back into a roar. I picture her raising her hand to shade her eyes from glaring sun so she could better watch him guide the big combine around the golden fields. Would she have been attracted to the deep tan of his forearms and ache to touch the muscles hidden under rolled-up sleeves? After returning his wave, she probably joined Lumir's parents in the car, and on the way home she might have sung along with Doris Day: "*I asked my sweetheart what lies ahead. Will we have rainbows, day after day? Here's what my sweetheart said . . .*"

It's just as likely, however, that she fought a rising sense of panic, wondered why she had come to Idaho and who this stranger was on the machine that severed wheat stalk from root in the front and spewed out clouds of chaff from the back. How much could she foresee about how their lives—and ultimately their deaths— would mesh as she sat next to him in the shade of the combine, watching as he set his cap back further on his forehead, as he sighed at the heat and propped one elbow up on a bent knee to eat a sandwich? If she did have fears, she surely hid them, giving in to them only in the darkness when she smoked a cigarette out by the back porch of my grandparents' home.

Keeping matters of the heart to herself was her habit. Even in those days when we were all cut down by news of my father's terminal cancer diagnosis, she hid from us that she had suffered the first of two heart attacks, a detail later revealed only by blood tests. "If she'd come in when the first one happened," the cardiac specialist told me as we stood outside the hospital room where she was failing, "I think I could have saved her."

"An actor must learn his part by heart. I must learn by heart my exercise," my mother wrote in a slim black notebook that I have from her years in Germany. With precise penmanship and that strange letter *t* my father complained about, my mother had written out her English exercises. Line after line records dutifully practiced responses to prompts like *"Which is the heaviest animal?"* and *"How do I get to the movie theatre?"* I may wish for some insight into what she feels in the liminal space of Germany, but I get instead *"She puts the vegetable into her basket," "Whenever I write my exercise it is always badly," "This dress matches my hair,"* and *"Don't cry, I am going to buy you chocolate."* These are interspersed with pithy quotes such as *"Who wants to be with the wolves must howl"* and a variety of colloquial phrases: *"It's all the same to me," "What's what?" Don't bother your head about it," "I am all in a sweat,"* and a whole page where she practices the conjugations of slang expressions like *"I'm gonna."*

But occasionally, in and among these mundane, sometimes comical sentences, the notebook reveals moments that seem to be in my mother's voice, where fleeting glimpses of her own thinking emerge. In the middle of a page of similar and therefore easily confused words (*"fly," "flew," "flown," "fall," "fell," "feel,"* and *"felt"*), she notes in capital letters "FLEE" and next to it underlines the synonym "ESCAPE." Notably, her attitude toward Munich evolves around this time; as I turn the pages, I see her go from *"This town is very strange"* and *"We are going to move soon out of Munich"* to, ultimately, *"In Munich I so feel at home";* however, later, after she has mastered complex sentences, she adds, *"Since the time I have been in Germany, I have not been so healthy."* Some sentences hint at her hopes, like *"Every girl want to be a bride*" (which is comically followed by "*Every spinster is cross and angry*"). But the number of such assumptions about romance pales in comparison to frequent thoughts about political freedom: "*Here you may go wherever you want to*," "*I could to do whatever work I want to*," "*We will fix it at the State Department*," "*The people turn rich in America very quick*," "*The people in America are going to vote the president.*" There are plenty of references to the political situation in the Czech Socialist Republic, too: "*In Č.S.R. we have national heroes*," "*Mr. Bursik was hero*" (in reference to Czech Resistance fighter Josef Bursik, who had worked against the Nazis and helped to liberate Kiev from the Germans before he was imprisoned by the Communists), "*Here is freedom but in Č.S.R. isn't*," "*The people in Č.S.R. must trying working very hard*," "*Our trip from Č.S.R. was very difficult*," "*Because of the communists we had to escape.*" This is followed by "*Have you some more news?*" a question that expresses a profound sense of yearning. But as if she expects no answer in return, the next line changes the subject: "*It is very good roast goose with sauerkraut and dumplings.*" The traditions of the Czech kitchen must have felt like a safe haven, although thoughts of savory recipes undoubtedly reminded her of the mother she'd left behind.

The number of entries referring to her mother moves me. Her father only merits, "*My father all at once died*" (a sentence followed incongruently by "*Your girlfriend has a kiss-proof lip-stick*"), and later the apologetic statement, "*You must for me it fix up with my father.*" Her brother gets "*My brother will be the heir to our farm*" (ironic, of course, since the Communists had already turned all the land around my mother's village into a farm cooperative where no one had individual claims to the land). But my mother's mother, Karolina, is everywhere in the notebook: "*My mother is somewhere in the garden*," "*My mother keeps a lot of geese every year*," "*My mother is cooking dinner*," "*Mother buys some vegeta-*

bles every day." Some of the sentences move beyond the mundane: *"I leave my mother wich lives in Č.S.R.," "My mother get old"* (which the teacher corrected to "is getting old"); *"Does my mother like her girl?"* (where the teacher crossed out in red "her girl" and wrote "daughter"), *"My mother wants to buy sugar and coffee"* (an obvious reference to shortages they suffered), *"My mother was shocked when I fled from Č.S.R.,"* and finally *"I am going to write letter to my mother."* She knew that although she could *write* a letter, she couldn't send it. Communication from outside the country would have been intercepted by the authorities and only endangered her family by raising additional questions about what they had known about my mother's escape.

How painful was it, I wonder, to copy out in English that empty promise when communication from either side of the Iron Curtain was essentially impossible? I keep coming back to that question *"Have you some more news?"* which suggests the longing she must have felt, so definitively cut off from her mother. Learning a new language in those months before she was granted a US visa put my mother at an emotional as well as geographic distance from her mother. With each new word that she memorized, she laid claim to a new place and, syllable by syllable, let go of her home village.

Eventually, after settling in Idaho, my mother was able to write to family in Moravia. Sometimes replies arrived at our house in fragments or with heavy black blocks of ink having savaged the delicate airmail paper, giving clear evidence that everything going in and out of the country still underwent careful governmental scrutiny. I remember a day in 1965 when a slim airmail envelope arrived at our farm from Czechoslovakia—an envelope, we would eventually learn, that contained the news of Karolina's death. My mother placed the envelope on the coffee table in the living room, and there it stayed, unopened, for weeks. Puzzled, my father nagged her, "Aren't you going to read it?" "No," she said simply and left the rest to explain itself. I used to think that by some instinct she knew what news the letter contained without having to hold a paring knife to the delicate blue paper. To refuse to slit open the letter would be to forestall the death itself. I have since learned that there is a folklore of signs—a certain kind of envelope, a certain mark as the seal—that indicates the letter contains tragic news, but I don't remember that letter, with its blue and red strips around the edges, looking in any way different from other letters she received from Czechoslovakia. My mother could be grateful that, for the most part, news of family deaths received a gentler hand from the censors. Still, my mother did not know if her mother asked for her in her last days, just as she did not know the reach of her mother's dreams or the extent of her regret. When my mother did finally open the envelope and pull out the single sheet, she read only the essential facts of the day her mother had died and that it had been cancer. The words telling her when and how were insufficient to compensate for the loss.

As a literature professor and writer I work under the assumption that the sum of lives can be neatly contained on paper and that emotions can be reasonably expressed by written words; however, the rest of my family puts no such stock in pen scratchings. A number of letters, including the one about Karolina's death, have disappeared in intervening years, and no one in my family ever thought their lives significant enough to keep a diary. Perhaps the closest my mother ever came to recording her daily life was the stack of more than a hundred weekly Weight Watcher food diaries that date back to the late 1980s. In these small blocks of space she meticulously recorded self-denial. Ask me, for instance, what my mother thought when she read about the 1989 "Velvet Revolution" in Czechoslovakia that peacefully removed the Communists from power, and I couldn't begin to tell you. But

I could tell you what she ate that November, and I could show you where she wrote each night in the block for dinner "TEA" in large, angled letters, as if she felt she needed to fill the space on the paper, if not her stomach.

My mother's one attempt at keeping a real diary was done only at my urging. In the winter of 1993 John Andrews, the owner of the seed company where my father always sold his grain, said it was a pity my parents had never gone back to Czechoslovakia, and one day, after he'd enjoyed coffee and kolaches at my mother's table, he pulled a thick envelope out of his coat pocket and handed it to Dad. It contained two plane tickets to Prague, thoughtfully dated for early March . . . just before the rush of spring would tie Dad to the farm.

Before my parents left for Czechoslovakia, I gave my mother a blue-flowered, cloth-bound journal where, I told her, she could capture her impressions of her return to her homeland. For my mother, however, it was an onerous assignment, not a gift, that I had given her.

Her first entry is dated March 29, 1993, and describes the days before they left the United States, when they were visiting my husband and me in Nebraska, where I was then in grad school. Mother notes where and what we ate in the two days before they left. She notes that they washed their clothes at our apartment the day before their flight out, and she writes, not once but twice on that first page, "Sure had a good visit with Evie and Mark," but she gives no further details about what specifically we talked about or why she enjoyed it so much. The next entry, which is dated two days later and discusses their flight into Frankfurt, Germany, and then on to Prague, is interesting not so much for what it says but rather for how the narrative switches back and forth repeatedly from English to Czech, often in midsentence, as when Mother writes, with some astonishment, that they paid five dollars for a glass of *pivo* (beer) in Frankfort. It is a glimpse of how, at that moment, she stood on a threshold between past and present, torn between the language of her youth and the life she had built in an English-speaking world.

The top of the next page is dated 4-1-93—the day they were due to arrive in Prague; however, the page below is blank, as raw and empty as a field before planting.

The remaining pages of the journal are untouched, achingly white, except for the last page, where she recorded the prices of crystal vases and other souvenirs they had bought, so that they would have a record of what they would have to claim at customs on their return.

After returning from Czechoslovakia, she hesitantly confessed to me, "I didn't write much in that book of yours." "Yours"—as if she couldn't lay claim to her own experience.

After her death I found a number of black-and-white photos of Toni's home village. Višňové, the village name, is printed in tiny, faint letters on the back, but nothing else serves to identify the view. I cannot remember my mother ever showing me these pictures, and I don't know how she came to have them. The images are not very sharp, but some photographic process gives them an odd, iridescent quality that glows gold as I tip them back and forth under the light. In one view I can see just the tile rooftops of clustered houses that stretch out across a draw and up the slight incline of a low hill; surrounding the village are flat stretches of farm fields that end only at the horizon, where the earth's curve belies a world beyond. In another view barns huddle around a neat and tidy courtyard, and in the distance a dirt road, flanked on both sides by bushes, vanishes in the haze of distance. Because Višňové has no mountains or towering buildings, the bird's eye perspectives of the village seem both surreal and oppressive.

I try to gauge my own response to this landscape and see if the pictures evoke any sense of connection or feeling that this is an ancestral homeplace. In one view of what appears to be a farm-yard, I can just make out the silhouette of someone—a child, I think—pushing a wheelbarrow across the yard, captured in the act of doing daily chores, and I try to imagine the child is my mother, off to feed the pigs after school in the late-day sun. But that figure seems profoundly alone. Evidence that humans in-habit this place—the man-made buildings, cultivated fields, and mounds of hay—is belied by views otherwise so empty that they are eerie. And I begin to feel—if I have any instinctive response to these views at all—that they are most certainly pictures taken during the Communist occupation because in their barrenness they convey a sense of the human spirit of the place gone "under-ground." The openness of the fields and expanse of the roads taunt citizens with a freedom they have no right to, and the build-ings convey no real, human claim to the landscape. This is what my mother must have felt in those years before her escape, when she looked around that familiar place that, by a set of political cir-cumstances, could not be her own.

My mother could not foresee that years after she became a natu-ralized US citizen in 1963 and shortly after the 1989 "Velvet Revolution" in her homeland, her name would be on a deed to a small parcel of land in Višňové. After the revolution the new Czech government enacted a series of programs aimed at restitution, and for a brief time Czechs could petition the government to restore to them land that had been taken out of private ownership and assumed by the Communist farm collectives. Mother and Dad's trip to Czechoslovakia coincided with the last days of the restitu-tion period. By that time, however, my mother and one of her sis-ters were the last living siblings who could directly petition to reclaim the small plot of land for the Kratochvil family. At a court-house in Moravia my mother signed papers that made that land hers again, and then, right after, she signed over the deed to her niece Silvia.

I did not know about this legal exchange, however, until months later, when my husband and I were visiting Mother and Dad in Idaho. We had spent the afternoon thumbing through their pic-tures from the trip and hearing about my cousins calling her the "aunt from America." And as she showed me pictures of them posed with dozens of relatives in the private courtyards and gar-dens of her home village, I remembered things she had told me over the years about her childhood there. In one picture she point-ed out the windmill where she'd gotten water for the family pigs. Every day after school it was her chore to feed and water them, but if she shirked the duty, she got the strap and, for days after, the sting of Karolina's disapproval. In another one of the pictures Mom pointed to the barren limbs of a tree. "The apple tree," she said simply, trusting that I would remember the story of this local variety of hard, black-red apples that her father buried every au-tumn in a pile of hay he kept in the cellar just outside their back door. By midwinter, they would mellow into a sweet fruit she loved and still hungered for. In the pictures my mother pointed out the children and grandchildren of her beloved brother Josef, who was dead now. I had been told the story of this brother often during my childhood, how during the Nazi occupation he was severely burned in a mine accident and suffered for weeks. I re-membered her saying how after the accident his thick, curly, red hair grew back straight, dark, and sparse, and that whenever she saw him, she was surprised anew to find that the waves of beauti-ful hair were gone. Clearly, the loss of Josef's hair represented something deeper about what they'd gone through under the Na-zis, but that was something Toni couldn't fully articulate.

Later in the day my mother took me aside, and looking solemn, she told me, "You need to know something. It's something I did while we were in Višňové. There was land," she went on, "in my name. A very small piece of ground from what my family farmed before the war." She shook her head dismissively as if to assure me it had little monetary value. "After '89 they got it back. And when we were in Czechoslovakia, I deeded it over to your cousin Silvia."

She paused while I soaked in the details. "Mom, you had land?" I was astounded, more by the miracle of the restitution policies than by her statement that she had given land that I had never stepped on to a cousin whom I had never met.

"By rights," she apologized, "it should have been yours. I know that. But I just didn't see how . . . " Her voice trailed off.

"No, Mom—" I protested, seeing that she had misunderstood my response.

"Your cousins, they are so poor, and they work so hard, and I just thought if I could help them. I just didn't see how you could benefit from it. I—"

"It's okay, Mom. I'm glad you did it. I *am*!" I assured her. She was gauging the sincerity of my statement. "What would I have ever done with that land?" I added. "I'm thousands of miles away. I just think it's amazing that you—your family—got it back." She warily responded to my smile. "What a miracle—after all these years. Silvia deserves it." My mother nodded, agreeing that legitimate land ownership demands proximity.

For those moments between signing one paper and then another, my mother had been an independent property owner. There is something important to me about that fact. With her name and identity notarized, a legal document had verified—however fleetingly—that my mother's birthright was there. Despite all the other places she had lived and the other languages she had learned, a small farm in Moravia had never left her. Although she was the "aunt from America," a visitor who would stay for a few days and then return to her "home" in a "foreign" country, she was able to reclaim a right to that place. Like wild oats itself she was as much a part of where she began as where she landed.

My mother was not typically forthcoming about her past in Europe. Facts revealed themselves to me layer by layer. Years ago, shortly after Jake's birth, she was sitting in my living room, and we were all half-watching some PBS documentary on hang gliding, when out of the blue she announced, "I did that once."

"What?" I asked, unable to picture my tiny, seventy-something mother soaring in the sky.

"Hang gliding," she said with annoyance, as if my astonishment were an accusation.

"When? Where?" I asked.

"In Europe. Germany. It was fun."

"Were you scared?"

"Sure. Of course," as if I'd asked the obvious.

But when pressed for more detail, my mother shrugged her shoulders, as she usually did when we asked about that segment of her life, and dismissed her story and our curiosity with, "That was a long time ago." Though I longed for a fuller narrative, she refused to offer additional details: why she was hang gliding, where this had happened, or who she'd been with, whether it had been a lark or something to do with her work for the Resistance or for Radio Free Europe, which I knew engaged in a propaganda war where leaflets were dropped by air behind the Iron Curtain.

More often than not the details of such incidents would have to be imagined, or I would have to discover them by doing the kind of historical research I've described here on the Eisenhower administration's refugee policies or how the IRO handled the influx of refugees into Germany. Toni selectively revealed the details of her life to a precious few people, and no one person knew much at all about those years. Once she told me about seeing the man in the New York subway. Another time she told me about stealing through the Austrian forest on the moonless night that they escaped, but I found out about the false-bottomed wine barrels from Frances's niece who wrote me after my mother's death. A family friend heard the story about Toni being a decoy for an escapee, for instance—again a story I heard only after her death. And while I knew that Pejskar had worked for Radio Free Europe, I only discovered how influential he was from a biographical sketch of him that cited the four books he'd written about Czech refugees and noted he also had been the editor of *České Slovo*, a newspaper read by Czech exiles around the world. In an online archive about Radio Free Europe's role in fighting the Communists, I discovered Pejskar's letter that describes the armed guards accompanying his wife and the family nurse, who was my mother. Even my father knew only a few of the bare details of Toni's life before she came to Idaho, and when he would urge her to tell their friends about her work for the Resistance—a gesture I always thought of as touching evidence of his pride in her—she would look at him sternly and refuse to talk about it at all. Her characteristic modesty prevented her from admitting how extraordinary these events were, especially when weighed against the especially ordinary life she led in Idaho. Naturally, this had been a terrifying time in her life, and I understand that life in such a totalitarian place makes people wary, even long years after the fact. Czech writer Arnošt Lustig recently said of the war years and after, "We collected certain experiences which do not permit us to give ourselves completely to anyone else. No one who survived the war is normal. It's impossible."

After my mother's death my father's sister, Gladys, surprised me by asking if I knew that Toni had once appeared on the cover of *Life* magazine—"or one of those magazines," she added vaguely. She thought Mother had been seated on or posed next to a tank, so perhaps this photo dated to the Russian liberation of Czechoslovakia, but she couldn't remember. When I looked for Toni the cover girl in decades' worth of magazines at the library, I did discover that noted *Life* magazine photographer Margaret Bourke-White had been in that part of Czechoslovakia during 1937, prior to the Nazi annexation of Czechoslovakia but not during the Russian liberation. I also found that *Life* had regular features about Czechoslovakia during the 1930s and 1940s. But I never found my mother's photo—either on the cover or elsewhere in *Life* magazine or any of the other popular magazines of the time. And as much as I have searched every drawer and cupboard of my mother's house, I never found such a magazine among my mother's belongings.

Things like the bridal-shower gift list, Mother's refugee identification card, and her English-language practice notebooks offer me the illusion that a continuing relationship is still possible, that there is still time to break my mother's silence. Every artifact and old story holds a potential message. I am the one to conclude, after all, that the silk robe came from New York, that the gypsy's prediction was a turning point that made the future seem possible again. Even in my dreams my mother is stubbornly mute and unresponsive, and I start wishing that I could believe in ghosts. Preserving the detritus from my parents' lives helps me believe that our attachment is ongoing and reciprocal.

The spring after my parents' deaths, at the urging of my husband, who suggested that it was time to move on from grief, I agreed to schedule a farm auction. According to the auctioneer mid-March was a perfect time because farmers would be anticipating a new season and would have the cash to buy Dad's machinery. Jo and I had gone through my mother's household things, and those neither of us claimed were also designated for the auction; those would be sold in the house in the morning, before the afternoon's main event moved to the farmyard and the tractors, planters, and a John Deere combine. During the weeks leading up to the auction, I desperately combed through everything. I passed up claiming Grandmother Funda's buffet hutch, with the wheat-sheaf brass handles, because Mark couldn't imagine where we would put it in our house. I urged Jo to take the set of flowered dishes Mother bought with Green Stamps. Dishes and furniture had nothing more to say to me. I focused instead on every scrap of paper, certain that the truth contained in these artifacts was full of potential, unvarnished by my mother's fear, modesty, or embarrassment. But without sufficient time to analyze all of it, I rubber-banded silly pop-up birthday cards that date back to the 1960s, and I added several of my father's farm ledgers to the "keep" pile. Anything that looked vaguely revealing with print or scribbles was saved. At night I dreamed that the auctioneer had come to the farm while I was out for a walk. He declared every bit of paper to be nothing more than trash and set a match to the fragile evidence. I returned to see it all—every grocery list and shoebox of meaningless receipts that I had packed—go up in smoke before I could read any of it. I singed my fingers trying to pull a curling magazine out of the flames. I woke from the dream with a sense of inescapable finality—that dismantling her home, not her death, was the real separation from my mother.

In the late 1970s my mother began a regimen of walking that she kept up for two decades. In the morning twilight she would circle the block twice, which, out in that part of the country, totals up to a distance of four miles; the distance between crossroads being a half mile each. Out of our driveway she walked west the short way to where my father's brother and his wife lived in a small house at the corner; turning south, she walked along the half-mile stretch along one of the fields that Dad farmed, along the place where the bachelor buttons bloomed on the ditchbank every summer. Then at the corner she turned left where she could see, across another field, the home where my grandparents had lived and farmed before their deaths. Going east, she had to pass the house rented by the woman who sometimes watered her flowers naked and who loudly responded to voices no one else heard. Then it was north at the next corner, where a barn owl nested in towering spruce trees at the Nasker place, and past the dairy that had changed hands with each decade but that everyone still called "the Carrolls' place." Finally she turned west again, where she could look across the road to see if Bob Stanley's tomatoes were as ripe and abundant as hers, then past the fence post that marked the eastern border of our property and past our own mailbox—to do the round all over again. She knew every dog along the way (which ones were friendly and which ones were not), knew every pickup driver who waved as they passed by in the early morning (knew which were headed to the sawmill for the morning shift and which were coming home from the night shift). She knew where the wild oats would send up lacy fronds near the fence line. She knew where the skunks secreted their young, where she had seen a snake this time last year, where the neighbor's dog had been hit by a speeding car, where the pheasants would scare up into awkward flight and the quails would call out to each other in their melancholy staccato, "Where-Are-*You*? Where-Are-*You*?"— a call so woeful, full of such yearning, it seemed to suggest they never expected an answer in return.

Back home again she would faithfully log on the calendar that day's mileage with a 4. I used to page through these calendars and add it up for her, imagining that the miles were carrying her somewhere away from our farm, instead of in the same circle that led nowhere farther than the next road over. By the end of January she'd be past Twin Falls; by the end of winter she'd reach the eastern state line; by midsummer she'd have crossed the divide and be into the plains of Nebraska; by fall just shy of Des Moines; by the end of the year it would be Chicago; by the end of the following year she'd be heading back from the East Coast. "How's Wyoming this year, Mom?" we'd all joke. Nearly every two years she'd walk enough miles to criss-cross the country, from Washington DC to San Francisco, neither being a place my mother had ever been before.

Instead, walking the weedy sides of those same roads, my mother deliberately circled those same fields, claiming, by the rhythm of her steps, this place, finally, as her home.

1. Lumir and Evelyn Funda, summer 1964.

2. Funda family, circa 1942, shortly after Lumir returned from college to take over the farm. Top row: Lumir, Gladys, James Frank; bottom row: Annie and Frank.

3. Toni Kratochvilová's International Refugee Organization card, issued just a month after her escape from Czechoslovakia.

Der Inhaber dieser Bescheinigung   CM/1 Nr. __974 749__

Name __K R A T O C H V I L O V A__

Vorname __Antonie__   Geschlecht __F.__

Stempel
und Unterschrift
des Inhabers
(teilweise über
die Photographie)

steht unter dem Mandat
der Internationalen Flüchtlings-Organisation
(Spezial-Organisation der Vereinigten Nationen)

Ort der Ausgabestelle __Control Center Munich__

Datum __28. Dez. 1951__

Unterschrift des Beamten
der Ausgabestelle

4. (top) Frances Pejskar and Toni Kratochvilová,
probably after their escape in 1951.

5. (bottom) Toni on holiday with Joseph Pejskar
(on the right) and friends, after her 1951 escape.

6. "The Kiss": Toni Kratochvilová on
vacation somewhere in the Alps with
unknown man. At right is Frances Pejskar.

7. Toni and Lumir Funda on their
wedding day, January 19, 1957.

8. Lumir and Toni, January 1969,
after the funeral of Annie Funda.

9. Frank Funda around the time he moved
to Idaho from Minnesota in 1910.

10. Cover of a promotional pamphlet for Gooding, Idaho, one of the communities in the Snake River irrigation district in Southern Idaho, circa 1910. The painting by William Bittle Bells was commissioned by the Oregon Short Line Railroad to promote Carey Act settlement along the Snake River. Courtesy of Idaho State Library.

11. *Winter Sport.* Clarence Bisbee photo of one of
the rabbit drives in the Snake River region near Buhl
and Twin Falls, 1913. Courtesy of Twin Falls Public
Library, Bisbee Photography Collection, #666.

12. Annie Martinek Funda, around the time
of her wedding to Frank in 1915.

13. Frank and Annie in Donnelly, Idaho, circa 1964.

14. Frank Funda's anachronistic flower
painting done on glass, circa 1963.

15. Frank Funda's Easter painting, circa 1963.

16. *Idaho Industry*. Clarence Bisbee photo, 1913. Courtesy of Twin Falls Public Library, Bisbee Photography Collection, PC2433.

17. (above) Kratochvil family. Nine of the ten Kratochvil children are pictured with their parents, Josef and Karolina, at a wedding of one of the sons, circa 1931. The man to the far left, in the front row, is Václav, Toni's eldest brother, whom she spoke to before she escaped. Karel is not shown. Toni is the youngest child, pictured at the far right.

18. (opposite top) Evelyn with the "two Sylvies," in front of grandparents' cellar, July 2007. "Little Sylvie" Adamová, who often translated, is next to Evelyn. On the far right is her mother, who is Evelyn's first cousin Silvia Adamová; Silvia was deeded Toni's land in Višňové in 1993. This photo was taken standing next to a cellar, the only existing part of Josef and Karolina Kratochovil's (Toni's parents) original home.

19. (opposite bottom) Detail from carved gravestones at Toni's childhood church in Višňové.

4

Sage

"[Sagebrush] is an imposing monarch of the forest in exquisite
miniature . . . .but as a vegetable it is a distinguished failure."

MARK TWAIN
Roughing It

To consider the facts of my grandfather Frank Funda's birth, you
might never imagine him becoming a poor Idaho farmer. In fact,
Frank's background in Europe was solidly upper middle class.
Born in 1882, he grew up in a picturesque, forested city alongside
the gentle Elbe River. Just outside Prague, Poděbrady is famous
for its curative mineral baths and for being a "royal city," so named
by Bohemia's King George, who was born there and built a spectacular chateau there in the fifteenth century. According to Frank,
his father, Václav, was a well-to-do shopkeeper in Poděbrady, and
Frank grew up in a large house, complete with servants' quarters
and the servants to go with them. When he came of age, he was
inducted to serve in the Austro-Hungarian army, and after that
he trained as an accountant, a respectable occupation in the late
Austrian Empire. As pleasant as all that may have seemed, the
late nineteenth-century Czech National Revival had heightened
already existing political and religious tensions with the Austrian
ruling class, and increasingly Czechs were leaving for America.
When my great-grandfather's business began to decline, Frank's

father, mother, and three adult sisters were lured to the United States by the promise of freedom from Habsburg tyranny and an opportunity to make their fortunes. They left in 1907, the peak year for Bohemian migration pre–World War I, and settled in St. Paul, Minnesota. Czechs like my great-grandparents were the target of propaganda efforts that were spread throughout Europe by American employers who needed laborers and were willing to stretch the truth. Satirizing the hyperbolic language of such propaganda, playwright Josef Kajetan Tyl wrote in *Lesní panna aneb cesta do Ameriky* (*The Forest Maiden: A Journey to America*) that America was a place "where dumplings grow on trees. Underneath those trees are lakes filled with butter and the dumplings can be dipped in butter. . . . Pigs are roasted and pigeons and birds are already fried when they fly, cakes and kolace bake by themselves and coffee pours straight into the mouth."

What my great-grandfather Václav hadn't foreseen about the family's immigration, however, was that class-wise, they hadn't gained any ground. Although being a baker was somewhat akin to being a shop owner in the old country, in America their family was just one among the masses of "greasy Bohunks" and "dirty immigrants" who struggled to assimilate in the early days of the twentieth century. That didn't stop Frank from following his sisters and parents from Bohemia to Minnesota in 1908, where he took up working in his brother-in-law's bakery in St. Paul. Still feeling unsettled, however, he began clipping stories out of the Czech American newspapers about Bohemian immigrants successfully homesteading in southern Idaho, and he voraciously read the "commercial club" pamphlets that were distributed in the Midwest and East by the western railroads. In these he found idealistic descriptions of a western paradise that could be his for the taking.

And so in the spring of 1910, less than two years after his arrival in the United States, he boarded a train going west. The first leg of Frank's trip took him 1,300 miles to Ogden, Utah, just 40 miles from where I now live. There he boarded another train, run by the Oregon Short Line Railroad, which took him 200 miles north to Twin Falls, Idaho, in the Snake River region, and finally, after hitching a ride from a fellow Bohemian to Buhl, he filed on a forty-acre homestead just outside of town that he eventually dubbed "Rock Creek Ranch." He stayed in the area for nearly a decade before he and his wife, Annie, moved 150 miles northwest to Gem County, where I was born.

According to family lore, when he came to Idaho, Frank Funda performed that remarkable magic trick, right out of the Book of Isaiah; even though he knew nothing at all about farming, eventually, with hard work and determination, he made the desert "blossom as the rose." This transformation of the land became a salient element in family mythology and represented how Frank reinvented himself from an aimless Czech immigrant into the land baron of his dreams. Ultimately, as patriarch of our agricultural family, Frank was proud of the fact that as a farmer he helped to "feed the world." He boasted that the fruit from our Emmett farm was shipped all over the country and that the rows in his fields of grain ran straight and true. For him farming was a creative act, a true alchemy more powerful than any sixteenth-century hocus-pocus practiced by Rudolf II's court alchemists at Golden Lane on the grounds of Prague Castle. In Idaho Frank could transform the relentless sun into acres of gold that swayed in the morning breeze and fell easily before the threshing machine.

Frank originally came west to the Snake River region because of second-generation homesteading legislation, the Desert Land Act of 1894, which offered expanses of irrigated Idaho land. Although irrigation is as ubiquitous in the West today as sagebrush itself, back in the early twentieth century the widespread use of irrigation beyond the one hundredth meridian was a relatively new idea, a successor to Charles Wilber's famous nineteenth-century "rain follows the plow" theory. An amateur climatologist, Wilber may have said in 1881 that "man can persuade the heavens to yield their treasures of dew and rain upon the land he has chosen for his dwelling," but by the turn of the century he had been discredited by the failure of the land to acquiesce to the authority of his theory. If rain couldn't be enticed from the sky by the plow, water engineers were certain they could change the course of rivers instead.

Supported by the Reclamation Act of 1902, the Snake River region's new irrigation projects applied modern technology and ingenuity to create for the first time in the West a large-scale, co-operative system of irrigation canals that offered human control over growing conditions. Known as the Carey Act, the homesteading legislation promised prospective settlers that they could "Plant Dimes—Harvest Dollars in Idaho!" With what appears to be complete sincerity, booster materials from the period claimed that irrigation was what made farming in Idaho far superior to any other place in the country.

Frank was primed, therefore, to a be persuaded by such rhetoric that claimed southern Idaho was "the most attractive, the most fertile and the most wonderful part of the world." In addition to promises of abundant land, the natural moral superiority of the citizenry, supportive infrastructure (with plenty of trains for getting crops to market), stunning views, and endless recreational opportunities (five trout streams make their way through the area), the pamphlets also expressed a pressing need: "During certain seasons of the year," one pamphlet admitted, "it is sometimes very difficult to obtain men and this brings us to the 'crying need' of the Buhl Country—MEN—men with money, men without money, with or without families, but we need MEN." Boarding that train for Idaho in 1910, then, must have seemed to the twenty-eight-year-old Frank like answering a call to serve, and ever after he saw himself as a poster boy for western settlement.

In the spring of 1915 he traveled briefly back to Minnesota, where he married his childhood sweetheart, Annie Martinek, who had immigrated in 1912, after she spent several years working as a servant and nanny for a wealthy German family. Frank and Annie's first son, my uncle, James Frank, was born ten months after their marriage.

It wasn't easy, of course. Overcoming hardship, as in all good homestead stories, plays a part, and I remember my uncle saying, "All that homestead would grow was rocks!" He liked to tell stories about how he helped his parents clear the land and build a rock fence flanking the long drive from the road to their small house. Once when I was camping with my uncle and his wife, we returned home by way of Buhl, and he drove by the old farm, pulling the pickup off the side of the road so that he could point out to me the original ranch. The ground sloped away from the road, and I could see the long rock fence that ran parallel to the lane that led to a clump of trees down by the draw where the original house once stood. I pictured my uncle heaving rocks nearly as big as he was into the back of a cart that my grandmother was pulling along the bumpy field.

My grandfather featured that homestead in cycles of his own oral narratives, which he used to tell and retell at family gatherings. These included the tale of the neighbor arriving at the ranch to find Frank standing on a chair in a dress as my grandmother pinned the hem of a new skirt she was sewing. Another story references Buhl being a dry town and describes the local minister inviting himself to lunch one hot afternoon; just as they sat down to eat, the corks on the homebrew began to loudly pop, so Frank burst out in song and began to stomp his feet in time to the music in order to disguise the noise coming from the cellar.

But one of Frank's stories stands out as his favorite. Rocky, unproductive land meant that he had to find additional income to support himself and his wife, and it has long been a source of considerable family pride to declare that in addition to farming, Frank used his prior work experience in Minnesota to open in Buhl the very first all-electric bakery in the whole state of Idaho. Living in one of the most progressive states in the union to develop extensive water-powered electrical facilities, Frank therefore was among the true visionaries of the early twentieth century, who foresaw the great revolution electricity would bring to the West. Moreover his expertise as a baker of savory breads and fine European pastries brought the wild town of Buhl a measure of culture and made him an important community member.

The work was hard, and Frank and Annie put in long hours at the bakery. Late one afternoon after working next to the ovens since early in the morning, my tired grandmother wanted to return to the homestead. Frank still had work to do at the bakery, however, so he hitched up the horse and absently helped my grandmother onto the wagon seat. The trouble was that Annie had never learned how to drive a horse and wagon; indeed, she was afraid of horses. No problem, Frank assured her. Babe, the big red bay, knew the way home, and she wouldn't even have to lift the reins. At the edge of the town, where the road turned right toward the ranch, the horse calmly turned left—and then slowed to a stop—right in front of a house. "Pokrač! Honem!" Annie hissed in Czech. "Go on! Hurry up!" But Babe was unfazed by her entreaties. She gave a sidelong glance toward the house, where the curtains stirred slightly. Mortified that someone might see and recognize her plight, Annie was about to reach for the reins when Babe moved on—and then stopped at the next house, for another excruciating moment, and then the one after that. Too much of a lady to yell at the horse, too much of a greenhorn to pick up the reins, Annie sat stiffly on the seat, staring straight ahead and feeling helpless as Babe circled the town, stopping at nearly every house. Nor was there any comfort in at last comprehending what the horse was doing: he was following Frank's daily bread route, pausing where he had paused that very morning and a hundred times before while Frank set freshly baked loaves on the stoop of nearly every house in town. By the time Annie and Babe turned at last onto the road that led out to the homestead, it was dusk. Frank had already walked home and, finding no wife and no horse, was imagining the worst until he saw the wagon coming down the lane with his red-faced wife fuming in the wagon seat.

My grandfather retold this story often as the family gathered around my grandmother's big walnut table for huge Sunday dinners. As he lit his after-dinner pipe and the women cleared the dishes, he would tell again the cycle of homesteading tales. Even though we had heard them all before, he was a skilled narrator who knew how to fully engage an audience. He puffed meditatively on his pipe, never rushing his performance. When he told the bread route story, he pretended not to notice my grandmother squirming in her chair, finding any excuse to leave the table—the coffee had finished percolating, or she'd forgotten to dust the kolaches with powdered sugar. He winked at me as the rest of us laughed at the moment in the story where Annie realized what the horse was doing.

The benediction of the story always included someone reminding us that years after Frank and Annie left Buhl, he wrote down the stories of his experiences on the homestead, and they were published in a regular column he wrote for the *Hlasatel*, a famous Czech-language newspaper that was published in Chicago and distributed to Czech Americans around the country. Thus, Frank's stories brought the family some measure of fame.

Among the stories the bread route tale remained the most popular, and my own parents, it is said, met as a result of its publication. Friends of my mother, who was then living in New York, had been reading Frank's stories and began corresponding with him after the bread route story was published; through them my mother and father began writing each other, thus beginning their love story.

My very existence, therefore, hinges on the certainty of a horse, a bakery, and a homestead in Buhl.

Trouble is, what I thought I knew as the facts about Frank's early days at the Rock Creek homestead, for the most part, have proven to be a series of downright falsehoods, dismantled one by one as I researched the details of Frank's homesteading stories. I had been utterly charmed by Frank's tales and how they made a compelling case for my family's relevance in the history of the West, and I wanted to know more. Even though Buhl was within a few hours' drive of both my hometown of Emmett (to its north) and my present home of Logan, Utah (to its south), I really didn't know much about the area. Lacking any more artifact than the stories themselves, I set out to read historical accounts and newspapers from the region and learn as much as I could about the privately funded irrigation projects of the Carey Act, which promised to domesticate that unpredictable Snake River for service to the greater good of agricultural success. The Great Twin Falls irrigation tract, which included the Buhl district, was the largest irrigation project in the United States in 1910. Moreover, under the Carey Act Idaho would bring more desert land into cultivation than any other state. Those facts are without dispute.

From here, however, the waters of the Snake River and its history get a little murky, and myth and hyperbole swirl in the current of family history like a fast-moving eddy.

Promotional pamphlets published by the railroads glossed over the harsh realities of this high desert and featured instead paintings on their covers that made Idaho look like the Elysian fields, complete with toga-clad and winged goddesses anointing the land with elixirs of fertility. Inside the text promised that "at the threshold of this great State, the goddess of GOOD FORTUNE has thrown wide the portals of OPPORTUNITY." Carey Act advertising likewise assured settlers that precisely 98 percent of the land is "level, has rich soil, is free of rock, lava reefs or gullies or coulees." Like a kid who adamantly denies he could have broken the vase in the family room because he's been upstairs the whole morning, listening to that techno-punk band he likes while was working on his chapter 3 math homework, the specificity of the denial is its own indictment. Although a rhetorical sleight of hand had labeled the Snake River Valley "Magic Valley," and nearby towns "Bliss" and "Eden," and the state as a whole the "Gem State," this is no paradise of easy living.

Idaho-born historian Leonard Arrington recalls his father telling a meeting of farmers in Hollister that "all this place needs is good people and lots of water"—to which the reply from the audience was, "That's all Hell needs!" Even today, decades after the Carey Act has transformed more than 630,000 acres in the state from sagebrush to marginally arable land, only a narrow belt of farms runs along the Snake River, and less than ten miles due south of the river the land is barren desert, dotted with the odd, wind-battered ranch house.

From the time of the earliest white explorers the landscape of the Snake River region mystified men who could only conceive of it in absolutes. Lewis and Clark took note of the "eternal sage," and explorer Wilson Prince Hunt described the "vast tracts . . .

[that] must ever defy cultivation." Hunt, who came to explore the southern Snake River region in 1811 for the Pacific Fur Company, warned that this was a place "where no man permanently resides," and he called it "a vast, uninhabited solitude, . . . looking much like the ruins of the world." The explorers who came after Hunt in the mid-nineteenth century thought of it as a "dead country" and "an aggressive wilderness," where "the conditions of survival required a whole new technique."

Look in any direction from Buhl, and it is true that within the circle of a hundred-mile radius you'll still find a bizarre and desolate land of inhospitable extremes: fire and ice, record-breaking heights and astonishing depths. In addition to sagebrush expanses that still dominate the area, the circle would encompass a series of lava tubes and ice caves, including the Shoshone Caves, which are reportedly haunted by a Indian princess buried in the ice; the Bruneau sand dunes, which claim the title of highest dunes in North America; the site of Wilson Butte Cave, which provided archaeologists with the first evidence of human occupation in the Snake River plain and is among the oldest human archaeological sites in North America; the spectacular Shoshone waterfalls, "Niagara of the West," which few know is actually fifty feet taller than Niagara Falls; Hagerman Fossil Beds, which contains the continent's largest concentration of horse fossils; and the 2.5-billion-year-old granite monoliths of the City of Rocks. Closer to Buhl you can find the strange, massive rock formation called Balanced Rock, which is a 48-foot-tall, forty-ton rock poised on a pedestal less than 4.5 square feet in size. The Snake River itself has a greater annual flow than either the Colorado or the Rio Grande, and crossing the river near Twin Falls is the site of the Perrine Bridge, once the highest bridge in the world and spanning the 500-foot-deep, 1,500-foot-wide canyon at Twin Falls, near the place where Evel Knievel attempted, and failed, to jump a

motorcycle across the canyon in 1974. These sheer perpendicu-
lar cliffs of the Snake River Canyon slash through the land, and
in some places you can look right across stretches of sage and rabbit brush without even knowing the canyon is only yards in front
of you. Walk through this country on a moonless night, and before you could even sense the danger, you might slip and plunge
through the chilled canyon air, hundreds of feet, past the raptors
nesting in the cliff walls, and smash on the rocky canyon bed below. But there's more. Less than fifty miles northeast of the bridge
is the edge of the volcanic lava field now called "Craters of the
Moon," with its ominously named sites "Devil's Orchard," "In-
ferno Cone," and the "Blue Dragon." As part of the "Great Rift"
volcanic zone the black expanse of this area is the largest and
deepest unbroken field of lava flows in North American. Seismic
activity in the area indicates this is a landscape still forming, a
geological infant, so to speak, and scientists claim the area, which
hasn't seen an eruption in two thousand years, is long overdue.
The ground is covered with shards of volcanic clinkers that make
simple walking a treacherous task, and even sagebrush has a hard
time growing amid the frozen swells of lava. Craters of the Moon's
eleven hundred square miles of cinder cones, fissures, and lava
fields (roughly the size of Rhode Island) create a black scar of volcanic land forms that can even be seen from space. It is appropri-
ate, therefore, that in 1969 *Apollo* astronauts, including Alan
Shepard and Czech American Eugene Cernan, came to Craters
of the Moon to prepare for future moon landings. Where else,
NASA officials thought, could they find any closer approximation
to the topography of that other world?

In 1910, however, when Frank arrived on that train, recognizing that the region had been from the time of the early explorers,
and remained, an uncongenial backdrop to the agricultural drama
wasn't the party line. Boosterism ruled the day. Although the town

of Buhl was less than four years old when he arrived, the newspaper was bragging that it already had a population approaching the fifteen hundred mark and had "passed from a small village to a modern little city" because it possessed all the big city's amenities, including electric lights, a new school building, several hotels and churches, two banks, and numerous merchants, as well as cement sidewalks, daily mail service, a volunteer fire department, a waterworks system, and a city sewer system. Resisting the western character stereotypes, the boosters claimed that the people of the area "are civilized, [and] you do not need to carry a six shooter or gatling gun, not even a pen knife. They are progressive, industrious, intelligent, peaceable people." Too much of this rah-rah talk, however, was perilous, and boosters walked a tightrope between such reassurances about how civilized the region was and their main message: that the Snake River valley was a cultural and environmental blank slate, full of "golden opportunities," as they said, for people hungry for a fresh start. Even though the promotional pamphlets like those Frank saw vowed a "scrupulous conformity with facts," writers of the time knew how to turn a phrase to dramatize that main message. In a newspaper editorial, for instance, the land's awe-inspiring transformation to agriculture was credited to "the hand of industry" that had "tapped the great Snake River . . . [so that its] waters gushed forth, and mingled with the rich soil. . . . The farmers came and sowed and reaped and were rewarded," and they would ultimately arrive "at the temple of success." Citing the "never-failing ditches," farmers quoted in the pamphlets demonstrated their unshaken belief in irrigation as a modern technology, borne of human ingenuity, certain to compensate for an imperfect natural world. Such optimism and faith in technology were not only ubiquitous in Idaho but were a nationwide phenomenon during the Progressive Era, prior to World War I. People believed theirs was a world without limits. And in

Idaho irrigation was a means of dominion over a wild land: "there is no saying how far, when the need arises, the engineering skill or the mechanical daring of man will go toward overcoming the obstacles that Nature has interposed." Unlike our nation's first Puritan colonists, who believed they would succeed only if God found them righteous and therefore blessed their efforts, the first white settlers of southern Idaho figured God had nothing to do with it. Since the 1890s western writers had been expressing what historian Hugh Lovin identifies as "the new irrigation gospels," in which Idaho was depicted as a man-made paradise, and their arguments were not subtle. Case in point, the masthead of one local paper, the *Filer Films*, laid claim to their settlement as "the Center of the Modern Garden of Eden." The same year Frank arrived in Idaho, C. L. Blanchard of the US Reclamation Service wrote in the *National Geographic* that irrigation was a "miracle" and that the deserts of the West were "the sleeping empires awaiting exploitation and development." With irrigation the Idaho farmer was "entirely liberated . . . from the caprice of the weather" by "an inexhaustible supply of water." Buhl farmer Gustave Kunze was quoted as saying, "When my pastures need rain, do I look anxiously at the heavens? Not on your life; I simply press the button (figuratively speaking) and can have a gentle shower or a gully washer at my option." To hear the boosters of the time tell it, "the farmer in the Buhl country invariably reaps bounteous crops, never experiences a crop failure to any degree whatsoever, and grows steadily prosperous in increasing measure, from day to day."

With such superlatives it should come as no surprise then that shortly after Frank first arrived in Idaho, a newspaper editorial insisted that Buhl was a "metropolis" where there was, "as yet, no need of a graveyard, [because] no one ever dies, and the city has not even a hatchet that needs burying." I can't help but think that the editor was only half joking.

Perhaps Idaho demanded exaggeration. Maybe it could only be conceived of in such broad strokes. If Frank is any measure, Idaho certainly inspired belief in the utterly transformative power of boundless imagination. If irrigation could make desert into an Eden, couldn't that Eden make Frank into anything he wanted?

The local newspaper never seemed aware of the schizophrenia evident in its portrayal of Buhl as a "progressive" community, but one also romantically beset by lawless horse thieves who rode through a landscape characterized by fierce coyotes, rattlesnakes, and cougars. Even while the newspaper was declaring in 1909 that Buhl was "no longer a sagebrush wilderness," it was also regularly discussing the twin scourge of jackrabbits and sagebrush as impediments to progress and portraying the homesteaders' efforts at eradication of both as a kind of Idaho Manifest Destiny.

Botanical surveys confirm what most of us already suspect: that sagebrush is the single most widespread plant in the West, and Philip Fradkin has written that it prefers "to dominate by pure ordinariness." During the early twentieth century Idaho farmers believed that huge stands of sagebrush, with some bushes standing chest-high, merely indicated the potential fertility of a virgin soil, but they nevertheless were quick to find ways to eradicate this impediment to their certain progress. T. B. Hendricks of Twin Falls was among the first of several inventors nationwide to submit patents for sage-grubbing machines, and in 1906 the Hendricks Grubber was advertised as the "acme of perfection," a machine that could "perform the labor of ten men" as it "thoroughly pulverizes the ground leaving it level and mellow, . . . a perfect seed bed."

If Hendricks's $100–$150 price tag was too much, there were other methods of grubbing sage. Some settlers experimented with "chaining" or "railing," which meant breaking the brush with heavy chains or timbers dragged by horses across the rough terrain. This worked relatively well on cold days when the sage would snap off at the ground, but still the roots of the plants would need to be plowed or dug up. Setting the sage afire might effectively clear the land, but settlers had to be careful not to start dangerous wildfires. However, the most typical method was hand grubbing sage with a mattock—difficult work, to say the least. If the parcel was relatively free of rock and the sagebrush was low growing (something that actually indicated poorer soil), a strong man might be able to clear an acre a day, but in the rocky soils of the Buhl area, where young men fresh off the train often took jobs picking up boulders for a dollar a day, settlers like Frank were not so fortunate. Carey Act homesteading laws took this difficulty into account, and unlike other homesteading laws the Carey Act required settlers to clear and put into cultivation only one-sixteenth of their land in the first year and one-eighth of their land within the entire three-year period it took to prove up.

But while farmers were out grubbing sage, scientists and inventors were pondering ways to make it useful. They were certain that sagebrush "merely awaited man's ingenuity to find new uses for it." The Buhl newspaper ran stories about promising research, and even Thomas Edison tried to rewrite the plant's story by arguing that the sage of Idaho and Nevada deserts was a valuable commodity that could yield millions of dollars, if we could just find the key to its worth. Scientists and entrepreneurs experimented with fruit and berry plants grafted onto sage stock; invented methods for making sage paper; mixed sage-based medicinal teas (based on indigenous people's formulas) and tonics for tuberculosis; manufactured a sage charcoal; hawked sage-infused shampoos for baldness and dandruff; and extracted tar, creosote oil, and rubber substances and distilled tannic acid and wood alcohol from the plants. But sagebrush resisted efforts to turn it into a compliant and profitable commodity. Instead the only real use settlers found for it was as hot and fast-burning fuel for their cook fires.

Once the land was cleared and planted, however, the difficulties still were not at an end. In 1911, the year after Frank's arrival, troublesome jackrabbits were so numerous that the local paper claimed they "travel in flock[s] like black birds." Capable of devouring entire crops in a day or killing orchard saplings by eating the bark, the jackrabbits were dealt with by various means including poisoning and fencing; however, the poisoning was indiscriminate in what it killed, and the fencing proved to be more of a scam to the buyer than an effective deterrent for the rabbits. In her memoir, *We Sagebrush Folks*, Annie Pike Greenwood wrote that the man who sold her husband, Charley, their rabbit-proof fence had "convinced Charley of its merit, but he had failed to convince the rabbits." In the spirit of making a silk purse out of a sow's ear, residents in nearby Jerome, Idaho, once killed, dressed, and packed in ice a train car full of five thousand cleaned rabbits that were bound for the meat markets of Detroit and Pittsburgh. According to a 1911 notice in the *Twin Falls Times* entitled "Market for Idaho Jacks," merchants got around the general skepticism of locals by announcing a six-cent bounty for each dressed carcass—"and the rest was easy. People turned out with all the shot guns they could muster." Certain that theirs was a creative solution to a perennial problem, the newspaper account concluded, "This is said to be the first commercial shipment of rabbits that has left the state." However, there was no second shipment of Idaho jacks, which remained plentiful but proved unpalatable. Serving Idaho jacks to the nation was just another one of those unfulfilled schemes.

The most effective method of getting rid of jackrabbits was tracking the beasts down and killing them one by one. For years the Buhl newspaper featured stories about rabbit drives where two teams of as many as two hundred men drove hundreds or thousands of animals into a fenced enclosure and then shot or clubbed them to death, or they drove them to the edge of a nearby bluff, where, says one writer, "the jackrabbits that were not shot at last committed suicide by leaping into the canyon." Historian Mark Fiege calls the drives a "masculine and overt demonstration of the desert conquest . . . a ritual in which farmers reenacted the subjugation of the desert," and although he suggests that the huge numbers, like the claim of twelve thousand rabbits killed in one drive near Hansen in 1906, were hyperbole, photos taken by Twin Falls photographer Clarence Bisbee still show a blur of hundreds of panicked rabbits running wildly in one of the enclosures. In contrast to these portrayals of conquest and mayhem, however, is how the local community set out to depict these rabbit drives as genteel events in which the rising middle class spent their Sunday afternoons at "enjoyable" gatherings of "sport" that exhibited "a prevailing community spirit." Greenwood describes one drive just north of Buhl where ice cream cones and "something more invigorating" were "passed around freely"; refreshments, she concludes, had become such a highly anticipated part of the rabbit drive ritual that they "never again can be omitted." Reporting one successful drive of June 1911, the Buhl newspaper noted that during the morning five hundred rabbits were killed, and then, without so much as a paragraph break, the account continues, "Lunch was then served, Mr. Beinz having a boiler of hot coffee provided." The paper even boasted that a writer from the *Ladies Home Journal* was in attendance that day and planned a feature on the drive. No one then questioned why one of the emerging women's magazines of the time would cover such an event, and no amount of free coffee or invigorating refreshments could make Idaho rabbit drives a palatable story for the readers of *Ladies Home Journal*, which never offered anything but a decidedly sanitized version of life, sans jackrabbit carcasses.

As I see it, then, Frank arrived in a place characterized by a culture of embellishment, where stretchers and whoppers and colorful tales were merely an expected part of the local rhetoric, both private and public. Maybe, then, he's to be forgiven, I thought, when a search of land records proved that, to be entirely accurate, my grandfather never in fact "homesteaded" but instead purchased one of the forty-acre parcels sold by local land speculator Oscar Boswell, who had actually been the one to file the Carey claim on that and several other parcels before he left Buhl for retirement in Washington state. This is no minor discrepancy, for within western mythology "proving up" on a homestead establishes your muster, and having the first white name associated in official documents with a tract of land bears witness to your involvement in a transformative act with national implications. That would have been doubly so for a poor immigrant like Frank. On the other hand, buying land in a fair and square exchange of money for deed remains on the level of a prosaic transaction, made all the more pedestrian in this instance by flowery legalese that has Frank promising, as the document reads, that "the party of the first part shall quietly enjoy the said premises." The closest Frank came to actual homesteading, I was to discover in the historical record, was when he served as one of the witnesses for Václav Miskovsky, a fellow immigrant, who was filing his "final proof" on Carey Act land nearby.

And that rock fence my uncle claims to have helped build? I discovered James Frank Funda was born sixteen miles away in Twin Falls, never even lived on the ranch (more on that in a moment), and he was only three years old—hardly rock-toting size—when he and my grandparents left the Snake River valley and moved to Gem County for good. But what's a little fudging when you're related to a man who rewrites regional history?

In addition to Frank's oral narratives both a 1965 newspaper announcement noting my grandparents' fiftieth wedding anniversary and Frank's own obituary claim that he developed a place called the Rock Creek Ranch and also purchased a bakery in Buhl, where he would become "known for his baking and culinary arts." Upon research, however, neither of these assertions holds up either. When I heard that a colleague at my university had actually grown up near Rock Creek Ranch, I thought I had hit the historical motherlode. Norm Jones was the head, mind you, of my university's History Department and therefore someone who banked on the absolute accuracy of historical detail. "Yes," Norm answered after I explained the family history of the bakery and the ranch outside town, he was familiar with Rock Creek Ranch. Pause. "It's a well-known locale in Twin Falls County." Another pause. "What years were your family there?" he asked. "The bakery was in Buhl, you say?" I got the sense he was being politely evasive, and Norm's questions were among the first signs that had me scrutinizing my family's claims more closely.

Historical records for Rock Creek Ranch were not that difficult to track down—and they were impressive. The stream that lent its name to the ranch flanked a portion of the original Oregon Trail. Moreover, the Rock Creek Ranch and the nearby town also named Rock Creek were subjects of local fame as a stage stop and mail station—during the 1870s. Homesteader Herman Stricker ran the Rock Creek Store and ranched adjacent land that, before his death, totaled a whopping 960 acres. His grand Victorian home is listed on the National Registry of Historic Places, and in 1984 that home and a five-acre parcel around it were granted by the family to the Idaho State Historical Society for use as an educational and cultural center, a homesteading mecca—Idaho style—complete with bus parking lot (already there) and a forthcoming visitors' center depicting life on the frontier at the turn of the century.

All of this proves that Rock Creek Ranch was, of course, there well before my grandfather's arrival in Idaho in 1910. In fact, the distance from the plot of land just northwest of Buhl officially listed in Frank's name to the real Rock Creek Ranch, just south of Hansen, Idaho, is nearly forty miles—no small distance when measured up against the story of Frank walking home from the bakery in Buhl to the ranch late one afternoon. And while it is true that Frank's little forty-acre parcel in Buhl was adjacent to a stream, topographic maps show it was the less than romantically named Mud Creek. The stream of Rock Creek itself never meanders closer than twenty-five miles to the northeast of what was my grandparents' land, although the "Rock Creek" name is ubiquitous throughout the entire region. A park in Buhl is so named, and innumerable businesses and other entities around Twin Falls County and nearby communities borrow the "Rock Creek" moniker, including an automotive shop, a coffee shop, a dairy, a church, a metalwork shop, and an upholstery shop. Frank, therefore, wasn't the only one who wanted to draw on the cachet of the name.

So what about that history-making bakery? Newspaper notices from the *Buhl Herald* never mention Frank Funda as owner of any bakery in town. Instead he would have found upon his arrival in Buhl two bakeries with thriving businesses. Already dominating the local scene were the Bon Ton Bakery (a name that is in keeping with the genteel image Buhl was striving for) and the nearby Buhl Bakery, which bragged about its modern oven and claimed that "Every Home is supplied with Bread and Cakes from The Buhl Bakery." In the vein of exaggeration I had, by now, come to expect, the bakery also made assurances that its breads were so "toothsome" that any child raised on the Buhl Bakery bread "won't be much [in] need of a doctor."

Electric or not, Frank Funda's bakery in Buhl never existed. In point of fact, just a year and a half after his arrival—and only one week after he'd served as a witness on his friend's homesteading claim—the newspaper revealed that Frank had moved north to Twin Falls, where he had "accepted a position as baker in a Twin Falls Bakery." "Accepted a position." In other words, he left Buhl even before his marriage to Annie, and while it is true he returned to work as a baker, he never *owned* a bakery—anywhere—either in Buhl or in Twin Falls, where I would also find evidence of several bakeries already in existence—all advertising their impeccable sanitary facilities, their modern packaging and delivery, and the world-class qualifications of their professional bakers. For instance, Mr. Stimson, who took over as the manager and head baker of Smith & Smith's Bakery at almost the exact time Frank went to Twin Falls, was said to be an "expert baker," who had a notable reputation for his fancy cakes and pastries. Down the road at "Graham's First Premium Bakery" Mr. Graham himself claimed to be "The World's Best Baker," a title from "the HIGHEST TRIBUNAL OF BREAD MAKERS in the World." Frank, on the other hand, was not newsworthy. In spite of his experience in his brother-in-law's bakery in Minnesota, the *Twin Falls Times* never made mention of Frank joining any bakery in town, which would suggest to me that he didn't even become the head baker at someone else's business.

Records do prove that Frank kept title to his land in Buhl until 1919. Apparently taking his cue from land developer Oscar Boswell, he somehow managed to buy two adjoining lots of land at some point, though there is no evidence he ever farmed them. According to the notice in the *Buhl Herald* about his departure for Twin Falls, he arranged to rent his land to another Czech immigrant family, the Zachs. That brief newspaper notice, barely two lines long, served to significantly unravel details of my family story about Frank's homesteading and his bakery. More important, for me, it indicated a significant and hard-to-swallow truth: Frank, like so many other settlers to come to Idaho lacking any prior farming experience, had admitted to failure on the ranch within just two years of his arrival. The myth of his blooming desert was just that.

Frank was among many who found out that making a farm successful in the Buhl area took more than just will, desire, and imagination. Without significant capital investment it was not something many single men managed alone. Land speculators were known to only improve land to the bare minimum—often tossing seed onto land, watering it once, and calling it a crop so as to qualify under the Carey Act's minimum requirements for cultivation. At best five cleared acres and a tar-papered shack might have been what Frank bought from Boswell; at worst, suggest local newspaper accounts, he was among the many new settlers during the winter of 1910 who had to resort to living in tents because the local carpenters couldn't build settlers' shacks fast enough. Frank might have thought twice about the move west if only he had read the well-respected magazine *Wallaces' Farmer*, which just months before he came to Idaho quoted one of the settlers as saying that the Carey Act lots in Idaho were "tremendous grafts," that the real estate men often underestimated the cost to clear sagebrush and bring a parcel into production, and that the advertising had overestimated the possible yield you could get from the land. Once lots had been sold, the story went on, the irrigation companies were quick to relinquish control of the projects, even before they were done building the head gates. Even if the infrastructure was in place, irrigation was a skill few quickly mastered, and some had to resort to hiring one of the itinerant irrigators to teach them how to most effectively manage their small share of the water available from the canals. Others struggled along, learning about culverts and corrugates and head gates as they went. If their land was level or naturally sloped away from the main ditch, they had a higher success rate, but the local newspaper regularly made jokes about greenhorns trying to coax water to run uphill. With all this against him it is no real surprise then that sooner or later Frank's complete lack of farming experience would be his undoing.

Even so, the community would have placed the blame for failure squarely at the door of the man, never the place or circumstances. In a column entitled "The Passing of the Sagebrush" the *Buhl Herald* reluctantly admitted that there was some percentage of attrition in the community: "Of course we occasionally find a man with a sluggish mind and tired muscles. This man makes a failure. It is not the fault of the country. The same man would have starved to death in the garden of Eden." Annie Pike Greenwood, however, had a different spin on the situation after her husband, Charley, admitted they too had failed to make a go of their homestead. "Most men long for the soil," she wrote. "Adam, I am sure, regretted the lost Garden of Eden, but I suspect that Eve fed him the apple in order to get off the farm."

If neither Frank's history-making bakery nor his homestead was real, I still had one slim hope—the stories Frank had published in the *Hlastel*, the Czech American newspaper. Finding those, I felt, would mean I could claim a legitimate literary heritage, even if I couldn't claim a homesteader in the family. And, if Frank's stories published in those pages turned out to be a fiction, well, so what? English professors like me don't think telling stories is a crime. Fictional stories I could forgive—as long as the pages themselves weren't a fiction.

That a Czech newspaper named the *Hlasatel* existed is true. But even a cursory look at the *Hlasatel* will confirm it was a conventional newspaper that published national and world news in the Czech language, not quaint or humorous stories about Idaho homesteaders. Although my family always insisted that Frank published in *Hlasatel*, another Czech periodical entitled *Hospodář* (which translates as "The Farmer") emerged as a more likely candidate. With its strong circulation in the early part of the century, both the time and the topic were right. But the focus was on *practical* farming matters, not sentimental ones. Advice on things like how to treat a bloated calf or eradicate weeds was its staple, and I never found Frank's stories anywhere in the bundles of the *Hospodář* stored in my parents' basement. Perhaps his stories appeared in issues not among my family's collection, but how, I thought, could a family that so prided itself on Frank's literary accomplishment not have kept copies of those stories? At this point I'd even be happy with a "letter to the editor" signed by Frank.

The one thing that still suggested the possibility of Frank's literary career were the letters that began my parents' relationship, which, I'd always been told, had its origin in my mother's friends reading Frank's publications. My mother's friends wrote to Frank about his stories, and then through them my father wrote to my mother. However, this was no smoking gun either. In a world where Czech immigrants had numerous ways of knowing each other, Mother's friends the Valentas might have first written to Frank for any number of reasons, especially given that they were part of a vital Czech subculture in New York City that sponsored refugees like my mother and prided itself on initiating new immigrants into the larger national community. And by 1956, when my mother was in New York, my grandfather was a member of a Czech lodge in Nampa, Idaho, which maintained close ties to the ZCBJ, a national fraternal organization that fostered connection among Czechs across the country. It is no stretch to assume that my mother's friends might have first heard of the Fundas through those ties. To assume my parents' correspondence is proof of the existence of Frank's published stories, therefore, isn't something the available evidence verifies.

Nonetheless, the existence of those publications is a story my elderly aunt Gladys, Frank's last living offspring, continues to perpetuate by telling me that she has the clippings tucked away in her antique safe, which is hidden in her home behind a false wall. Because I want to believe those stories exist, I ask her repeatedly if I can have copies of them; however, she makes excuses: they are in Czech, and with our limited abilities neither of us would be able to understand them; they would be troublesome to find among all the investment paperwork and collectible coins she has stuffed on the shelves; I will be able to find them for myself when I inherit the safe and its contents—which means, "Soon enough. Next subject, please." She guards those secrets with the kind of vehemence she uses to guard herself, even still, against unpleasantness. Only a few months ago she wrote me that she still desperately missed her parents, even though, she added, "it's been almost 20 years since they passed." For the record, Frank died more than forty years ago, and Annie followed just three years after that, in 1969. These are indisputable facts, etched in my memory, verified in newsprint and public records, and chiseled in the granite of their gravestones.

I stopped researching Frank's life for months after I uncovered the lies in his Buhl stories. Finding out more felt risky since my concept of my family and of my own place in an agricultural West had already been rocked by my discoveries. But neither could I let go of what I'd found. Every time I'd take hikes through the sagebrush stands on my favorite local mountain trail, I thought about Frank and his narrative sleight-of-hand.

Reasoning that "myth has often been mistaken for reality in the West," writer and environmentalist Philip Fradkin has said that when western settlers ripped out the native sagebrush and replaced it with grain and beans and other crops, it "was like tearing out history and replacing it with fantasy." As an academic studying the West, I could recognize and intellectualize such conclusions in their broad historical context. As a member of a family where such fantasies had been perpetuated, however, I felt betrayed. It was like believing that the beautiful designs of a crop circle had been created by intelligent life from the heavens only to find they had been crafted by a drunk pair named Doug and Dave.

So Frank and I remained at a stalemate.

That fall I attended the Western Literature Association conference in Boise, and I sat in on a discussion where colleagues whom I admired and trusted talked about the surprises and perils of writing biographies. Panelists Judy Nolte Temple and Mary Clearman Blew, who had written biographies about several western men and women, talked about the "otherworldly communication," the "thrill," the "mystical experience" they had felt when taking on-site trips to research the lives of their subjects. Susanne Bloomfield maintained that there is no substitute for going to the place where the subjects of your biography actually lived. Arguing that the physical act of being in these places is important "in order to understand elements about a life that you don't find in texts," she told a story of writing Elinor Pruitt Stewart's biography: "In her letters, she talked about how she couldn't go to a church, but if she looked at the mountain across from her room, there were gullies and the trees in the fall would turn into a cross of gold. And I walked in the room, and I looked out at the site, and there was the cross of gold. It was meant to be, and it just totally took my breath away."

As I talked to these women privately after the panel, I admitted to myself that I'd been reluctant to do the on-site research for Frank's life, even though Buhl was less than two hundred miles from where I lived. On that very trip I had driven within twenty miles of it on my way to Boise, and as I drove by the interstate exit again on my way home, I knew I needed to take up Frank's story again. Because nothing before now had proven stable, I hoped that the constancy of the land itself might feel like a fixed and reliable touchstone. I wasn't expecting the kind of apparitions or "cross of gold" visions that Susanne and the others had been talking about, but I did hope that taking the time to find the farm and look at that ground for myself would give me the chance to come to some resolution about what I had been finding. I sought something simple and unequivocal.

Later that month Jake had a fall break from fifth grade, and he planned to join me on what he was calling our "vacation." I'd only been to Frank's farm in Buhl once before, nearly forty years ago, when my uncle pulled off the road to show me the rock fence, something that I now had to question if I'd actually seen. But this time I was prepared with plenty of legal documentation and maps to pinpoint the farm. I had an address for the homestead provided by the Twin Falls County courthouse, where someone in the county clerk's office had kindly translated the tangle of the property description—sections and quarters and coordinates—into a real address for me. She had even provided a picture of the modest, single-story house, taken for the assessment paperwork when the owners built on an addition to the original structure in the 1980s. We were also equipped with topographic maps, geographical maps, tourist maps, and two satellite maps from online sources, both of which had been taken only months prior to our trip. In one satellite image I could see the rooftop and the shadows of the trees at the end of a dead-end road where Mapquest unmistakably indicated the address I'd been given by the Twin Falls county clerk's office. I could pull back one frame on the satellite image and see the lay of the land and the nearby creeks, and with the click of another button I could see these creeks overlaid with their names: Deep Creek about a quarter mile west and Mud Creek running alongside the north boundary of the property. With the help of these maps and documents I knew I was much better prepared than my grandfather had been in 1910 for what I would find in Buhl.

On our way to Twin Falls Jake and I took a brief detour just off the interstate to Eden, Idaho, where Jake thought it would be fun to have lunch at the "Garden of Eden," a food court inside the combination gas station and tourist gift shop at the travelers' complex. The artificial garden looked neon green under fluorescent lights, and we ate tacos next to a plastic palm tree while a little girl at the next table giggled at the mechanical parrot that wagged his head back and forth and warned of the dangers of Eve. Jake snickered and pointed to the place between two huge synthetic boulders where the red eyes of a python glowed on and off. The truck stop made no apologies for being a cheesy, neon version of the Garden of Eden, but from the looks of all the people around us, it attracted visitors, nonetheless—just as Eden, Idaho, itself had attracted settlers with illusions of a garden.

From there we took Highway 50 south to Hansen, Idaho, and on to the real Rock Creek, where the terrain was rough, sufficiently like something out of a John Wayne movie, and I could see why Frank would have been attracted to it as the setting for his stories. We drove winding roads, and I took photos of the landscape, even though I had no claim to this place. Late that afternoon we stopped at the Rock Creek Gas Station & Store for sodas. The building was almost new, but with its false front, log construction, and boardwalk porch, it obviously aspired to a touristy version of the Old West. Before we went into the store, Jake paused next to the nearly life-sized, chainsaw-carved statue of a moustachioed cowboy, and as he leaned shoulder-to-shoulder against the frozen figure, he asked me to take a picture of the two of them. Just before I snapped the photo, he slyly gave the cowboy two-fingered rabbit ears. Inside a bulletin board was posted with newspaper clippings written by a local historian about what a "Wild West" place this had been during the late nineteenth century—an Idaho version of Tombstone, complete with shameless desperados and violent shootouts. A far cry from the region's attempt back in 1910 to portray itself as a utopian civilization with modern cities, the clipping recapped the story of a dead man paraded around town in his coffin by the same drunk revelers who had shot him in the first place. While I scanned the bulletin board, Jake lingered in a candy aisle that featured "old-time" treats like horehound candy and Necco wafers, but finally he made his decision and fingered cellophane-wrapped beef jerky out of a plastic jar as I slid the ten-dollar bill across a varnished wooden counter at the cash register. Thus far it had been a day of illusions.

Buhl and the land once in Frank's name was still another hour away. That night Jake and I went only as far as Twin Falls, where I planned to spend the following morning doing additional research in the county library. For some reason I was putting off the trip to the site of Frank's place on Mud Creek. I knew it, but I was unwilling to consider why. Although libraries hadn't proved safe haven from ambiguity in my search for Frank, at least I knew my way around them.

Always a good sport, Jake was happy as long as the motel had a pool and a free, all-you-can-eat breakfast buffet. He even indulged me when the electronic game he'd brought along ran out of battery power in the middle of my stint in the library's special collections room, so obligingly, he fed my copy machine with the coins, and while I skimmed a biography of I. B. Perrine—one of the developers who had raised funds to build the Southside irrigation project—Jake flipped through a huge US atlas that illustrated the history of the evolving boundaries of the nation.

That afternoon we finally drove to Buhl, through the town, and out to the stretch of road where I expected to find Frank's place.

It was still harvest time, and big trucks heaped with sugar beets barreled down what is now a two-lane, blacktop highway. As I slowed and searched for the right address, an empty truck, headed back to the fields, loomed up behind me, and I pulled over at a driveway. I thumbed through our maps and squinted at the number painted on the nearest mailbox. Frank's place should be somewhere near here, I thought, somewhere after Highway 30 curves west out of Buhl and before it takes a sharp turn north again toward Hagerman.

On the topographic map the place looked to be the second dead-end road past the first curve, and I turned the car down an unmarked narrow dirt road and drove past the first house on the left, where two ranchers stood in the driveway and talked at the muddied tailgate of a truck. They watched us pass, no doubt taking note of my Utah license plates. I considered stopping, but they didn't look any friendlier than all the "No Trespassing" signs posted along the fence lines. I knew these were meant to keep out pheasant hunters, but for all the connection I felt to this place, the signs might as well have said, "Keep out, you pesky writer, you nosy academic." And even if they didn't say it, I could imagine how the story would go around the coffee shop in town the next morning, the two men pushing back their seed caps and saying, "Yeah, she was some English professor looking for the place she thought her granddad used to own. She finally stopped and talked to the wife up at the house. You know those university types. She's got the front seat covered with maps and still can't tell her ass from a hole in the ground." The risk of looking stupid—the eternal curse of a farm daughter—kept me from stopping to ask.

At the end of the dirt lane was just a single house that looked nothing at all like the picture I had, so I turned the car around and came back down the lane, past the ranchers, who eyed us once more. I figured Frank's place must have been on the lane east of where we were, so I turned left back out onto the highway and then left again onto another dirt road, also unmarked by any sign. As we bumped along the lane, I could make out large black boulders, piles of them along the way, with weeds and tall grasses nearly completely hiding them. It wasn't actually a rock fence, however, just some piles of boulders randomly placed, perhaps a century ago by a Bohemian immigrant named Frank, I thought. But perhaps not. There was a miserable grove of trees at the end of the drive and an abandoned house, which, again, looked nothing at all like the photo I had from the county clerk's office. Besides, I realized, this lane couldn't possibly be the 1150 East I was looking for because as far as I could tell, it was too close to what should be 1200 East, that is, if the roads were laid out with equal distance between them.

Finally, Jake reached up front and took the maps from the seat, announcing that he was good at this kind of thing. "I never lose my way," he said, citing his electronic games, where threats loom around every corner of those virtual worlds of dark forests and stone labyrinths. His best buddies get hopelessly lost, he went on as he shuffled through my papers, "because they don't have the big picture. They can't tell where they are from where they've been."

Still, armed with a multitude of maps, a photo, an exact address from the county clerk's office, and a personal guide who never gets lost, I couldn't find anything that I felt with any certainty was Frank's place. I was sure that the highway we were on was right, but none of these houses looked even remotely like the house in the picture, and it didn't seem feasible that the house had been torn down or remodeled again to the point of being unrecognizable from the 1988 photograph I had. The maps served only to further disorient both of us. They contradicted each other, we finally realized—the topographical map saying Frank's place was on the last dead end and the geographical map identifying the one east of there.

Back out on the highway we drove again west and around the bend that headed north. About a half mile from the curve I pulled over so we could look south toward the backside of the farmlands where we'd just been. From this vantage point we could see the boundaries of both potential properties, and we could get a good sense of how the farms abutted a rocky cutbank that dropped down precipitously, probably twenty feet or more, to the edge of Mud Creek, where only scrubby, stunted trees survived. In spite of the promises that Buhl land was level, free of rocks and coulees, this land looked as if any minute it could slide off and be swallowed up by Mud Creek. On the north side of the creek, across from the farmland, sagebrush still covered a huge piece of land that had never been brought under cultivation.

I turned the car around. Near the lane with the rock piles I pulled off the highway again and took a few pictures of the landscape without even getting out of the car. I zoomed the camera in on the abandoned clapboard house, too, which had probably been built in the 1920s, from the looks of it, and perhaps built by the people who moved there after Frank and Annie moved to Emmett. Still, I couldn't be certain this was the place.

"It's a dump," Jake said, his good spirits flagging. I slowly pulled back onto the highway, reluctant to give up the search without definitive answers. "No wonder he left," Jake added. It was obvious that neither my son nor I felt any bond with this place, certainly not the kind I was secretly hoping for. No apparitions or sunlit crosses. Not even the certainty of a rock fence to point me in the right direction. It was as if Frank had never even been there. What was clear, though, was that the people who came after Frank didn't prosper. In fact, I couldn't help but think this was some of the worst farmland we'd seen around the southern Snake River country for the last two days.

Had he bought the place sight unseen? I wondered. Had Boswell been a con man who had told him some "You better buy it while you can!" story and made him as much the victim of lies and exaggeration as I had been feeling? Frank had arrived relatively early in the settlement of the Snake River region—surely there had been better land available. Perhaps, though, he saw the creek running on the north side of the property and thought it suggested some promise in an arid landscape that was otherwise so unlike the ten thousand lakes of Minnesota where he'd just been or the healing waters of the Elbe River back in his Bohemian hometown.

I pulled the car onto another spur road, clearly marked this time with a sign that read 1300 East—not Frank's road. I parked again and shut the engine off, planning to look at the maps one last time. Instead I stared out across the pasture next to us. We were two or three fields away from where Frank probably lived in 1910—that is, depending on which map you believed. Another "No Trespassing" sign hung askew on the barbed wire, and next to the road there stood a small, squat stone cabin, no glass in the window frames, no door in the doorway. The horses and cows could walk right into the building and then out again to the flimsy shade of two scraggly trees nearby in a pasture where every blade of grass had been gnawed down. Even though it was now little more than shelter for the stock, someone who might have known Frank had once lived there. I told Jake that from the looks of it, I was pretty certain that it must have been built around the time his great-grandfather Frank was here.

Jake looked up from the map he was studying and said again, "It's a dump," in that "my final word on the subject" way of his, and to prove his point, he said, "Look," and indicated a huge mountain of trash littering the edge of the north field. A toilet seat crowned the pile of splintered wood, twisted metal, and the torn black garbage bags that flapped in the wind.

I'd come to Buhl with the expectation that at last I'd be able to pinpoint the *where*, if nothing else in this crazy web of stories. I just wanted the dot on the map where governmental records said Frank had first landed in Idaho. One certainty in all this absurd confusion was all I needed. The closest I'd come, however, was this broken-down cabin and a toilet seat on a pile of trash.

The afternoon was getting late, and Jake and I could see a storm coming in from the west. We had already spent more time than I had expected driving up and down this road, and although we had originally planned to drive out to Balanced Rock after we found the ranch, the approaching thunderheads reminded me we still had a three-hour drive home ahead of us, and tomorrow was a school day. The last thing I wanted was to get stuck on some remote dirt road where rain could turn the soil into a slick, sticky gumbo and we would have to walk out in the dark. "Next time," I promised Jake, and he generously did not ask if there would really be a next time.

We were quiet as I drove back to the interstate and then took I-84, which veered off south just past Burley. Minutes later we were surrounded by nothing but sagebrush that stretched as far as the base of the mountains. Only miles from Mud Creek we were in a landscape where, with the exception of the interstate, the entire circle of vision undoubtedly looked much like it did back in 1910. The settlers may have harnessed the power of the mighty Snake River, but its waters didn't go far, I thought. Jake pulled out a magazine to read, and I put in a Dave Matthews CD to break the silence. We stayed just ahead of the storm the whole way home.

Over the next few days I couldn't shake the feeling of failure.

I hadn't even managed to pinpoint Frank's place, and I felt like it
was one more event in a conspiracy to prevent me from finding
out anything I could trust. But then, I thought, why should I be
surprised that I couldn't precisely locate Frank's first Idaho ranch
when I'd already gone down so many historical dead ends with
him and been forced to circle back along so many wrong roads in
my research? Why should I think Frank wouldn't try to elude me
one more time or that I would find in Buhl anything more than
illusions, half truths, and faded dreams?

I realized I'd been angry with my grandfather for a good, long
time. As my research had unearthed embellishments and falsehoods, I felt more and more duped by Frank and his stories. Even
the claim that Frank had been an accountant in Bohemia proved
ultimately untrue. Among some papers my aunt sent to me was
a certificate, dated 1900, that once translated confirmed he had
completed an apprenticeship at a dry goods store in Poděbrady.
There was also a letter of reference from another shopkeeper for
whom Frank had worked for five and a half months in 1902. Post-
cards from 1902 to the time he left the country in 1908 show him
living in more than half a dozen cities, from Domažlice, in eastern
Bohemia, to Trest, more than three hundred kilometers to the
west in Moravia. A letter from his sister to my aunt claimed that
just before he emigrated, he was working in a haberdashery, dressing the mannequins in the shop windows. This didn't indicate
the stable life of a well-respected accountant. I had begun to even
question whether he'd really served in the Austro-Hungarian army,
although I did have a picture of him in a uniform. When my aunt's
husband told me that Frank used to claim that he and his family
had owned their village in Bohemia, I threw up my hands. Lies
is a four-letter word, and Frank's lies called into question everything that I believed about my family and about him.

But anger with Frank didn't feel comfortable any more than it felt like a resolution. I couldn't simply dismiss him out of hand as some western P. T. Barnum, a huckster who thought of his family as easy marks, rubes who would buy tickets to any sideshow that came to town.

I couldn't reconcile that image with the image I had of him serenading his wife with Czech folksongs while they sat in a tiny boat in the middle of our pond. That kind of tenderness was also on display in a March 1964 letter to his daughter in Portland that read, "The roads are mudy but I have to go every day to see my little darling Evlen. She like me so much, she hug me and kiss me when ever I get there. Now we can have soon picknick outside. It was very hard for her to stay all time during the winter in house." His affection seemed genuine.

Nor, in the end, could I dismiss Frank's ultimate achievements. Eventually, he did make a relative success of the farm where I grew up in Emmett, that is, if you think of "success" in the broadest terms. We had food to eat and money to pay the bills, and as a family we had set down spiritual and economical roots in that land. What made the difference in the intervening years between Buhl and Emmett I can't know. Maybe the difference was that he now had a family, or maybe it was just that he'd learned more about farming. Before his death we collectively had deed to the most farmland we ever would own. In Emmett he had bought one parcel that was an orchard and another that was the hilly, sagebrush parcel near the foothills that had been originally owned by the Crane Creek Sheep Ranch. Like Buhl Emmett was a high desert area just poised for the kind of transformation that irrigation could perform, and in 1924 the damming of the Payette River at Black Canyon Dam made Gem County's irrigation district another one of the biggest irrigation projects in the state. Over the years Frank stripped the sagebrush; leveled the land; dug a runoff pond; participated in digging local canals and irrigation ditches; planted another small family orchard of apple, plum, and pear trees near the sheepherder shack; and began growing barley, wheat, potatoes, and beans in the fields. He set up beehives in the orchards, quite literally turning this into a land of milk and honey where the fruits of your labor could be shipped to locales all around the country with "Funda Farms" proudly stamped on the box. Although a horseback ride half a mile straight north from the sheepherder shack would take you up into the foothills where sage still bloomed and coyotes still hunted jackrabbits and punctuated the night with their wild yelping, there on our farm the land had been reclaimed from such wildness. The other parcel of land changed too. After the market for Idaho plums dropped and the trees played out, the commercial plum orchard was also turned into farmland, and the packing shed was converted into my grandparents' white, two-story home that was surrounded on three sides by Frank's gardens.

My grandfather *had* made the desert bloom, and his front yard was planted with pines and ornamental shrubs, a tulip tree, and dozens of roses. In the 1964 letter I quoted above, he mourns that the roses he'd been grafting had frozen over the winter, a fact that had him saying "I would nearly cry . . . I had lots of them buddet, but every one is gone. All my work for last 3–4 years was waisted." In one reel of the family's 8mm films, which I think was taken the summer before this devastating loss, Frank happily gives a tour of his garden. The prolific roses stand nearly as tall as he is, which was just under six feet, and in one scene he playfully twirls the stem of a yellow rose. He then points the camera to the huge blossoms of his peace roses, which he loved more than any other type of rose. Even on this single bush the colors on each blossom offer a remarkable variety as the petals transition from yellow or cream at the bud to peach or pink at the tips. In the background I can see a field of grain behind Frank, but he never turns to look in that direction. He was always too dreamy and quixotic to be bothered by the kind of farm practicalities that pre-occupied my father, who enjoyed calculating yield per acre, fussing over the seed drill, adjusting the planter's gates to give optimal coverage with the least amount of waste. How do you calculate the yield of a peace rose?

Although my grandfather bragged about being a farmer in his stories, I never remember him dressing the part. His uniform was typically white shirt, suspenders, vest and suit coat, pocket watch, and felt Fedora or straw hat. I have a picture of him dressed like this, standing with my grandmother in the middle of a field that I think is one of the fields my father and uncle leased in the mountains near Donnelly, Idaho. While the photo probably dates to the late 1950s, it looks like the early twentieth-century historical photos of farms that often show people standing knee-high, waist-high, or chest-high in the middle of fields of grain, alfalfa, or corn. This was a common motif in the early-century promotional pamphlets advertising southern Idaho that Frank probably saw. The thinking was that human figures provided a point of reference that emphasized the vigor of the crop. But in this photo, even with the vegetation up to his knees and towering mountains in the background looking sufficiently wild and western, I think Frank looks every bit the nineteenth-century clerk. Hands casually clasped behind his back, he looks as if he had never spent a day doing the kind of manual labor demanded on a farm.

When I look at this photo or watch those movie scenes in my grandfather's garden, I can't believe that my family history, and the history surrounding my Frank, in particular, was defined by some elaborate scheme of conscious or malicious lies. Understanding his stories within the context of southern Idaho and its early twentieth-century culture of exaggeration may offer some sense of historical perspective, I think. In Idaho truth was as precariously poised as Balanced Rock itself, that improbable landmark just a few miles south of Frank's place on Mud Creek. After all, who among my family knew that Frank's cheeky granddaughter would grow up to use that university education of hers—the education a small bequest from his estate helped pay for, by the way—to research and correct the public record?

Context, however, doesn't fully explain Frank's own motives. I still find it curious that his mythology never drew upon some of the additional, colorful facts I did discover in newspapers of the time. Neither my aunt nor I ever heard stories of those bizarre rabbit drives that the newspaper relished, even though it's more than likely that he was in attendance at one or more of these popular, community-wide events. I discovered a series of brief notices he put in the "Lost and Found" section of the Buhl paper about a stray bay who was "heavy with foal" (ten-dollar award offered, it read). The notice suggests that he, like numerous others for a six-month period, fell prey to a pair of horse thieves who were caught, tried, and sentenced to fourteen years in the penitentiary in Boise—but we'd heard nary a word about that in family mythology. At least that confirmed he *had* a horse, I suppose. The biggest surprise was a notice that he had trapped a mountain lion "in a peculiar trap of his own invention." Although we all knew he enjoyed building things, no one I know had ever heard that story. For unknown reasons these details of his life didn't appeal to him as fodder for his narratives. The stories of the bread route, the ranch, and the bakery in Buhl, and more broadly of the whole southern Idaho chapter of Frank's life, were shaped narratives, products of an absolutely creative act. His fabrications show a consistent effort to refashion the world around him into something that better pleased his keen aesthetic sense, rather than accommodate himself to that world, and in the process the stories also became a "peculiar trap of his own invention," a myth he had to live by.

For Frank creativity always trumped fact. He had a deep need to craft that fanciful portrayal of himself and, in turn, to perceive of and imagine the world around him in ways that were true to his desires for beauty and order. His stories are not the only evidence of this, either. My father used to describe the elaborate gingerbread houses Frank would bake with his own honey and construct for his children during the Depression. For me he built beautiful doll furniture carved with scrollwork and painted with flowers. After he retired, he designed, built, and painted birdhouses. I remember one in particular that was a little white church with a steeple and handsome stained-glass windows. And then in his seventies he took up painting.

The family story is that he only realized his talent when his daughter-in-law Viola (wife of James Frank) began to take a china painting class. Viola had always loved her crafts and had created everything from tabletop Christmas trees (made by folding down at an angle each page of the Sears catalog) to tea towels embroidered with perky Scottish terriers cross-stitched in red and black thread. However, her artistry was more *Reader's Digest* than Monet, and apparently her attempt at china painting wasn't any different. One day Frank was watching her struggle to copy a flower design, and finally, in frustration, he grabbed the brush out of her hand, told her she was doing it all wrong, and finished the little painting without even looking at the original design. Before that, as far as we knew, he had never touched a canvas. After that he was never far from his battered tackle box of oil paints, and his works typically feature emblems echoing the themes and subjects of his life. One is an oil painting of a mountain lion perched high on the branch of a tree, watching some unseen prey. For as long as I can remember, it was hung in a bedroom in my aunt's home, where I often slept when I visited her, and at night I would feel strangely safe, as if the mountain lion were watching the bedroom door, guarding me—not a threat or a predator. Another canvas is an Easter painting he did for me of an egg-laden wagon being drawn by a caricatured banty chicken and driven by an impish-looking jackrabbit in a stylish gray suit coat. While the mountain lion painting seems so real it makes me catch my breath, this painting turns the reality Frank once experienced in Buhl entirely upside down, placing the reins of the delivery wagon in the paws of a serene rabbit who looks strangely like my grandfather himself.

Frank's favorite subject, however, was still-life arrangements of flowers, and most of these paintings use a folk art technique called glass underpainting in which layers of translucent paint are built up on the back of a glass sheet instead of a canvas. The technique, which is one Czech artists used to create luminous light and a depth of color in religious pictures, required Frank to paint in reverse: the highlights and the most delicate details first, then shadowing and the flower's main color, and last the backgrounds. It was as if he were painting his way away from you, backing down the road toward the distant vanishing point. My most treasured of his flower paintings is a huge one on glass that is half an inch thick and surrounded by a darkly stained wood frame that Frank handcrafted with rounded corners. Side by side across the painting, growing out of a grassy floor, is a line-up of flowers: large red, pink, and yellow roses in full bloom with their petals fully open; a bunch of freckled orange tiger lilies with a hummingbird poised at the throat of one of the blossoms; and deep purple irises with velvety pistils. The row also includes daffodils, sunflowers, columbines, forget-me-nots, poppies, foxgloves, and hollyhocks—each individually depicted with precise, realistic detail. As any gardener will tell you, however, this picture is anachronistic, pairing early spring flowers with late-season bloomers. Call it another of Frank's fictions, but obviously, in spite of the mimetically accurate details of individual flowers, he wasn't aiming for realism here. Surrealistically floating above the whimsical row is a miniature portrait, just four inches square, of my grandmother calmly arranging a bouquet of flowers where she sits under the shade of a parasol umbrella at a small bistro-style table. She isn't the least bit concerned or even aware that right below her is a large monarch butterfly, proportionally twice her size, about to land on a sunflower as big as her parasol. Her untroubled presence in the painting, therefore, suggests to me Frank's own complete acceptance of anachronistic fictions. Whether in his paintings or in his stories, Frank's artistic expressions, therefore, used selection, arrangement, omission, and manipulation of materials to effectively defy the boundaries of time and truth.

While Frank lived in Twin Falls from late 1911 to 1918, he may well have met the local photographer Clarence Bisbee. Bisbee had been commissioned to work for the railroad's promotional pamphlets, taking inspiring pictures of thriving local farms and impressive crops, splendid new buildings and city streets in the county, and important cultural events. It is Bisbee who took the photos I'd seen of the Buhl rabbit drives, and he is given credit for systematically documenting the history of southern Idaho from his arrival in 1905 until the 1950s. In his studio in Twin Falls he also did portraiture photography, and in fact I have one photo of Frank that I suspect may have been taken in Bisbee's studio just before he married Annie. But that's not why I mention him here. Clarence Bisbee was, like my grandfather, an artist. When he had his studio built in Twin Falls, he instructed builders to carve in the mantel over the fireplace one of his favorite sayings: "Life and Art are One." Although his work is rarely recognized for its artistic merits, he is an interesting figure who used his camera to shape the reality around him. For instance, one of Bisbee's undated photos that I found in the Twin Falls Library archive on my trip with

Jake is a posed composition he entitled *Early Settlers*. However, this isn't a portrait of the first homesteaders or the irrigation project developers or even the local Shoshone Indians. No humans appear in this photo at all. Instead it's an uncluttered tabletop still life of a glass vase filled with branches of sage and a young jackrabbit crouching next to it, looking very much like he is about to bound away. Like Frank's Easter painting Bisbee's *Early Settlers* turns the preconceived notions of his time upside-down. The photo is a study of the trials and aspirations of that particular moment and place, and the composition draws upon the codified expectations of the still life as a particular art form. Still-life artists artificially arranged ordinary objects, both natural and manmade, into vignettes in order to express subtle and allegorical messages about profound ideas (such as the search for beauty or the transitory nature of human life). Another objective of the genre was absolute verisimilitude—trompe l'oeil, painters called these depictions that were so real, they could "fool the eye." A living fly might hover near painted grapes, for instance. Executed in close-up, these domestic scenes often portray an array of sumptuous, sensual pleasures (food, wine, flowers), and they are a study in how these objects relate to each other, in terms of both light and shadow, and meaning and sensibility. In other words, an empty wine glass might cast a shadow onto an open book, thus suggesting something about the intoxication—or is it the dissipation—of intellectual pursuits. Elements in still-life paintings have symbolic values that were known to everyone: a rose means love, a tulip signifies nobility, and a poppy foretells death.

Everyone in Idaho also thought they knew exactly what sagebrush and jackrabbits meant. They were so ubiquitous that they had become objects of many contemptuous jokes. But Bisbee's mischievous study of them in his still life takes these figures out of the context of the southern Idaho landscape and renders them with the scrutiny of a close-up perspective. In so doing, Bisbee uses the still-life genre to transform sage and jack into something we must respect as having aesthetic value. The photo is, in effect, the 1910 Idaho version of Andy Warhol's Campbell's soup can—art because he tells us it's art. Moreover, Bisbee's composition challenges us to rethink the dismissal of rabbit and brush merely as impediments to agricultural progress. If these living things can be art, what else can they be? The rabbit looks decidedly innocent—small and bunnylike rather than menacing—and by putting the sage branches in a vase, Bisbee forces us to challenge the scientists who failed to make the plant conform to the agricultural imperative of commodification. Once a wild, useless brush, in Bisbee's still life sagebrush is just like any other ornamental plant. A sage by any other name would smell as sweet. And although this is a "still life," the rabbit's crouch suggests that at any second he will dart away in an explosion of movement, this time escaping all efforts to confine or define him. Bisbee's posed scene, therefore, is as mutable and precarious as our interpretation of the Idaho landscape itself. Bisbee's title adds an additional layer of irony: homesteaders like Frank might have imagined themselves as the Adam in Eden, but they did so only by ignoring the genuine "early settlers," the flora and fauna that had been there long before I. B. Perrine had his vision of an irrigated Eden.

For me Bisbee's photo is an objective correlative about the transformative powers of perception in Idaho at that time. It's a bold joke that reminds us that art can be constructed out of the materials you have at hand. After Frank left Twin Falls County, for instance, another Czech immigrant, Anton Suchan, began to carve sculptures, animal figurines, and jewelry out of sagebrush and sold his pieces around the world. If jack and sage can be art, as Bisbee and Suchan demonstrated, can other realities be as easily reversed? What about the life of an aimless Bohemian who fails to make the desert bloom or to make himself into a somebody in a place where those transformations were practically guaranteed?

Every few summers, in the valley where I now live, a spate of crop circles appears in the golden wheat fields nearing harvest. After a set of circles appeared north of Logan in 2001, the county's sheriff's department jokingly speculated that the designs "could be the work of hungry gophers." Inspiring jokes about alien visits and comparisons to Stonehenge, these crop circles serve the typical folkloric function of uniting a community around a common story, and they become a fascinating type of folk art in which the farm is the canvas and the crop is the paint. Serious literature about what some call "cereology" identifies crop circles as "cereal art," "agrarian graffiti," and "large-scale land art." A recent *National Geographic* article suggests that someday they may well be considered "as the most remarkable artistic innovation to emerge from the twentieth century." Whether you believe crop circles are hoaxes pulled off by drunk pranksters or the work of some otherworldly artist, anonymity is the key to the power of the crop circle. No name is signed in the corner, and therefore no one can say definitively where the design originated, unless or until someone confesses. And circle makers have become increasingly cagey in their execution and sophisticated in their designs. One admitted crop circle maker claims, "You think about art in terms of authorship and signature. . . . But circle makers never claim credit for specific formations they created. To do so would drain the mystery of crop circles. . . . The art form isn't just about the pattern making. The myths and folklore and energy [that] people give them are part of the art."

While I never knew Frank to create crop circles, I wouldn't have put it past him. He was a mischievous practical joker, and the mysterious emergence of crop circles with all this talk of aliens would have made him chuckle. I can imagine him whistling as he looked for just the right size for a crossboard, drilled the holes, threaded and knotted his rope through. Annie would have scolded him, knowing full well he could not be dissuaded from a practical joke. The contraption waited behind the back porch door for some moonless night. But he was patient. An old accounts book from the orchard business provided graph paper where he could plot out his design. As much as he would have liked to make a rose, that might be too difficult for his first try. No, he needed a design beautiful in its simplicity. A cross was too ecclesiastical for his freethinker tastes. A heart was too cliché. But a cluster of grapes seemed possible, reminiscent of the intoxication of wine. He couldn't wait to hear the neighbors talk, and he imagined how the party line would ring and excited voices would tell of the pattern that appeared in the Skoros' grain field last night, stalks laid down neatly at an angle.

Crop circles would have fit the pattern of Frank making the elements of the thing at hand, his own life, into a series of creative acts and then disguising the artifice by a succession of false leads. The best art, of course, is enigmatic. It straddles the fence between what we've learned to trust and the unexpected. It surprises, shocks, challenges our very ideas of what art ought to be or what it should be made of. Art is participatory—the believing (or unbelieving) audience creates its meaning as much as the artist does, giving the creation a life of its own after its inception. Crop circle makers have no control over how others interpret their creations, and if a maker is good, we *want* to suspend our disbelief and accept that the design is real and has its origins in another dimension, in a wider, better world where beauty and order come to those who are worthy.

In some way crop circles help me understand Frank, why he chose to tell the stories he did, and what my role is in interpreting them. The famous British crop circle maker John Lundberg draws upon the folklore term *ostension* to explain the phenomenon of those who attempt to verify the otherworldly origin of crop circles; he writes that ostension is "where an individual draws from a legend and claims it to be their own experience [thus] transforming legend into an apparently verifiable first-person account." Ostension, he says in short, is when "narrative becomes action: action becomes narrative. Legend as life: life as legend."

Even if Frank didn't homestead or write stories for a Czech newspaper, my family heard his stories and wanted to believe those things were true. Recently my aunt tried to convince me that Frank served as Buhl's postmaster for a time—an utterly improbable assertion, given the national prejudice against "Bohunks" that I know existed in the early part of the century, when Americans were especially suspicious of Czech religious practices. In 1910, when anti-Catholic sentiment was already running high, 40 percent of Bohemian immigrants identified themselves as Catholic, while slightly more than half of all Czech-speaking immigrants were Bohemian freethinkers, like Frank, and therefore suspect because they were atheists or agnostics often tending toward socialist politics. Thus, Bohemians, who more often kept to themselves in the settlements of the West, rarely chose to pursue or were accepted to hold any public office. But I didn't bother to point this out to my aunt. She needs her picture of her father to remain unchallenged, something I realized when I sent her, among other things, copies of the sales agreement with Oscar Boswell and the Buhl newspaper notice about Frank leaving the farm less than two years later. She tells me how meaningful these artifacts are to her, but she resists laying them out side by side and piecing together what they mean. And doing it for her, pointing to the conclusions those dates insist upon, wouldn't be doing her any favors. I have to let her interpret those facts for herself, if she will.

Frank's own life was like a crop circle: the stories may have turned out to be some practical joke on me, but he couldn't deny my power to now participate in the deconstruction of his art. And so I try to circle back to what I know to be true. Truth was, Frank wasn't the postmaster, or the founder of Rock Creek Ranch, or the owner of the first all-electric bakery in the state. He wasn't even a big fish in a little pond. He and so many Czechs like him in the Snake River Valley were practically invisible.

In my study of nearly two decades' worth of Buhl and Twin Falls newspapers, from 1905 to 1920, I rarely ever saw a Czech name mentioned, let alone one associated with a public position. This was especially true of the Twin Falls paper, where the "Local and Personal" column was filled with names like Green, Smith, Brooks, Bradley, all the bon-ton folks of town. Nothing more ethnic than Monahan was put into print (and he was a local attorney, so he was to be forgiven such an Irish name). A few German names showed up on occasion, in those years before World War I would wipe away even those. By contrast every sneeze suffered or picnic celebrated by the Perrine family was documented in the papers. But when James Frank, my grandparents' first child, was born on leap year day in 1916, the paper made no mention of the event. It did, however, report that twins were born on that day to a family named Howard or Bradley—I can't exactly remember the name.

It seems brave to me now—at the very least forgivable—that in the face of such erasure Frank drew the line and chose to narrate himself right into the golden center of the myth. When the reality is a dried-up disappointment, the story needs to be all the more grand.

A Bohemian freethinker, Frank believed that "truth" was not passively accepted from some institution. Rather, truth was a thing made—it was participatory. And, I suspect, Frank began the creation of his truth not for the benefit of me, his progeny. The origin of his myth was backward looking, not leading forward to a suspicious granddaughter. In late 1911 he still had elderly parents residing in a small, crowded house in St. Paul with one of his sisters and her family. I wouldn't be surprised if my conservative great-grandfather had originally advised Frank against leaving his steady job in the bakery and chancing the wilds of Idaho. So when Frank faced failure, he had to choose between returning to Minnesota like a prodigal son or initiating a performance that would color the rest of his life.

I've pictured the moment when Frank faced the facts. He stands in the middle of a small field, trying to coax a meager trickle of water down corrugates crookedly carved in the rocky soil. But the water wicks into the dirt, and soon the trickle diffuses and then just disappears. He looks up the field to the half-irrigated rows of stunted oats, wilting and looking gray. He looks toward the shack that has been his home for less than two years—not even the horse is there anymore to provide company. He looks to the north where beyond the perimeter of this field all he sees is sagebrush and swells of rock. *All that place would grow was rocks!* He is still for a moment, and then in disgust he throws down the shovel. As he tramps back to the shack, he thinks how the time to make his mark is short.

And at that moment Frank's life as a homesteader both ended and began.

5

Cheatgrass

"I listened carefully about clues for whether the West has accepted
cheat as a necessary evil, to be lived with until kingdom come, or
whether it regards cheat as a challenge to rectify its past errors in
land-use. I found the hopeless attitude almost universal."

ALDO LEOPOLD
A Sand County Almanac

Summer 1965. July in Emmett can be miserably hot, with day
after day of one-hundred-degree weather. Sometimes the air is so
dry it seems almost brittle. It was too hot to swing on the hammock or play house in the little kitchen I'd improvised on a stump
with old boards and chipped cups my mother had given me. So I
was just sitting in the shade, plucking tiny clover blossoms out of
the weed patch Mom insisted we call a lawn. She came out the
back door and fingered the last batch of laundry. As she pulled a
sheet off the line and folded it, I stated the obvious: "I'm hot." She
didn't reply to my complaint, but the curls at the back of her neck
were damp with sweat. Across the yard Tippy, the curly-haired
mutt, climbed out of the ditch, energetically shook himself off,
and then settled into the shade. My mother eyed him suspicious-
ly. More than once on hot days like today she had cussed him as
she rewashed mud-splattered laundry.

The wind started to rustle the leaves of the black poplar trees above me. My grandfather had planted the trees close to the house to provide shade in the afternoon, and they were huge, with a tangle of dead branches in the center that clicked in the wind. The sheets and towels still on the line began to snap. With a sigh my mother turned to face the breeze that was coming from the west. Within a few minutes the sky darkened in a ring of thunderheads to the north and west, and lightning flashed. Because such afternoon storms rarely produced any rain that offered sustained relief from the heat, they were called "dry" lightning storms. Often they lingered over by the Owyhee Mountains far away, providing a show of jagged strikes, but often as not they petered out as they moved across our valley.

Dad was still custom-combining at the backcountry ranch twenty miles north, so Mother and I were home alone. "Count," she instructed when a strike flashed, and we would "one-Mississippi" our way to the rumble of thunder. I was so enthralled by my mother's magic trick of gauging the speed of the storm that I didn't immediately realize how fearfully she watched the clouds. These storms always had my mother worried that lightning or a bad wind would send one of the poplars crashing onto our little house. As the winds picked up and the dust devils swirled in the farmyard, she hurried us into the house, threw down the laundry basket, and rushed to slam the windows shut. When the last window was secured, she stood there watching branches sway for a moment and then rushed to the other end of the house. We waited out the storm in my parents' bedroom, huddled together on her chenille bedspread. The room was really a sleeping porch, with windows on three sides, so we could see the darkening sky and hear the wind rattle the windows. Although it was still warm, my mother pulled out a blanket and threw it over our heads—a new game, she said, and we lay face to face in the eerie turquoise light cast by the blanket. We jumped when a lightning flash was followed a breath later by the crack of thunder. "Close now," she whispered.

"Tell me a story," I begged, relishing the intimacy of our little cave. "The story of your doll." And as the storm ebbed away, she told me about receiving a porcelain-faced baby doll one Christmas. Just days later she was running with the doll in her arms. She fell, and the doll's face shattered. When she sought out her mother for sympathy, however, she got a scolding for being careless.

Although the storm was dramatic, it had subsided within an hour, having produced only a commotion of wind and lightning. My mother opened the windows again, and my father returned home for supper. Up at the Van Deusen, he said, the storm had produced a terrible dust storm, but nothing more. By bedtime the air was stifling again, and we were all wishing for some reprieve from the heat as we lay sweating in our beds.

Late that night I woke to the sound of my father rushing past my room, pulling his pants on as he went. As I jumped out of my bed to follow him, I could smell the smoke of a grass fire.

"There!" he said, as my mother and I followed him out the door. I could dimly see the shadow of his arm pointing north. The storm had started a foothill fire that had hung back until nightfall, but now an eerie red fire line was advancing down the foothills just half a mile away, and in the moonless night the fire blazed and glowed ominously. The smoke from the burning cheatgrass and sage was considerable, and in the quiet we could hear the crackle of the flames.

"The wheat?" my mother asked. As usual my father had been too busy with his custom-combining business to bring in his own crop, and the field between us and the county road leading up into the foothills was dry as tinder.

"No wind," he observed as I leaned against his leg. "We should be all right." He lifted me up on his shoulders, where I could get a better view of the fire and then the flashing red lights of the county fire truck zooming by on the county road. But there wasn't much you could do with a foothill fire. The fire crews would use shovels to clear brush out ahead of the fire and keep it contained as best they could. If the winds came back up, though, the fire could jump a break or even set fields ablaze. In that case the only plan was to get in the truck and drive south away from the foot-hills as fast as you could.

My parents and I stood out in the yard, swatting mosquitoes and watching the creeping line of red. No one said much more than the occasional surprised "Oh!" as the fire reached a new stand of sage, which was instantaneously engulfed in flames. At some point I flagged, and someone put me to bed. I woke up the next morning with the sun shining into my eyes through my win-dow. The smell of fire wasn't as strong, but it was still evident, and outside, where my mother was working in the garden, the air was gray with a haze that burned my eyes. To the north huge parts of the hillside were covered with an ugly black scar that would remind us of that fire until snowfall.

Such foothill fires happened every few years, especially if we had a wet spring and the cheatgrass thrived through early sum-mer. Stands of it invaded our ditchbanks, where irrigation water had distributed the seeds. No matter how hard we tried to eradi-cate it, by July we were picking the prickly awns out of our socks or out of the dog's paws and ears. Day to day it seemed like just another nuisance.

If sagebrush is the most iconic wild plant in the American West, in the last 150 years cheatgrass has given it some stiff competi-tion. Now the most dominant grass in the West, it was originally a Mediterranean immigrant that likely stowed away in European grain seed or ship ballast sometime during the late nineteenth century. The Latin name of *Bromus* for its broomlike shape and *tectorum* for its tendency to grow on thatched roofs makes it seem like a poor refugee from some quaint medieval village. But cheatgrass (aka "cheat") is a real con artist that got its English name because pioneer wheat farmers complained it "cheated" them out of their wheat yield. Another of its many aliases, "June grass," refers to the brief period when it is green and can offer an early forage for livestock, but within days the soft fronds dry into awns equipped with one-way barbs that cling relentlessly to the fur of grazing livestock. Pernicious tooth-shaped barbs work their way into the ears, eyes, and mouths of cattle or, worse, needle their way into lungs, internal organs, or abdomens. Cheat takes advantage of ecological disturbances like overgrazing and is so prolific and fast growing that it has displaced native bunch grasses in over one million acres of the West (roughly the size of Utah and Colorado combined). Aldo Leopold called the proliferation of cheatgrass in the West a symptom of a "sick landscape."

The changes brought about by cheatgrass are so considerable, widespread, and devastating that Utah state representative Steve Urquhart has characterized the grass as "a 6' 8", 250-pound, tattooed, heavily-armed, escaped-from-death-row, invasive species." In addition to being an ecological threat with economic implications, cheatgrass fires threaten thousands of acres and dozens of lives every year. Few weeds are as dangerous as cheatgrass. "When lightning strikes a bed of dead cheatgrass it's like dropping a match into a lake of kerosene," writes journalist Bettina Boxall, who regularly covers wildfires for the *Los Angeles Times*. Where once lightning strikes may have ignited wildfires once a century, now the fire patterns in cheatgrass lands are every three to five years. Because it is the first wildlands species to recover after a fire, it has changed the natural wildfire patterns in the West by creating a vicious cycle of fire-recovery-fire that has taken over from species like sage and bunch grasses. In 2008 a power transformer sparked a cheatgrass fire just outside of Boise, and before the evening was over, ten homes were gutted, another ten were damaged, and one woman was dead. A year before most of the wildfires that burned nearly five million acres in the entire West were cheatgrass fires. The largest fire in Utah history, the 567-square-mile Milford Flat fire, resulted in two deaths, and while the record-breaking Murphy Complex fire that started in Idaho—and burned just twenty miles southwest of Frank's original farm in Buhl—resulted in no loss of human life, it burned 1,020 square miles in Nevada and Idaho and was recorded as the worst western fire in a century.

Strictly speaking, the original introduction of cheatgrass initiated another instance of ecological succession similar to the example of purple loosestrife displacing cattail habitat in irrigated waterways. If dodder, purple loosestrife, wild oats, and sage have taught me anything about my family's relation to land, it is that we pioneers have a natural desire to root ourselves in our environment, even if we may not be able to foresee or ultimately survive the consequences of that desire. No certainty is so great as the certainty of change. Cheatgrass, however, reminds me that our human attachment to land is constructed on a tremendously complicated set of claims that at any moment may betray us: we make political assertions and then legal declarations about land, we plant it, we people it with our offspring and our community, we will it to family or sell it to strangers, we narrate and imagine it, we envision it through our religious and sentimental convictions, we groom it in ways that reflect our cultural mores, we come to know it through habit and longevity, and we protect it from encroachment and natural disaster. And sometimes we fail in these things. Sometimes our lust for land burns with a physical and psychological violence that disregards legitimate human claims.

The deeper I looked into my familial and ancestral history, the more I saw that wanting land wasn't always a noble thing. Beyond the homesteader's dream or the refugee's fear emerged stories of power, destruction, manipulation, and betrayal. As I considered recent family history and then looked on into ancestral history, I saw how my forebears played the role of the cheated or the cheaters, by turns, in stories that range from the petty to the profoundly brutal. Let me be clear: I am not talking about the lust of the flesh here. Sexual infidelity isn't the kind of cheating I found in both my familial and my ethnic history. The lust for land seemed to be a much more compelling desire. Contested space has been a theme throughout Czech history, from the land conflicts during the Habsburg monarchy to the occupation of the Nazis during World War II and the Communist rule after that. Sadly, it was a theme in my history, as well. Lined up, side by side, these stories seem like rows in a wheat field, all leading inexorably to a vanishing point off in the distance.

Frank Funda always claimed that he came from nobility and that once our family had owned considerable property in his home village of Poděbrady, just outside of Prague. The estate included an attractive manor that had been divided between comfortable family living quarters and smaller servants' quarters, and our claim to this estate dated back generations. "We were rich like kings," he railed indignantly, "until the Catholics stole it!" The Catholics "stealing" that estate was the reason the family emigrated from Bohemia, he said. Harassed by Catholic officials who demanded money at every turn, my great-grandfather Václav finally gave up his homeland and came to the United States in defeat, not in hope. "Katolík!" Frank spat in conclusion.

It was an old grievance that Frank often brought up, usually in the presence of my mother, who had been raised as a strict Catholic in her little village in southern Moravia. He knew that she chose to give up her Catholicism when she was forced to give up her homeland, but still, he seemed to hold her in some measure responsible for this great loss. Her religious upbringing in the backwaters of southern Moravia forever tainted her in his eyes, and she, in turn, resented his tirades. "He was happy enough when I *married* Lumir. I was good enough *then*!" she used to complain, referring to the early days, when Frank bragged to his friends that his new Czech daughter-in-law could bake like an angel—all the old, traditional pastries like fruit kolaches, the braided Christmas bread *vánočka*, and poppy-seed-filled babovka. At the monthly Czech lodge meetings in nearby Nampa my mother's grace on a dance floor matched his, and the pair were legend among the local Czechs. While my grandmother preferred to listen to the music from the sidelines, and my ungainly father had shied away from the floor since he broke a knee dancing, Toni and Frank were natural partners, as proficient at the intricate polka steps as they were elegant during the waltzes. "He treated me like a queen back then," I once heard her say bitterly. But in his last years emphysema made Frank ill tempered and unreasonable, and if my mother dared voice any stories from her childhood, he would answer again with his claim that the Fundas had been nobles in Bohemia, forced from our rightful claim to land by the Catholics. My mother, the recent immigrant who had been directly involved in the Czech fight for autonomy, seemed to present some kind of challenge to Frank's Czechness, and his voice would swell with anger and indignation as he retold the story of being cheated out of that estate. My mother would go silent for the rest of the afternoon, brooding over the fact that my father never came to her rescue in these uncomfortable moments.

Although I knew my grandfather used the story to hurt my mother, I used to fantasize about a return to my noble roots. Like something out of a Dickens novel my great-grandparents Václav and Dorthea Funda and their three children (my grandfather and his two sisters) were cast out from their sizeable stone house by someone wearing priestly robes. In a small wagon piled high with a few belongings they had managed to salvage, they drove away from the only home the men of Frank's family had ever known. Could this tragic story mean that I was descended from Czech royalty? Was there some crumbling castle just outside of Prague that needed only to be reclaimed by me, the rightful daughter of the family?

As I learned in adulthood, however, Frank never was a reliable narrator. All evidence suggests that his father was and had always been a shopkeeper—a thoroughly middle-class occupation. As I tried to tease out the threads of this family history through my research, I realized that Frank's story wasn't exactly a lie; it was just that the "we" he was referencing was misleading because it did not refer to the Funda family specifically. Rather, he had conflated personal history with national history that dated back to the Counter-Reformation of the seventeenth century and the Hussite Wars from the fifteenth century before that. The injustices were real, but that my family played any direct part in them is highly unlikely.

Private property was indeed seized and Catholicism was proscribed under King Ferdinand II, the Habsburg ruler of the Holy Roman Empire. This led to a significant but short-lived protest in 1620, when Protestant Czechs took up arms at the site of Bílá Hora (White Mountain) against an army of mercenaries paid for by Ferdinand and the church. Their defeat was the beginning of a dark chapter in Czech history, and the events at White Mountain are as well known in Czech culture as the Boston Tea Party is in American culture. It is true that most Czech nobles went into exile in other countries at this point rather than face retribution and certain death. According to historian Derek Sayers, "The estates of Protestant lords were confiscated on a grand scale, and gifted or sold cheaply to Catholic loyalists. Over three-quarters of the land in the kingdom, Church and crown estates excepted, changed hands in the 1620s. Out of this a largely new—and often foreign—aristocracy emerged." For the next three centuries the Czech Lands as a whole were the site of serious clashes between the Bohemian Protestants and the Roman Catholic Habsburgs, who controlled land, dictated religious worship, and demanded that all civic and public matters be conducted in the language of Vienna rather than the language of Prague. During the last half of the nineteenth century, until Habsburg absolutism was ended at the close of World War I, cultural rhetoric rekindled these stories about White Mountain, precisely at the moment when Czechs like my family began to emigrate to the United States in greater numbers, bringing with them these old resentments about feeling exiled from their homes. But the actual events at White Mountain happened nearly three hundred years before the Fundas emigrated.

Additionally, the trope in Frank's story of the church's unrelenting demands for money probably came from an entirely different century. It's as if Frank's ideas originated in the story of Jan Hus, an early fifteenth-century priest, reformer, and philosopher who was burned at the stake in 1415. Hus had protested vehemently against the practice among Catholic priests of selling indulgences and demanding payment for every rite from cradle to grave. For this and other heresies, including preaching his sermons in Czech rather than in Latin, Hus was tried by church officials in Germany and sentenced to the stake. He was stripped naked and chained, and then his accusers used two wagonloads of wood to build a pyre around him that reached up to his chin. After fire consumed his flesh, Hus's bones and skull were next broken up and burned again, and finally the ashes from the fire were scraped from the ground and thrown into the Rhine River so that absolutely no trace of him could ever return to Bohemia. But as with Bílá Hora, Hus was not forgotten, and his martyrdom became a defining event in the nation's history, one that led to the Hussite wars, where, in a reversal of the Book of Isaiah, the poor Czech peasants used their pitchforks, threshing flails, and scythes as weapons, thus turning their plowshares into swords.

In appropriating these stories into family myth, Frank was filching stories from history about Catholic thievery and then claiming them as his own, and his revisionist history reminds me of a famous nineteenth-century novel by Horatio Alger that tells the rags-to-riches story of Ragged Dick, a poor, uneducated bootblack living in the slums of New York City. Dick often jokes that his tattered, oversized coat once belonged to George Washington, who had worn the coat during the Revolution. In thus "lying" about the man who could not tell a lie, Dick quite literally aims to cloak himself in an archetypal national myth. He boldly makes that story of honor and revolution personal and relevant right there in the slums of the city.

Like Ragged Dick, Frank created a way for myth and history to coexist. If his Rock Creek Ranch stories were framed according to the outlines of the quintessential American immigrant homesteader myth, his story of his family's ouster at the hands of the Catholics ignored historical anachronisms and allowed him to assert his claim to a political ancestry.

Unlike his sisters, who ironically converted to Catholicism upon their marriages to devout husbands they'd met in Minnesota, Frank maintained no church affiliation. Having no formal religious affiliation was not unusual for Czech immigrants, who, writes Kenneth D. Miller, "have seceded from their old country faith more extensively than any other immigrant race. . . . Other races have drifted away into indifference, but the Czechs have broken with the church and fallen into uncompromising hostile attitude towards Catholicism in the first instance, but incidentally towards Protestantism also." However, Frank did think of himself as pious. He had committed long passages of the Bible to memory, and he was known to chide his family for not being as familiar as he was with the "who's who" of biblical stories and Bohemian religious history. When pressed to identify a religious affiliation, Frank would say he was part of the Bohemian Brethren Church in Nampa, which was founded on the traditions of Jan Hus, but I never knew him to attend, nor did he have his children baptized in it. Rather, he left them to make their own decisions about religious affiliation, and all three of them experimented with membership in different churches. Oldest son James Frank attended the Lutheran Church for a time, but he admitted to choosing that church only because the prettiest girls in town attended there. My aunt Gladys "endured" Sundays at her best friend's "holy roller" church until she was publicly humiliated by a minister who chided her for painting her fingernails red. My father briefly tried and soon drifted away from a Methodist church, and long before my mother came to Idaho, he dated a Mormon girl until her parents put an end to their romance because my father wouldn't convert. The truth was, the Funda siblings were apathetic about church affiliation, mostly because Frank had raised his children within the tradition of the Bohemian Freethinkers, who were a uniquely American group, often associated with the Czech Benevolent Lodge societies like the one my grandparents belonged to in Nampa. Bringing together the social, cultural, nationalistic, and philosophical needs of the immigrants, they resisted any doctrinal creed whatsoever, preferring to be agnostics who remained suspicious of any organized religion. For Frank keeping himself independent of any organized religion was a state of exile he was proud of because, as he saw it, religious institutions represented fraud and outright theft.

My paternal grandmother grew up as Annie Martinek in the affluent mining village of Kutná Hora, just east of Prague. The oldest of just two children, Annie was a good and dutiful daughter. By the beginning of the twentieth century she was of age and fulfilling her promise as a genteel lady of an emerging middle class. She was quiet and obedient, educated only to the level women of her station were—that is, she was literate, knew how to sing and to be pleasing. Her father adored her, and with thick brown hair that she piled on top of her head and the fashionable hats and dresses that her station in life afforded her, she looked like a Czech version of a pretty Gibson girl. But when her father suddenly died, shortly after her mother's death, she discovered that his regard was not expressed in his final bequests.

In Bohemia, where the medieval notion of primogeniture still lingered, the oldest male inherited the entire estate. Annie was disappointed to find that neither her father's written desires nor the laws of the land allowed her any claim to her family's belongings or estate. Without money, or any promising prospects for marriage, Annie was like a boat cut from its moorings. While her younger brother, Josef, just eighteen himself, assumed claim to all their family's possessions, she was given only her clothes. When she appealed to her brother to let her stay at the family home, he coldly refused, and when she begged for a small portion of money until she could find lodging, he simply laughed at her. Her survival was no matter to him, he said.

Homeless, her outlook was grim. Only marriage would offer real security, but without a dowry she was no longer considered marriageable by men of her own class, and she had no other prospects. Although she had shown a gift as an herbalist—a folk healer—she was essentially unskilled and had little chance to set herself up as a midwife or nurse. Finally, to avoid starvation or prostitution, she was forced to find employment as a "hired girl" for a wealthy German family living in Prague. Among her duties was to serve as a nanny for their unruly young son. She tried her best to teach him the complexities of Czech grammar and polite table manners, but he was defiant and insolent. He played tricks on her, hiding when she called and sneaking up behind her to yank hairpins out of her hair to let the loosened curls fall around her shoulders. When Annie complained of his behavior to his mother, she raised an eyebrow and said simply, "Perhaps he misbehaves because you are a poor excuse for a nanny." Thus fearing that she would be turned out, Annie tried to remain calm in the face of the boy's misbehavior, even when he shouted at her in German, as he often did, "Goddamn lady! Goddamn lady!" One day, when his taunts were just too much, she turned to face him, shoved him into a dark closet, barred the door with a chair under the doorknob as he shouted after her, and went off to her own room to await being sacked. Although her employers reprimanded her, she was not fired, but the incident convinced her that she had no future as a nanny. She decided to leave Prague, and in 1912 she immigrated to the United States.

At Ellis Island she was questioned about why she wanted to come into the United States, and she was required to provide the name and address of her closest relative still living in her country of origin. Should officials ever decide that she was unsuitable for entry into the United States, they wanted to know where to send her and whom to contact. She must have felt a bitter irony when she spelled out for the examiner her brother's name: "That is Josef, with an *f*, not a *ph* like the American spelling."

Young, single women traveling into the country alone faced many hurdles. They were typically detained for weeks or months by immigration officials, who worried that, because there were so few jobs available to them, they would become wards of the state, or worse, they would be forced into prostitution. While immigrant families could clear the Ellis Island system much more easily, sometimes within hours, neither the promises nor the protests of single women could sway the officials; they could not leave Ellis Island unescorted or in the company of single men. Like hundreds of other single women Annie was confined to one of the huge dormitories to wait until immigrant friends in America could be contacted and confirm their willingness to sponsor the new immigrant. In Annie's case she listed my great-grandfather Václav Funda as her sponsor and St. Paul as her final destination. She had been best friends with Václav's daughter Beatrice during their childhood, and she'd heard the Fundas had emigrated to Minnesota. The Ellis Island documents say that she claimed Václav was her uncle, which would mean that she and my grandfather Frank were cousins when they married, but other evidence about her family contradicts this claim, and I suspect she named Václav as her uncle because someone had advised her that people with family in the United States had an easier time of being admitted. She arrived on April 20 and was cleared for entry on May 1 of that year.

Years later, during the Depression, my grandparents returned to visit Beatrice and Frank's other sister, Lizzie, in St. Paul. There, to Annie's surprise, she discovered that the naughty German boy's family had also emigrated and settled in nearby Minneapolis, where the boy himself, now a well-mannered and contrite adult, was president of the family's thriving department store. When he and Annie met again, he apologized profusely for cursing her and laughed about the time she'd locked him in a closet, and in order to make amends, he insisted on giving her the finest dress in the store.

There would be no such reconciliation with Annie's brother. She heard from him just once—also during the Depression. He found out where she lived in the United States and wrote her a letter about how he had lost their family home and almost everything their father had willed him. Now that she was living in the United States, he wrote, surely she could see her way to send him some money. He had children, he wrote, and they were without resources. She had an obligation to help, he implored, because they were family. Annie and Frank and their three children were just scraping by themselves, but Annie dutifully packed two trunks full of clothes and dry goods for her brother's family, anything they could spare and some things they couldn't. I don't remember a fancy dress being in my grandmother's possessions when she died, so I wouldn't be surprised if that, too, ended up in the trunks that were bound for Czechoslovakia. But Annie never heard from her brother again.

When Frank sat down just months before his death to draw up his final will, I doubt that he could have predicted how the decisions he made in those early weeks of 1967 would set into motion family squabbles that would last for the next thirty-plus years. His bequest consisted of two main parcels of land. One part was what we called "the forty," which had originally been the sage-covered sheep ranch, later converted into the farm where I grew up and out of which the tiny corner lot was carved for my uncle's house. A half-mile southwest of this parcel was "the thirty," the original site of the Italian prune orchard business Frank bought in 1919 and the location of the two-story house that had been made over from an orchard warehouse into my grandparents' home sometime during the late Depression. In short, Frank's was a modest estate. But read the documents that survive from those years— the file folders containing dozens of personal letters, steno pads filled with notes scratched in my grandfather's handwriting, and thick packets of legal documents—and you would think we were fighting over Howard Hughes's millions, instead of less than half of a quarter of a section situated in the backwaters of Idaho.

Frank was absolutely serious when it came to determining the control and ownership of the farm. Agonizing over how these two plots of land were to be divided equitably among his three children, he drew up several maps of the land, each designating different parcels to different heirs. He used the current fair market values to calculate their worth, and then he scratched out his figures and started again. He carefully differentiated between the value of the farmland and what he designated as "waste ground"— that is, the land where the family houses, shops, and gardens stood. He factored in various outstanding loans among family members, in particular a small farm loan of just over one thousand dollars my father had recently gotten from his sister to buy farm machinery and an old, unpaid three-thousand-dollar loan James Frank had gotten from his father many years prior (although the purpose of this loan remains unclear).

He also factored in individual strengths and lingering concerns about his children. Because my aunt Gladys had business and accounting experience, Frank and Annie appointed her as executrix. Second, my good-hearted father had never been compensated for coming home from college at the University of Idaho after just one year when Frank was seriously hurt in a farming accident during planting season. Back then, in the spring of 1942, my uncle James Frank was working in the shipyards in Seattle and had no intention of leaving a good-paying job for work on our penny-ante farm, and so my father was forced to leave college less than a year after he'd started, take an agricultural deferment, and come home in time for irrigating season. Since then my father had stayed on the farm and increasingly been called upon to take care of his parents' daily needs as they aged. Frank wanted to reward his loyalty. My uncle, meanwhile, only briefly went back into farming after the war, coming up with making-it-rich schemes that took him away from Emmett to farms in the central mountains of Idaho (where he loved to fish and hunt) or to the remote deserts of Nevada (where he could go rock hunting or do absolutely nothing at all). As for the Emmett farm, he had little to do with it. Also, my grandfather was profoundly hurt that his namesake rarely drove the half a mile to even visit him, and my grandparents couldn't count on him for any help; in fact, they suspected Vi simply took the phone off the hook so that no one could call to ask for a ride to town or to beg for a scoop of coffee for the percolator. Frank was particularly distrustful of James Frank's "greedy" wife, Vi, who goaded her husband to buy new pickups and camping trailers, on one hand, but always brought the poorest-looking hot dish or the tiniest present to family gatherings, on the other hand.

Letters that Frank wrote to his daughter during this period predicted that Vi would convince my uncle to sell any land he might be willed rather than stay on it, that they would squander the money they got from the sale, and that then they would end up no better off than they were. With this in mind he considered just giving his eldest son money in the will—letting him cast it to the winds in any way he wished—rather than risk the family losing any of the land. But the problem was that my grandparents were cash poor. The money they might give James Frank would have to be raised by selling a parcel of the land anyway, so that idea was abandoned. Instead Frank compensated in other ways that he hoped might be insurance against the breakup of the farm. Under these terms James Frank's outstanding loan and the accrued interest, which Frank doubted would ever be paid off anyway, would be completely forgiven; in exchange for this writing off of the loan, my uncle would receive a much smaller portion of the land than his siblings. Frank instructed that any remaining difference was to be made up by a cash award to James Frank from my aunt, who was heir to the largest parcel and was the most cash solvent of the three siblings. Thus taking into account interfamily debts, Frank accounted for what he thought of as the fair distribution of sixty of the seventy acres in this very logical manner.

The division of the remaining acres was less logical and revealed Frank's lingering pipe dream for complete family harmony. The last ten-acre parcel on the thirty was to be "divided equitably . . . to share and share alike" among his three offspring and me, his only grandchild. James Frank, Lumir, and Gladys were instructed to "completely cooperate in obtaining surveys if necessary" to divide that parcel. Beyond saying that, my grandfather did not specifically designate who would get which of the two-and-a-half-acre lots, but he made clear in a family meeting of the siblings and their spouses that his plan was for four adjoining plots where each of us would someday build our own dream house and we would live side by side.

Although the meeting took place at the same table where we'd all shared hundreds of meals and stories, this was neither a dialogue nor a communion. It was Frank's speech, which he gave in English, to make sure that even his American son- and daughter-in-law understood. Accordingly, everyone remained quiet while he outlined how he had arrived at this division, showing the siblings details of his calculations that put the value of each of the three main bequests to his sons and daughter at twelve thousand dollars. While my grandfather's oxygen machine sighed in the background, Gladys took notes and wiped away her tears. Uncharacteristically still, Annie sat in the chair next to her husband, looking down at the hands folded in her lap. My father and uncle remained stoic as their wives hovered at the kitchen door, whispering for me to stay quiet with my coloring books. Pausing to rub his forehead, my grandfather looked up and motioned to me, and I escaped from between my mother's and aunt's legs. As I crawled up onto his lap, Vi refilled coffee cups and went to sit beside her husband. "You two," Frank said, pointing at first James Frank and then Gladys, "you vill lease that ground to Lumir. No meddling, you hear? Lumir has been doing a good job." Bristling at this implied criticism, James Frank shifted uncomfortably but said nothing. Frank continued. "Lumir, you vill give dem a fair part of the profits. And if anyone should vant to sell their part of the ground, you must gif the others first chance. Dis is my vord on this. I haf put 'no contest' in my vill. Your maminka vill do the same." Annie looked up long enough to nod at her children. At this moment Frank motioned for Aunt Gladys to read the exact language from the document, and with a shaky voice she read, "and they shall take nothing pursuant to this will or otherwise, except for the sum of One Dollar, which shall be paid by the executrix." It was the one-dollar clause. Everyone knew this disinheritance threat was being leveled at James Frank and his wife, but at the meeting they mounted no protest.

What we were to learn, however, was that Vi and James Frank were not going to accept the terms of the will without a fight, especially the manner in which it distributed the land. In fact, in the years that followed Frank's death that summer and Annie's death just two years later, each of the family members predictably played true to character. Aunt Gladys used her role as executrix of the estate to make up for a childhood in which she had been indulged by her father but never given any real power or agency; she endlessly fired off letters that consistently proclaimed she alone had the power to disinherit anyone who questioned her mother's or father's intentions. "Daddy said I could give you just one dollar!" she threatened again and again. Always the family

chameleon, my uncle pulled his usual pranks and good-natured-
ly joked with us all while secretly meeting with a shyster lawyer
to plot ways around how the will allocated the acreage. And my
father—the quintessential middle child—was desperately trying,
and hopelessly failing, to keep the family peace.

As a result the final distribution of the seventy acres wasn't
made until early 1973, over four years after my grandmother's
death and almost exactly six years after my grandfather had so
carefully outlined his wishes at that family meeting. Tensions that
dated back to Frank's will continued to ripple through the family
until the last of the farmland was sold in 2001. I didn't know the
full extent of those conflicts, however, until I had sorted and read
through these documents. Even then, with letters that testify in
indisputable black and white to the nuances of each individual
grudge, I remain mystified by how petty it all seems—such spite
and drama over such small fields of land.

James Frank was at the center of the conflict for much of the
time. Because of his outstanding loan Frank's original bequest just
apportioned a seven-acre field south of his house to him, while my
father was slated to get the twenty-one acres that surrounded where
we were living. My uncle—assuming a first-born's sense of entitle-
ment—vehemently protested; even before my grandmother's death
he had persuaded Lumir to go to Annie to change her will so it
would be more favorable to him. My father, who operated by an
unyielding sense of fairness—whether it benefited him or not—was
willing to give up the extra acreage. As much as he loved that land,
he thought family unity was more important, and, he reasoned,
he'd be farming the land anyway because James Frank had no intention of giving up his sawmill job to return to farming. Although
Aunt Gladys argued that their father had had good reason to dis-
tribute the land as he had, Annie, once herself the victim of an un-
just bequest, conceded and changed her will so that both sons

would receive an equal allotment of fourteen acres of farmland, over and above the acreage where our houses stood. Moreover, James Frank convinced Annie that he should have the field to the east of his house rather than the one south of his house, which he complained wasn't as fertile as the lot that fronted the highway.

After Annie's death James Frank argued that Gladys had unfairly influenced their parents during their last years, and he accused her of taking advantage of their aging minds and planting seeds of suspicion about his motives. While the family was trying to probate Annie's will, Gladys and my father discovered that James Frank had secretly sought out the town lawyer to get the courts to probate his *father's* will in place of his mother's. Because Frank's will lacked the exact land descriptions—only saying things like "acreage west" or "acreage east of the Garmon ditch"—James Frank now seemed under the impression that his father's will allowed for an interpretation that would favor him. He argued that the acreage split gave my father an unfair advantage, in part because it included the acreage with the pond, and he believed that my father owed him money to make up for "more waste ground," which James Frank calculated to be worth as much as farm ground (unlike his father, who had calculated the "waste ground" at a much lower value). Gladys got wind of these back-door tactics and threatened on multiple occasions to invoke the one-dollar clause.

Another set of battles was waged over the ten acres that had been set aside for the family to be "shared and shared alike," as Frank's will so momentously put it. James Frank accused my father of double-dipping—that is, of unfairly getting an additional 2.5 acres because he was the only one to provide my grandparents with a grandchild. I was a minor daughter, my uncle argued, and had no legitimate claim to the land I was being allotted from the ten acres set aside by Frank for our dream houses. My father and his sister united on this front, so James Frank then questioned how the ten acres were to be divided. Neither of the wills was explicit about whether it should be divided into a four-square configuration—in which case one of the lots would have no access to the road except through another parcel—or whether Annie and Frank had intended four narrow, side-by-side parcels—in which case the question remained who would get the most desirable parcel, with frontage along two roads, and who would get the middle parcels, where the field still dipped slightly and irrigation water pooled. After months of haggling James Frank won the corner lot. Gladys argued that naturally her lot should abut her other ground, where the big house stood; for symbolic purposes, she argued, her parents would have wanted my land to be next to her land—all of which meant that once again my father got the last pickings, the middle lot that was hard to irrigate.

As nasty, petty, and mean-spirited as all these disagreements seem to me now, the remarkable thing is that during the four years it took to probate my grandmother's will, when all this dissension was an undertow in our family, life on the surface functioned as it always had. We all exchanged presents at Christmas time, fussing over what would be just right for each other. We often ate Sunday dinners together at my mother's table, and at Vi's birthday my mother would make Vi her favorite meal and bake her favorite rum cake. When my mother and I had an argument, I'd seek sympathy at Vi's kitchen table, where we'd leaf through magazines, and Vi would feed me one of our favorite meals: buttered toast dipped in coffee with lots of cream and sugar. Several times a year I went on weekend rock-hounding or fishing trips with Vi and James Frank. My father regularly stopped for coffee at his brother's house. Vi and my mother permed each other's hair. James Frank borrowed my dad's tools, and Dad sought out his brother's advice on everything from crop rotation to whether or not he should "shoot the moon" during a pinochle game. Nothing seemed out of the ordinary. There were no heated arguments. As usual, when Gladys bought new furniture, she always gave her castoffs in equal measure to James Frank and Vi or to us, and she freely doled out her advice on everything from curing a cold to putting away money for retirement, the last of which was rather like offering vacation tips to a condemned man. Dad and James Frank continued to partner on the doomed Nevada ranch until 1975, although they always argued about who devoted more time or money to the project, and in their darkest moments they bitterly accused each other of a failure to abide by the spirit of their partnership. The two sons who had grown up on their father's stories of homesteading worked to the very end under the illusion that the Tonopah Ranch provided a genuine opportunity to make the desert bloom.

Shortly after the final settlement of Annie's will issues over the land flared up again. Like James Frank my father had taken a job at the sawmill in town, and my mother began dreaming about moving out of the tiny sheepherder shack she'd been living in for fifteen years. With a small loan from the bank my parents built a modest ranch-style house in 1972 on the narrow strip of ground between the ditch boundary with my uncle's parcel and the dirt road that led back to our shop and farmyard. But the bedrooms of our new house faced west, and after the first sweltering summer on that side of the house, my father decided we needed trees to provide some shade. However, the house was less than six feet from the Garmon ditch that marked the dividing line between James Frank's acreage and ours. To have space for shade trees, the ditch and the property line would have to be moved. After a typical Sunday dinner Dad sketched out his request. He proposed taking over a narrow strip, less than a quarter of an acre, for our new yard; in exchange for the land he offered to do the work of canceling out the Garmon ditch that irrigated James Frank's field and moving and replacing the ditch with gated pipe.

"Hell, Lumir, I don't want gated pipe," my uncle argued.

"But it'll make irrigating that field much easier. No more broken ditchbanks. Faster and better control over the water."

"I'm not the one irrigating it," James Frank answered. "You are. Why should I go to the big expense of getting gated pipe to make *your* job easier!"

"I said *I'd* put it in. It won't cost you a damn thing. But what it will do is increase the value of *your* land at no cost to you." Dad didn't bother to remind his brother that the portion of land they were arguing over had originally been designated to go to my father, but no doubt he thought of it.

"Christ, Lumir, if you want it that bad, I'll tell you what. I'll do what the old man said in the will. I'll sell that land to you. You get first option to buy. Fair market value." He named a price.

"What about the ditch?"

"You do with that what you want. Put in pipe or just move the ditch. It's all the same to me."

In the end my parents bought the land, and my father put in the gated pipe at his own expense. They planted a lawn, a fast-growing pin oak tree that stubbornly held its leaves all winter long, and a row of three white pines, like those that grew in the mountain valleys where he and James Frank had hunted as kids. As the trees grew, they provided cool evening shade and blocked the view west to Vi and James Frank's. But the best thing about them, my father once told me, was how the wind whispered through their long needles, "Wish, wish, wish."

Mark and I decided to marry in 1986, but it was a match my aunt Gladys clearly disapproved of. Although she had never actually met Mark, she told everyone in the family that he was no good and that she was going to do everything she could to stop the marriage. So every Sunday she phoned me with the same litany, as if playing out the cards in a hand that never changed. He was ten years older than I was and had been married before. We should be ashamed of ourselves that we were living together already. He was from the East. He had left a good job in the air force in order to get two "worthless" degrees in history and anthropology. "What on earth is he going to do with those degrees?" she demanded. And on and on. The more she talked, the more I dug in—telling her that at age twenty-six I certainly had a right to choose my own mate. But I knew my aunt was used to getting her way. She always had a talent for plotting and coercing until family members agreed with her. So I should have known that she hadn't done her worst yet.

By late that summer Mark and I were weeks from the wedding date when Gladys called at the little house where Mark and I were living in Boise. "Evelyn, I want you to know," she began without any prefatory greeting, "that if you go through with this marriage, I will cut you out of my will." Her icy tone brought a rush of heat to my entire body. "You'll never see an acre of my land. You will never see a dime from me," she warned. "None of it. Do you understand? You were going to get that land, but now . . . never! Do you understand?" She was confident she had her ace. Essentially, it was the "one-dollar clause" all over again.

I sank down into the nearest chair. I couldn't believe that she would try to bludgeon me into submission with her own father's farmland. "Oh, I understand," I replied at last. "I understand that you're trying to blackmail me back into line with what you want. And you're using your father's land to do it. I understand that. I just can't believe it."

"Not an acre. Not a dime," she repeated. I could just picture her pursing her lips in that nervous way of hers. She was breathing hard, and I could tell she was working herself up to continue the tirade. But I was done listening. I lowered the phone into the cradle. I had never argued so openly with her, but I felt a small victory in hanging up on her. The phone rang again almost immediately, but I didn't answer it. Her disapproval of Mark wasn't even the issue anymore. And for me Granddad's farmland never had been the issue. All I wanted was autonomy and a degree of respect for the decisions I made. But now we had crossed some kind of boundary of familial decorum. We had stepped off a cliff and were free-falling.

After a pause the phone rang again, and I thought about picking up to tell her to just give my inheritance to the Humane Society. If the land was mine in theory, didn't that mean that in theory I had the right to designate who got it? Puppies and kittens—that seemed safe. But I never answered.

When my aunt realized that I wouldn't pick up, she called my parents, who called me that evening. My mother, who had had her own run-ins with Gladys, sympathized as far as she could. My father, on the other hand, told me I was overreacting, and he pleaded for me not to "make trouble."

"I'm not making trouble," I said. "I'm reacting to trouble. And I'm never speaking to her again. That's it."

Mark and I eloped, instead of having the backyard wedding we had been talking about. We went to a courthouse in another county and waited for the judge to get out of traffic court to marry us. Since we hadn't brought along any witnesses, the judge designated a clerk to sign on behalf of "the court."

After we returned from a camping honeymoon, my father kept trying to get me to talk to Gladys. "Don't let this tear the family apart," he implored every time we saw each other. He was caught in the middle again, and we both knew it. But for my part I felt that was a decision he had made.

In accordance with Frank's wishes Lumir kept the agreement with both his siblings that he would split the yearly net profits from the crops that came off their portion of the land. He liked the symbolism of a "family partnership" rather than a "lease," which suggested an inequitable relationship. At the end of 1987 my father made his final accounting to Gladys for that year's crop, but there had been a run of bad years. The price of grain hadn't held, even though the expenses for seed, spraying, and harvest had gone up. My father explained in his letter to Gladys that he had taken the cost for seed and spraying out of the profits, but, he assured her, he hadn't taken out money for his hours irrigating or for the cost of him combining the grain with his own machinery. Those were not out-of-pocket expenses; still, they were at a three-hundred-dollar net loss. He enclosed an accounting of the expenses and income for her to look over, and as always he closed with a wish for a better crop next year.

Days later my aunt fired back an angry letter, accusing him of misleading her and taking advantage of her goodwill. After all, she said, she'd been "letting" him farm her land—as if the land were some toy he could be amused by. Complaining that she should have sold the land right after the wills had been probated, she said, "with the interest all these years I could have been sitting pretty now. . . . But I wanted you to have a better life." She was "just sick" that she still wasn't seeing a profit from the land. "I feel I helped you all these years letting you work my farm without charging you." She was putting the land up for sale immediately, she said, and she instructed him "that we *absolutely do not* put in any crops this spring . . . as I don't want any bills against my farm—just let it got to weeds or untouched." The letter closed with an incongruous thank you to my mother for sending kolaches and a note that she still had to write her Christmas cards.

Weeks later and just after the new year she listed for sale her twenty acres down on the thirty-acre parcel. When my uncle James Frank heard what his sister was doing, he too decided that he would put up for sale the tiny corner 2.5-acre lot down on the thirty. "If she thinks *she* needs the money!" he complained, as if needing money were a horse race and she was nosing ahead. The two remaining lots, mine and my father's, lay in the middle of that field between my uncle's and my aunt's lots. Resigned to the impracticality of farming just five acres on that parcel, my father suggested that both he and I put our lots up for sale too, in hopes that someone might buy the whole thirty-acre parcel. "There's no point arguing with her," he said of his sister.

My father felt betrayed by both his siblings. They had forced his hand, and there was nothing I could say. I felt sad that he wouldn't be farming that land, but he'd still be farming James Frank's fourteen acres on the forty, along with his own acres. And if sale of the thirty-acre parcel meant he no longer had to feel accountable to Gladys, well, I thought, that was for the best. My aunt and I hadn't been on speaking terms for months (indeed, we wouldn't speak to each other until my father was dying fifteen years later), and so selling my little lot, which she had originally fought so hard to see abut hers, was just one more way of saying I wasn't coming back.

Relations with Vi and James Frank went on much as they always had. My father had capitulated, and that temporarily bought him some peace. He continued to farm, and farm prices began to inch up in the early 1990s. Dad always hoped that in the end his patience would win out, and these family schisms over the land would be genuinely repaired. In 1993 that almost happened.

Sixty years of smoking meant that my uncle's heart and lungs were giving out. He was on oxygen twenty-four hours a day, and he was weak and gray. Dad now stopped by Vi and James Frank's house twice a day to check if he needed anything. One day, when my mother had taken Vi to town for groceries, James Frank brought up the land.

"You know I ain't gonna live long, Lumir," he said breathlessly. My father began to protest, but James Frank waved off his words. "I've had a talk with Vi. I've made her promise . . . " He gasped between puffs of air from the tank. "She will leave this land to you. With the idea that someday it will go to Evie. It's not to be sold. It's to go to you. I've made her promise me." When my father didn't say anything, he added, "This was the old man's place. It stays in the family." For now, the brothers agreed, the land would stay in Vi's name, and my father would continue the leasing arrangement. Corn prices had been going up, year after year, and that would give her a small income that would supplement the money the two of them had squirreled away over the years in CDs. The amount James Frank named seemed like a king's ransom to my father. "She's got enough that she shouldn't have to sell the land." My father promised he and Toni would help take care of Vi for as long as she could manage to stay in the house, given her advanced age and her steadily failing eyesight. Then upon her death the deed to James Frank's acreage would go to Dad.

As Dad recapped this conversation to me, it was obvious that he felt vindicated. "He said he hoped it would make up for the Tonopah thing, too," my father added, referring to extra money Dad had invested on his own over the years in developing their failed Nevada venture. "He's trying to make things right," he said with emotion. "I know he's sorry about the whole mess."

But after James Frank's death that winter Vi had a different agenda. The land my uncle had promised my father became a source of power that allowed her to make new demands. Having already spent years counting on my parents' generosity, she became even more dependent on them, calling at all hours for this or that. Rather than stay in the familiar surroundings of her own home across the field from my parents, less than a quarter of a mile away, she wanted to buy a single-wide trailer and move it into their yard, right where my mother planted her garden every year and on the land James Frank had once sold to my parents. "I'd be steps away from you. It would be easier," she argued. When my mother put her foot down, leaving my father to say lamely that it wouldn't be a good idea, Vi became petulant. "I'll disinherit you," she warned. My father thought it an idle threat and tried to calm my insulted mother by arguing that Vi was just lonely. He took it upon himself to spend extra time at Vi's house, fixing up broken appliances or oiling hinges that creaked. Temporarily placated, Vi apologetically gave him a copy of her will during one of these visits, and my father was pleased to point out to my mother that it not only made good on her promise to leave the farmland to him but made my mother and me beneficiaries of the largest portion of her remaining estate.

"Dad, she's just showing you the will so that she can keep you at her beck and call," I told him one day on the phone. That week alone they'd taken her to two doctor's appointments, twice to the grocery store, once to a hair appointment, and to a funeral forty miles away in Marsing.

"She's family," he insisted. "I don't much like her. It's true. But Vi and my brother were married for sixty years!"

Just months after my uncle's death Vi quite suddenly put most of the possessions in the house up for auction. She claimed she had no choice, even though my father was sure that the money his brother had left Vi was still largely untouched. "I'm poor as a church mouse," she whined. It was too soon, we all argued, as she coolly designated for auction much of the furniture, tools, jewelry, and china she had once been so proud of. Post-it notes, which meant "sell," were stuck all over the house and shop. She hemmed and hawed over what to do with James Frank's clothes because no one could convince her that the tattered shirts and pants wouldn't bring any money at the auction. At one point my father picked a small set of his tools that James Frank had borrowed out of a sale pile. "Prove it," she demanded. "You can't prove their yours!" My father pointed to the "L.F." stamped onto a big wrench. She squinted and moved to find the best light to verify the initials. He'd learned over the course of many years to label any shop tools he bought for this very reason; otherwise James Frank was prone to carry off anything that he fancied. Even as Vi reluctantly let go of the wrench in her hand, however, she protested that she needed the money.

When my father saw one of James Frank's hunting knives, originally belonging to their father, in one of the sale piles, he asked Vi if he could have it as a memento of times when they all went hunting together. But sentiment didn't sway her. "That's an antique," she protested, citing an unreasonable price she thought it would fetch at auction. Both Gladys and I offered to buy the knife for Dad, either from Vi directly or to pay whatever it took at the auction to get it back for him. However, this time Dad was the one who was insulted by Vi's actions. At the auction he stubbornly refused to raise a finger when the auctioneer held up the hunting knife.

After the auction, however, my father still kept his promise to Frank to take care of Vi. The calendar next to my parents' kitchen phone became covered with Vi's appointments, including doctor's appointments for vague ailments, which usually meant a drive to Boise and a half day lost. My father maintained her house and mowed and irrigated her yard. If Vi went to the grocery store, it was with my mother, although typically she just phoned my mother and added her list to Mom's. "Whenever you get to town," she'd say, "but I need the milk by tonight." And when my mother brought the groceries, she argued about the bill—"You paid *what* for oleo?!" she'd exclaim—or she would chide my mother for buying a brand she didn't like, and then she'd count out the money, down to the exact penny, never offering to pay for gas.

After more than three years of caring for Vi and weathering her tantrums, my parents were exhausted by it all. Although she was almost blind now, her health was stable, even though she used every twinge to manipulate them. When they suggested that her ever-increasing needs might warrant moving into a care facility, she simultaneously pleaded poverty and accused them of being lacking in family love. "Now that my husband's gone, you want to throw me out with the trash," she cried.

"What does she think we've been doing all these years!" my mother objected. My father had no response. For once my mother and her sister-in-law Gladys were on the same side. According to my mother Gladys recognized that my father was taking care of Vi with the same solicitude he had shown during the final illnesses of James Frank and their parents. She accused Vi of being ungrateful and insisted that my parents come to Portland for a vacation. "Let Vi see what life's like without you," she reportedly told my father.

Stubbornly ignoring Vi's pouting, my parents arranged for a few days away. My mother left Vi with a refrigerator stocked with microwavable meals and assurances that they had instructed a network of neighbors to check in on her. "You'll be fine," Toni said. "We'll be back by Saturday," she added. Vi was silent.

The second night after Lumir and Toni left for Portland, Vi went outside in the middle of a storm—none of us ever knew why—and she fell just outside of the back door, off a half flight of cement steps. She lost her glasses in the fall, and it was too dark to find them again. Apparently dazed, she just curled up on the gravel of the carport, where she stayed until morning, when a neighbor found her. She was hospitalized for almost a week. My parents rushed back home from Portland, and I came up from Utah. She appeared to be slipping in and out of consciousness. Although she was bruised from the fall, the doctor told us that nothing was seriously wrong with her physically, and he saw no reason why she wouldn't make a good recovery.

Vi was discharged and brought home by my parents, but she stubbornly said little to them, except "I had my accident because of you." Days after she came home, she secretly called a friend of hers who lived in Boise, and she disappeared with her for an entire day. The next day the local realtor's car was parked in her driveway. That evening she called over my parents and told them that she had changed her will, had written every one of us out of it entirely. She had also listed for sale the house and the fourteen acres where Dad's corn was already knee-high. Feeling avenged, she told my father that just as soon as the land would sell, she planned to use the money to go to one of the nicest retirement homes in Boise.

At first my father tried to reason with her, asking if the money she had in the CDs weren't enough to cover a retirement home, then telling her that if she sold their house alone, rather than the farmland with it, she could comfortably live in the retirement home for many years. Maybe by then he'd have the money, he said, to buy the farmland from her. "Of course, you have the first option to buy," she said coolly, mimicking the instructions from Annie's and Frank's wills. "But I'm selling it all now. If you want to buy it, you can buy it all—farmland and house, to boot."

"My brother promised me that ground," he implored, " . . . for Evie. She was the closest thing you ever had to a daughter. How could you?" But she held firm. He reminded her of the capital he'd invested in the Nevada venture and then added, "I used to combine that ground of his up in Donnelly without ever charging him." He hoped that she could be persuaded by accounting records, if not by family loyalty and promises. When she didn't reply, he ranted, "I've taken care of you for the past three years, day and night, like James Frank asked me! Christ, Vi! He's turning over in his grave. A stranger would treat me better!" She was unmoved.

Gladys joined in the argument from afar, sending Vi letters outlining how much the family had done for her and James Frank. She sent my father copies of these letters, in which she listed every can opener and hedge clipper she'd given Vi over the years. She even argued that she had been the one to pay for James Frank's funeral flowers. What she didn't say in writing, however, was what she'd been saying privately for years: that her parents, Annie and Frank, had never liked Vi, thought her a greedy, manipulative wife who had done everything she could to turn James Frank against the rest of his family.

Finally, she reminded Vi of that old dispute: that according to their father's original will James Frank had actually been granted only half of what he'd gotten, and that when that estate was being settled, Lumir had "insisted," as she wrote, that the acreage be split equitably and that James Frank get his full share of the acreage. Therefore half of the land Vi was now selling *rightfully* belonged to Lumir, she said, if they had followed the original wishes of their parents. "Lumir was very generous to you to give up his *own land* legally given to him by Dad. . . . We know you will do the right thing by us," she concluded, "and we wish you health and God speed."

In the end my father had to fight with Vi to even agree he could harvest the crop he'd planted. If the fourteen acres sold during that summer, the agreement said, he would at least have the right to get his crop off without interference. Gladys's argument about Frank's original wishes didn't hold any legal weight because my father had agreed to the change all those years ago without any stipulation. He'd had no crystal ball back then to foresee this betrayal.

Still, after the sale of the land in 1998, my father helped move Viola's belongings to the nursing home. Even though the land was gone, he tried one more time. Whatever her grudge with him, he tried to tell her, Toni and Evie should remain in her will, just as they had been in the will she'd once shown him. They'd had no part in this, he said.

"I've cut them off," she said flatly, and that was that.

My father never saw her again. Thereafter he refused to even say his sister-in-law's name and called her only "that bitch."

After Vi's death six months later, at Gladys's insistence, she and my father filed a creditor's claim against Vi's estate. In it my father had to enumerate each thing he'd done for Vi since James Frank had died—page after page of handyman chores or trips to the doctor that totaled more than $6,000, which was probably a conservative estimate, especially since it didn't take into account any of the meals my mother had prepared or sewing she'd done for Vi. In another list my aunt enumerated her claims, which amounted to $9,400 and included the prepurchase of their gravesite, a cash gift of $2,000 she'd given them when they were threatened with a suit for nonpayment of medical bills, and the purchase of their house, which had been moved onto their corner acre before I was born. In the end Lumir and Gladys were granted half of what they claimed was owed them, an amount that couldn't half make up for how cheated my father still felt.

My father never got over the conflict with Vi. Physically, he seemed to age overnight, getting weaker all the time until farming the very last parcel of that land completely exhausted him. My mother, in turn, worried over him and renewed her pleas to sell, adding that he should sell the last fourteen acres, if it caused such heartache.

The following spring, for the first time, he accepted my offer to help open corrugates during the first irrigating, always the hardest irrigating because it meant cleaning out ditches, digging out the last yard or so of each row between the gated pipe and where the corrugator had come as close as possible and scratched out the little furrows in the clods of clay. We had a matter of days on the fourteen-acre field before the ditch rider came and sent the water on down the line to the neighbor's place. If you didn't do this first irrigating right, you'd have trouble all summer long. During those days when the Idaho summer was heating up, my father and I slogged down the muddy fields over and over again, watched with eagle eyes as the water progressed down the corrugates. We made sure the water wasn't going to break by going down a gopher hole or get diverted by clods of clay into another corrugate, thereby leaving some rows dry and withering while others flooded out and suffocated the emerging crop with stagnant pools of murky water. You couldn't predict which way the water would go. You could only react.

While I was busy congratulating myself that I'd finally proven I could be useful on the farm, I was too busy to see that asking for my help had cost my father something. He expressed his gratitude for my help that year and when I opened corrugates the next year, too, but he had become more remote and detached. The truth was, he had lost at every turn.

I had wanted to write a hero's story about my family on the Idaho farm. Instead I was ashamed of us all now. Down to a person the facts pointed to pettiness, ugliness, and disloyalty that Frank could have never predicted when he first signed his name to this land.

When the 143 surviving women of Lidice, Czechoslovakia, were released in April 1945 from the Ravensbruck concentration camp for women, located outside of Berlin, their only thought was to return to their small rural village just a few kilometers northwest of Prague. They hadn't seen their families or home for nearly three years, since they had been loaded in trucks by the German ss on the evening of the 9th of June, 1942. The ss soldiers had entered the rural hamlet and separated the women, children, and men of the village over the age of fifteen. Although they were told by officials at the camp that their husbands and children had been sent to camps in Poland, they set off for Lidice not knowing if they would ever be reunited with their families.

Sick and malnourished, they walked for almost a month before they arrived at the site of their village; however, they saw nothing but blue-green fields of young barley and sheep grazing in pastures. Disoriented, they wondered if their memories had failed them. Had they forgotten a turn? It was as if their home had vanished. If someone at that moment had handed them the latest maps of the region, they would have seen that the name of Lidice had been geographically erased. All roads and paths going to Lidice had been rerouted, and the town itself had been completely leveled. Their houses and church had been set on fire, their horses and cattle taken away or destroyed, the orchards of cherry, pear, and walnut trees pulled down and buried, the granary at the village center demolished, the pond filled in with rubble from the buildings, and the stream diverted away from where it ran next to the village. Even the bodies in the village cemetery had been disinterred, looted for gold and silver, and then the bones burned. Plows had been driven back and forth across the ruins of the village until everything was turned into a fine dust. Finally, the dust of the village was buried under new topsoil, where barley was planted. The very crops that had once sustained the villagers were now used to disguise the fact that their community had ever existed.

The only trace of the village was where the barley in one of the fields grew taller and greener. That spot, they were told by villagers from nearby Kladno, was where the 173 bodies of their husbands and adolescent sons had been interred in a mass grave.

At sunup the day after the women had been sent to Ravensbruck, the Nazi firing squad had escorted the men out into the farmyard next to the Horák barn. The men watched their village being set ablaze. Groups of five or ten men at a time were lined up in front of the barn wall and shot while their fellow villagers watched; then the next group of men were led to stand in front of the fallen and meet the same fate. That task in the obliteration of Lidice's men was over by noon.

Next Jewish prisoners from the death camp at Terezin were brought in for the gruesome task of burying the dead. As they were driven up to the Horák farmyard, they first thought they were seeing hills of potatoes rather than nearly two hundred corpses strewn about the farmyard. As the Nazis looted for valuables, mutilating the bodies and even gouging out gold teeth, the Terezin prisoners were ordered to strip the men's bodies, dig the hole for a mass grave, and gather the human remains for burial. At some point over the next few days a Gestapo film crew set up to document the town being burned. At night the flames could be seen from the outskirts of Prague, and the smoke hung over the village for days, reminding the entire region that Hitler would go to any lengths to exert his power over the people and place.

Stunned by this account, the women asked about the fates of their children. As far as anyone knew, they had indeed been taken away to a children's camp in Poland, but eventually only 17 of the 104 children who left Lidice in 1942 would be traced to the German families who had adopted the blond-haired, blue-eyed children in an "experiment" of "Aryanization." The rest were untraceable, and the women could only presume they had been gassed at the Polish camp.

Hitler had ordered the complete "liquidation" of Lidice in retaliation for the assassination by Czech dissidents of his number-one man in Czechoslovakia, Reinhard Heydrich. When Hitler first proclaimed to his advisors in May of 1938 that "it is my unshakeable will that Czechoslovakia will be wiped off the map," Heydrich was among the Nazi elites in the room. Heydrich was the main architect of what he termed at the Wannsee Conference "the final solution to the Jewish problem," and it was Heydrich who established Hitler's system of concentration and extermination camps in German-occupied lands. Heydrich remained among Hitler's inner circle during Hitler's expansion of power, while the Führer negotiated the "Munich Agreement" with British prime minister Neville Chamberlain, who called giving a horseshoe-shaped area along the borders of the Czech Lands to Germany an "appeasement" that would bring "peace for our time." Called the "Mnichovská zrad," or the "Munich Betrayal," by the Czechs, the agreement was negotiated without the presence or input of the exiled Czech president, Edvard Beneš. In fact, Chamberlain, fearing further escalation on the European front, categorically warned Beneš that no one would come to the aid of the Czechs if they chose to resist Hitler's annexation of the borderlands. By the spring of 1939, of course, the Germans had invaded the whole of Czechoslovakia. In the early morning hours of March 15, Hitler announced on German radio that "Czechoslovakia had ceased to exist," and he renamed it "the Protectorate of Bohemia and Moravia." The next day Hitler, accompanied by Heydrich, toured Prague, and that night they both stayed in Prague Castle, the home of Bohemian kings since the eighth century. In the autumn of 1941 Reinhardt Heydrich was appointed deputy Reich protector of Bohemia and Moravia, and he immediately made it clear that he thought Czechs were little better than Jews. His ruthless campaigns in the early weeks of his appointment quickly earned him the name "the Butcher of Bohemia."

Since his arrival in Prague during the autumn of 1941, Heydrich had been carrying out a plan to "racially map" Czechs, Germanize the few youth who passed the racial examinations, and then ultimately rid the country of up to 60 percent of the Czechs. In a speech to Nazi officials that echoed Hitler's pronouncements, he said, "The Bohemian-Moravian area must never be left in such a state that the Czechs might be able to claim it as theirs. . . . This space must be German once and for all." Heydrich had also been successful in creating a compulsory labor system in the Czech Lands that supported the German war effort with munitions and other war-related goods.

Heydrich was a vital component of Hitler's overall plan, and the Czech Resistance movement struck a crucial blow when they assassinated the man who had declared himself an "untouchable." The men of "Operation Anthropoid," who were responsible for the 1942 car bombing that killed Heydrich, were part of a Resistance unit of former Czech soldiers who had escaped after Hitler's takeover of the Czech Lands and, under the orders of exiled Czech president Edvard Beneš, parachuted back into the country to participate in covert operations to sabotage the Nazis and ultimately assassinate Heydrich.

Immediately after the bombing of Heydrich's car the Czech paratroopers went into hiding, and when Hitler's men couldn't immediately find them, Hitler toyed with the idea of destroying the entire city of Prague in retaliation for Heydrich's assassination; then his plan was to kill thirty thousand Czechs, but he was advised that this would have an adverse effect on the nation's workforce, which the Germans needed in the war effort. Still, less than a week after Heydrich's death eighteen hundred Czechs had already been killed in Hitler's effort to seek out the men who had bombed Heydrich's car.

Enraged, Hitler set out to find a scapegoat to prove his power over the Czech people, and that is the moment when Lidice's extermination was determined. Since the Nazis knew that at least one young man from Lidice, Josef Horák, had escaped and subsequently joined the British Royal Air Force, Hitler targeted the little village just outside of Prague on trumped-up charges that Lidice was harboring the killers, distributing anti-German propaganda, and keeping one of the radio transmitters that connected Resistance soldiers to the outside world. Hitler knew these were ridiculous accusations, of course. Specifically, Horák, a trained pilot still working with the Brits, had nothing to do with the assassination. But Hitler was invoking the Nazi law of *Sippenhaft*, literally "kin liability," which was based on the principle of collective responsibility, asserting that relatives of persons accused of crimes held a shared responsibility for those crimes. Hitler put Karl Frank, the new minister of state of the protectorate of Bohemia and Moravia, in charge of completely erasing every trace of Lidice, and it was Frank who promised Hitler that grain would grow where the village once stood.

As far as I know, no relatives of mine were among those killed or ousted from the village of Lidice, and I recognize no family names on the village's published list of the dead. By the summer of 1942 the Funda side of the family had all immigrated to the United States, and because no Martineks appear on the list, I can only assume that Annie's only brother, Josef Martinek, was still safe in Kutná Hora, well east of Lidice.

Although my mother's family was clustered two hundred kilometers to the south of Lidice, members of the Kratochvil family realized that their little village of Višňové was no bigger and no safer from Hitler's indiscriminate threats than the demolished village to the northwest. No Czech was untouched by Heydrich's rule, and now no Czech was safe from Hitler's wrath.

In that summer of 1942 Toni was sixteen and old enough to understand the magnitude of stories being passed from village to village about how the fires at Lidice were still burning. Her life had already been changed by Heydrich's policies that targeted young Czechs. She had been subjected to the racial examination all Bohemian and Moravian youth underwent on the pretext of tuberculosis prevention. Her blond hair and blue eyes meant that she was acceptable for "Germanization," and she was, therefore, forced into Heydrich's "reeducation" programs, which aimed to "produce Czechs with a German outlook." But she was lucky that she hadn't been sent to Germany, as many other young Czechs were. However, under Heydrich's compulsory labor laws, as an unmarried woman of sixteen, Toni had been compelled to leave school and go to work twelve hours a day in a munitions plant, where at one point she was hospitalized for some type of heavy metal poisoning. Heydrich's influence had been far-reaching, and the news of his death brought Višňové no real relief from their worries.

Just nine days after the executions at the Horák farm and the razing of Lidice, the next chapter of the story unfolded. One of the men involved in the plot against Heydrich betrayed the location of his fellows to the ss. The seven paratroopers of "Operation Anthropoid" were cornered in St. Cyril and St. Methodius Church in Prague. After a brutal gun battle that lasted for hours and involved seven hundred German soldiers, the ss finally resorted to using fire hoses to flood the basement, where the remaining men had taken refuge among some of the church's empty crypts. At that point those still living shot themselves in the head rather than be captured and tortured by the Nazis.

As details of the siege at the Prague church slowly emerged, some around Višňové began whispering that the men who had died that day had local ties. Indeed, among the seven men to die were two Moravian boys: Jan Kubiš, the man who had actually thrown the grenade that killed Heydrich, and Adolf Opálka, the commander of the operation. Kubiš's hometown was just forty kilometers (twenty-five miles) from Višňové, while Opálka had been born and raised fifteen kilometers (less than ten miles) away. As proud as they were of what these patriots had done, the continuing reprisals of "kin liability" made everyone in Višňové fear for their own lives.

Over the next weeks Hitler continued a campaign of terror. Hundreds of sympathizers in Prague were executed straightaway, while more than two hundred other collaborators were sent to concentration camps, where they were shot or gassed. A tribunal was held in Brno, the capital city of Moravia, which lies sixty kilometers to the north of Višňové, and over two hundred men were condemned to death in revenge for Heydrich's death. Hitler also ordered more raids on any villages he thought might be associated with the assassins or with the Resistance fighters, who continued to communicate with the Czech government-in-exile. Four other villages were plundered, and the tiny village of Ležáky, like Lidice, was burned to the ground and leveled.

But Višňové was spared.

Within days of the extermination of Lidice the story escaped the borders of the country, and Hitler's desire to erase the village from public memory was thwarted by an international community that vowed, "Lidice shall live." People of Czech ancestry throughout the world, whether they had been related to one of the dead or not, felt the tragedy of the events in the tiny village. Cities and neighborhoods were renamed Lidice, and the *New York Times* asserted that the name of Lidice "is written in blood in every free man's atlas."

After the liberation of Czechoslovakia from the Nazis, when the widows of Lidice returned to their razed village, they organized a committee for the rebuilding of the village; many remarried and moved into new houses and planted trees. It took two years, but by their efforts the seventeen "Aryanized" children of Lidice were tracked down and repatriated.

Four hundred people now live in a Czech village named Lidice that was rebuilt near the ruins of a town dating back to the fourteenth century. At the site where the Horák barn once stood, town officials planted a rose garden of "Peace and Friendship" with varieties from around the world, including a specially developed white rose named after the village, as well as the now famous pink and yellow "Peace Rose," which had been developed during the war and was coincidentally introduced to the world the day the war was declared over. The eighty-two children who never returned to Lidice are honored at the site with a cluster of life-size bronze statues that portray each individual child, just as each stood on that morning when they were first separated from their mothers in Horák's barnyard.

Those who study such concepts as national character say that the Czech character is shaped by a distinct sense of absurdity, that Czechs readily accept the ironic blurring of tragedy and joy, disaster and desire. In the years since the end of the war Lidice has come to embody that. Once the site of massacre and wholesale destruction, the rose garden has become a popular destination for weddings. For years after the widows of Lidice even helped officiate at these marriages, offering their good wishes to couples poised on the threshold of an uncertain but hopeful future. Lidice in June is a bittersweet confluence of time, where white rose bouquets represent both the anticipation of lovers and the murder of loved ones. Where else can barley fields grow so insistently in the certainty of the reaping hook?

6

"The True Point of Beginning"

"We all carry within us our places of exile."

ALBERT CAMUS
"The Rebel"

According to ethnographer Helen Papanikolas Greeks immigrating to the United States often brought with them a pinch of homeland soil in an amulet that they wore near their heart. Whatever their joys or successes in the new world, that amulet always called them home, even as they were determined to settle elsewhere. More than just a sentimental reminder, that soil was the measure by which they assessed all other landscapes and experiences.

Other cultures similarly reverence the soil. A few years ago I had a Navajo graduate student from the desert of southern Utah who became both physically and emotionally ill during the cold foggy winters in Logan. One day Alan's grandmother, the matriarch of his family, drove for seven hours from her home on a reservation to the state's most northern tip. Her mission was to deliver to him a Mason jar full of desert sand from the red rock country south of Blanding, where he grew up. She handed him the jar and then returned to the cab of her pickup and drove away without saying a word. Alan, however, didn't need words to understand the nuances of her message.

That jar of sand contained all the sunsets and all the sacred songs of his homeplace made portable. It offered solace when he was profoundly homesick and second-guessing his decision to enroll in a graduate program. Here in Logan he could pour that salmon-colored sand out of the jar, let it sift through his fingers, and reconnect with everything he believed he was. He could be of a place, even when he was not in that place. For Alan, who suffered from debilitating asthma attacks during our cold winters, that gift was also a curative, a psychological link to a place where, quite literally, he could breathe. Call it placebo effect, but that offering eased the symptoms of both his asthma and his homesickness.

Yet it was not a gift freely given. The jar of sand was also meant as a talisman of the familial and tribal traditions his grandmother expected him to honor. In handing him the earth of his home, she was holding him accountable to that land and community, obliging him to remember that he had made her a promise to return. The jar held, then, both a gift and a conscription. It was as binding as any contract, as compelling as any desire. Thus, Alan would always be a man of two hearts and two homes. Like the Roman deity Janus—the double-faced god of literal and symbolic thresholds—he would always look backward and forward simultaneously.

Such stories remind me that the deeper meaning of "belongings" has nothing to do with our portable, material acquisitions; rather, our "belongings" are the people and places that claim us as their own. Since my parents' deaths and the sale of the land in Emmett in 2001, however, I had been troubled by the sense that no land or tribe claimed me.

That feeling of homelessness led me in late June of 2007 on a trip to my ancestral homeland, where I'd come to participate in a writing workshop whose theme was, appropriately enough, "There's No Place like Home(land Security)." Teetering between the sacred and profane, the workshop's title situated Dorothy's hope that her ruby red slippers would carry her back to the farm within the cultural landscape of a post-9/11 world, with all its concerns for safety and sanctuary. Certainly for me personally the year 2001 had brought the sudden collapse of the towers of family and homeplace, as well as a destructive, disorienting tornado that dropped me into a life that seemed weird and strange. I could not escape the irony that I was "coming home" to the Czech Lands, a place I'd never been before, to work on writing a book about Idaho, a place from which I felt exiled.

An unfulfilled desire for a homeland is as central to Czech cultural thinking as is the long Czech history of disputed claims to land. For Czechs there is no certainty of a "Home, Sweet Home." Instead their national anthem is that old song my grandparents used to sing, "Kde Domov Můj?" or "Where Is My Home?" J. K. Tyl's 1834 song expresses the Czechs' profound sense of estrangement from their own land and a heartbreaking longing to be restored to the *domov*—a word that conflates the concept of home and home*land* so that domestic space, nationality, and personal identity are all inextricably linked for a people who are, according to Tyl, "tender souls in agile frames."

The question of why a collection of American writers and students should be studying such a theme in the Czech Republic was addressed by Richard Katrovas, director of the Prague Summer Program, when he cited Tyl's song and argued that "it is telling indeed that the shared aspirations [of the Czechs] were encoded as an interrogative" about "the metaphysical location of an intimate, familial space." By contrast, Katrovas emphasized, the American anthem, with its proclamation of this nation as the "home of the brave," expresses "no such charming wistfulness, no residue of introspection, no thoughtful doubt clinging to its own apotheosis of familial space."

Most of my two weeks in the country were spent in the capital of Prague, where the lively city life allowed me to think of the specific locale of "home" as something that was vague and distant, having a fainter pull on me. There was comfort in such abstractions. After morning workshops my afternoons were free, and although other workshop participants invited me to go on excursions with them, I chose to wander the city alone. I learned to negotiate the city's efficient and modern metro system that took me into quaint neighborhoods where little grocery shops sold fresh apricots that were as sweet as honey. I also visited the iconic sites like the Czech National Museum, the hilltop Hradčany Castle, the astronomical clock in Old Town Square, and the St. Charles Bridge, which is the main pedestrian route connecting Old Town with Lesser Town. Thirty statues of Czech saints flank the bridge, and I paused at the statue of St. John of Nepomuk to touch with my left hand the figures of the dog and of St. John being thrown from the bridge on the burnished brass plague. The figures have been polished gold by millions of such caresses because legend says that touching them is supposed to bring good luck and ensure a return to Prague.

Several afternoons I ordered coffee and ate fine Czech pastries in a café at the foot of Wenceslas Square, that long boulevard and marketplace where conflicts about national sovereignty had so often come to a head. In 1918 writer Alois Jirásek chose the site to read a proclamation to the Czechs that declared their independence from the Habsburgs after centuries of the empire's rule. The invading Nazis in 1938, and then again the Soviet Communists in 1968, chose the site to demonstrate a show of force by parading their tanks up and down the boulevard. In January of 1969 a young university student, Jan Palach, set himself on fire at the head of the square to protest the continuing Soviet occupation. Then twenty years later and in a happier time tens of thousands of Czechs marked the overthrow of the Communists throughout Wenceslas Square. They greeted the playwright and former political prisoner Václav Havel as their new president by chanting "Havel to the castle!" From my café table I could see where he had stood on a balcony waving to the crowd as they jangled their keys in the air to signify that at last they had a clear right to claim the royal residence for their leader. As I poured thick cream into my coffee, I thought about what kind of house-warming party Havel must have held that night when he arrived at the castle across the river from where I sat. I could picture the short, square man waving a broom in the air to sweep out linger-ing evil spirits and hanging a sampler that read "My Castle Is My Home."

I was staying in a dormitory that belonged to Charles Univer-sity and was located in the northern part of the city, away from these tourist centers. I ate dinners in the corner of a local pub where the *knedliky* and *zelí* (that is, dumplings and sauerkraut) were traditionally prepared, much like my mother had made them. Although I'd been fluent in Czech during my early childhood, I had mostly lost the language of my ancestors since Frank and An-nie died, so as I listened to the conversations at nearby tables, I was able only to catch a phrase or two that I understood. Still, I was content to quietly absorb it all rather than seek out company.

Late each night I called Jake and Mark in Utah just in time to ask them what their plans were for a day that had already unfold-ed for me. In Utah they were looking forward while my existence in Prague was decidedly backward looking. Reassured that all were fine and happy and that Jake missed me "only a little bit," I hung up and then slipped between the covers of my narrow bed to dream of jangling keys and tanks rolling down cobblestone streets.

My stay in Prague wasn't entirely solitary, though. My mother's niece Silvia, with whom I'd been corresponding since my parents' deaths, called at my dormitory room the first night I was there and invited me to Višňové in Moravia for the upcoming holiday weekend. Our cousin Zdenka would accompany me there, she said. Zdenka was one of my few relatives to live in Prague, while most of my cousins still lived in the Moravian province, two hundred kilometers to the southeast of the city. Silvia joked in broken English, "Be prepared. We are like *Big, Fat, Greek Wedding*. Many of us. And noisy!" I laughed and told her I looked forward to it.

Later that week cousin Zdenka invited me to dinner at her home. She and her husband, Jarda, were both retired and living on pensions, and they rented a small apartment located near my dormitory in a complex that dated back to the sterile architecture of the Communist era. But the inside was tidy and homey. Lace curtains decorated the windows, and family pictures were hung everywhere.

Zdenka was welcoming and motherly, while Jarda was broad-shouldered and quick to laugh. Although she knew very little English, and Jarda knew even less, we communicated well enough with the help of our Czech-English dictionaries and a fair amount of charades. Even without the ease of a shared language I quickly came to love the pair. During our first evening together Zdenka began correcting my pronouns, urging me to forego the polite *vy* form of *you* and instead use the informal *ty* form, which one only uses to address close family or dear friends who have bestowed their permission. My mother had been very strict about teaching me to use the polite pronoun, and since I'd never met or corresponded with Zdenka before now, I felt I had to earn the informal address. But Zdenka insisted that we were *rodina*—family—and that was that.

Jarda refilled my beer glass at every turn, and remarkably, he found ways without words to make me laugh. He and Zdenka squabbled in a good-natured way, with Zdenka rolling her eyes and then cocking her head to look at him accusingly. Or she would chide him by waving her open hand back and forth, as if slicing the air at an angle with a cleaver, before she relented to his teasing with a laugh. Her gestures were achingly familiar. Many times I had seen my mother laugh at the same time she scolded my father with that same hand wave, but I had never thought of it as a product of family or culture.

After a dinner of pork chops and a tour of the common garden out front, where Jarda had planted perennial flowers and berry bushes, Zdenka and I began to tentatively map out the family tree of the Kratochvils, starting with the names and birth order of our mothers. Zdenka's mother, Anna, was the oldest daughter of my grandparents Karolina and Josef. Cousin Silvia was the youngest daughter of the eighth child, daughter Žofie, while my mother, Ántonia, was the youngest of the family's ten children. We filled in the blanks with names of the other seven Kratochvil siblings, and the names of some of their children, our other cousins. However, Zdenka ultimately claimed she didn't know how many of us cousins there were in total because, quite simply, no one had ever bothered to count. Silvia, she said, was planning a gathering of the cousins in Višňové that weekend, and everyone had been instructed to bring records, photos, and stories with which to document our generation as the grandchildren of Josef and Karolina. I silently marveled at a family so large that it took its numbers for granted.

Before that trip to Moravia, however, Zdenka and Jarda generously offered to escort me on a short day trip to visit one of my paternal grandparents' hometowns—either my grandfather's hometown of Poděbrady or my grandmother's birthplace of Kutná Hora, the very place that Tyl had been picturing when in the national anthem he characterized the Czech countryside as a blooming

orchard and a paradise on earth. As tempting as the luxurious resort spas of Poděbrady were, I thought the cultural history of Kutná Hora seemed much richer. Home to a huge silver mine that
had once minted the national coins, Kutná Hora had served as
the economic center for the entire eastern European region and
was the second-richest city in the country from the thirteenth to
the sixteenth century. However, by the time my grandmother was
born in 1883, the mines had mostly played out, and the village
had fallen on hard economic times. My grandmother had always
identified her home village as a dirty, run-down place that she'd
been happy to leave. A hundred-plus years later, however, tourism had revitalized the town. We joined the visitors who strolled
by the fountain in the courtyard of the Italian-style palace where
the coins had been minted, and we were awed by St. Barbara's
cathedral, which has been called the most spectacular church in
the country. The opulent architecture includes three grand, tent-
style roofs topped with turrets, a dozen double arches, and outer
flying buttresses on each side that connect to slender spires surrounding the entire structure. Inside the church large glass windows encircle the soaring heights of the interior, and light refracts
into the room, shining on the tableau paintings and frescoes, the
dark woods of the elaborately carved pews, and the gold- and sil-
ver-leafed statuary throughout that testifies to the city's mining
history.

Next to the church a mining museum advertises tours down
into the mine's twenty levels below ground, and Jarda tried to get
me to join him for a visit into the tunnels. I saw other sightseers
suiting up in white paper jumpers and hard hats for their descent
down the two-hundred-meter shaft into what local Czechs call
"the soil of eternal night." As much as I knew going down into
the land of my grandmother might have been a fitting and poetic
experience, just the thought of the close, dark walls of the mine-

shaft and the stale, humid air made my throat clench. Such burial held no appeal.

I mumbled "claustrophobia" and automatically started to thumb
my dictionary to try to find the Czech equivalent.

"Sure, sure," Zdenka nodded, picking up on the Latinate word.
"*Klaustrofobie*. Me, too," she said and waved off Jarda, who
shrugged his shoulders and chuckled.

Besides, I hadn't come to Kutná Hora to see either the spectacular cathedral or the "ageless darkness" of the mines. My real
aim was to visit a modest little church that my grandmother must
have known, located less than two kilometers away in the adjacent village of Sedlec. Originally a monastery meant for quiet
contemplation and prayer, the Church of Our Lady of the Assumption is a little chapel that doesn't look very special, especially when compared to hundreds of spectacular churches in the
country that represent the very finest of architectural periods dating back a millennium. But what makes the Sedlec church unusual are its history and the art that it houses. In 1278 King Ota-
kar sent an abbot from the church to the Holy Land, and the monk
brought back with him a handful of holy soil from Golgotha, which
he sprinkled over the church's cemetery grounds. Thus conse-
crated, the Sedlec cemetery became famous, and people from all
over Central Europe desired burial in that sacred place. During
the plagues and the Hussite wars the demand was so high that
thirty thousand were reportedly buried there in one year alone.
Even though the cemetery was enlarged, some of the bodies were
eventually disinterred to make room for additional graves and for
the building of a new chapel in which the church's lower level
was to be used as a charnel house to store the human bones. While
such ossuaries were not uncommon in Europe, what happened
next was undoubtedly out of the norm. In the mid-nineteenth
century a member of the Schwarzenberg family, the most signifi-

cant noble family in Bohemia and the whole former Austrian Empire, commissioned wood carver Frantisek Rindt to decorate the ossuary with the exhumed bones. Completing his commission just over a dozen years before my grandmother was born there, Rindt used the bones as his medium to epitomize the transitoriness of human life.

Undoubtedly, Annie knew this place and had walked past the entryway wall where Rindt's signature is fashioned out of bones. A century earlier she might have descended down the same long flight of steps to the small basement chamber of the Kostnice, or "bone church." This chamber, I recognized, is dramatically different from the light and soaring spaces of the St. Barbara cathedral across town, but still it is a popular site for both Czechs and foreign travelers, admitting an average of 450 visitors a day. The muted grays, soft beiges and yellows, and age-bleached whites of the bones are the only colors in the palette of the ossuary. The chapel contains the bones of an estimated forty to seventy thousand people in the various bone sculptures of a royal crown, a chalice, a crucifix, several bell chambers made out of thousands of skulls, and—in honor of Rindt's patrons—a huge Schwarzenberg coat of arms. Yet I could tell that the whole chamber is smaller than the main floor of my own 1950s ranch-style house. The scene was as mesmerizing as it was macabre, and the room was decorated with several pyramidal stacks of skulls and crossbones, topped with trumpet-blowing, cherubic angels. Oblivious to the ghoulish nature of their posts, these ceramic angels are among the handful of the room's artwork not crafted entirely out of bones. Rindt's masterpiece, a huge chandelier that reportedly contains at least one of each of the 206 bones in the human body, ominously hangs in the center of the room, with garlands of bones draping to the corner vaults of the nave. In the hush Jarda, Zdenka, and I mingled among groups of people who indicated to their friends specific portions of the creations, pointed to their own bodies, and then in various languages argued over which bone was which: finger or toe, femur of a child or humerus of a mother.

Meaning, however, is sometimes greater than the sum of the parts. The bone church proves that, as Helen Paris Reimer writes, "indeed, dead men do tell tales." These bones weren't merely Rindt's medium, like abstract shapes and shades of color to be fitted into a mosaic. Looking in the chambers where stacks of skulls stared straight at me, I couldn't help but feel that in some way Rindt was in fact the medium by which these unearthed bones told their stories. I had to wonder to what degree, during the ten years it took to complete work on the chamber, Rindt speculated on the lives once housed in the bones he held. How did he know that he wasn't handling the femur, coccyx, or mandible of his own great-great-great grandmother? It takes a village to make a coat of arms, and I wondered if Rindt made up stories for the bones he chose, polished, and carefully set into place.

This is the ulna of the village priest who filched coins from the offering; this, the sternum of the big-chested, big-hearted baker who left loaves of stale bread at his back door for the widow's children. This is the pelvis of the woman leery of the world, mistrusting of love, scarred by rape. And there, cupped in the bowl of her pelvis, lie the metacarpals of the man who used those fingers to stroke her thigh before returning to a crippled wife whose cranium, as worn away as she was, watches from up there among the chandelier membership. By now, however, the marrow of her jealousy has turned to dust.

Any of these bones, I realized, could have once belonged to my own kin. I had no idea where Annie Martinek's ancestors were buried, but I was sure they had been buried in the region. As I stood eye-to-eye with one of the skulls in the Kostnice, I was tempted to defy the "Do Not Touch" signs and stroke the jagged stitching of a skull or the place where a brow once furrowed with worry. How did I know that I didn't share DNA with this polished forehead? How did I know that Annie, perhaps on the eve of being ousted from her father's home, hadn't stood here and wondered something similar? I wanted to whisper into the ear cavity little assurances that in addition to being part of Rindt's beautiful arrangement, their bones had enduring meaning for me, that they continued to participate in the give and take of human interaction. I suppose I hoped as much for my own bones. Gone but not forgotten.

Even so, the Sedlec bone church made me wonder about the ethical dilemma of turning our ancestors' bones into art. On the bus ride back to Prague I kept thinking about Rindt's signature, crafted out of the fingerbones of plague victims. Could it be regarded as a morbid appropriation, even an act of plagiarism? He used those hands to say what he wanted, without regard to the sanctity of their graves or the message they would have written themselves. Was telling the stories of our ancestors, either in Rindt's way or in mine, a resurrection or a violation? I didn't know if I was fulfilling an obligation to my elders or unearthing their bones, stealing their stories, and manipulating the details to fit mine.

The cosmopolitan city of Prague has been called the "Paris of Eastern Europe," and although Prague's greatest sites are buildings and monuments that date back centuries—in some cases almost a millennium—you never forget that you are in a decidedly modern city with an efficient metro system, world-class museums, and signs written in both Czech and English. The region of my mother's birth, on the other hand, was decidedly Old World. Our hot two-and-a-half-hour bus ride south was rather like going back in time. The roads became rougher. The weathered signs were written only in Czech. We stopped to pick up passengers in small villages. In between stops the dwellings were distanced farther apart, and fields of barley, sunflowers, and grapes dominated the landscape. A scenic area known for its family-run vineyards, southern Moravia is like a rustic Czech version of Napa Valley, where wine and bike tours attract travelers from all over Europe. More than three hundred vineyards are located in the area, including one, I was to discover later, owned by one of my second cousins.

About two o'clock in the afternoon we pulled into a dusty, tree-lined bus station in Znojmo, a cultural center of about thirty-five thousand people just a few kilometers from the Austrian border. As Jarda pulled our overnight bags down from the luggage racks, Zdenka waved through the window to a group of half a dozen people gathered at the stop. Among them I recognized my cousin Silvia from pictures and her thirty-year-old daughter, "Little Silvie," a graduate student in music theory at the university in nearby Brno. I knew that Little Silvie was as self-conscious about her English as I was about my Czech, but since she knew more English than her mother did, she'd been appointed to be one of my main interpreters. Typically, few people in Moravia speak English. With the region's proximity to Austria the German language tends to be the more practical choice made by schoolchildren choosing a second language. As I came down the stairs of the bus, my cousin Silvia rushed forward to greet me. *"Big Fat Greek Wedding!"* she said as she waved her hand to indicate everyone else. I laughed and nodded as I hugged her and Little Silvie. Silvia introduced me to her oldest sister, cousin Anna, who was the spitting image of my mother. Her hair, nose, eyes, even her frame took me aback, and when I communicated this, Anna seemed especially pleased and linked my arm in hers. She turned to a man who looked to be in his early thirties whom she introduced as her son Milan.

"Just like the city in Italy," he said to me in perfect English. I had expected Silvie to be the only fluent English speaker, and when I expressed surprise, Milan told me he was in fact an English teacher at a nursing school in Brno. Because of a student exchange program that had placed him in Britain for a year, he spoke English with more ease than Little Silvie. "The English of my students is only rudimentary, of course," he said, "so I'm looking forward to talking to a native speaker." The plan, Milan told me, was that Silvie and I were going with him to his mother's apartment there in Znojmo for lunch. Afterward we would drive the last twenty miles to meet everyone else in Mother's village of Višňové.

Milan directed Silvie and me to an old German car, and as he turned the ignition, I heard the familiar music of *West Side Story* from the stereo system: "I like to be in America! Okay by me in America! Ev'rything free in Amer-i-ca! . . . " I could barely suppress a laugh, and I wondered if he'd cued the tape up to the verse of that particular song for my benefit. As he put the car into gear, Milan looked sideways at me, smiling sheepishly. "I like American musicals," he admitted and added, "This one is my favorite." In that surreal moment in which the legacy of my mother's emigration story was overlaid with the pulsating music of Bernstein and Sondheim, I wouldn't have been surprised if I saw a young Rita Moreno dancing through the dusty streets of Znojmo.

Later that afternoon we drove on to Višňové, a village of about a thousand people located on a tertiary side road, miles from anywhere. This was decidedly off the beaten track, and I realized I was probably the only American citizen within miles. The famous wineries that attracted the tourists to Moravia lay slightly to the north of here, and Višňové and the surrounding rural areas were mostly planted with grain. It was the first weekend of July, and I had come just in time to see combines crawling through the fields for the harvest. Over coffee I said something to Silvia, via her daughter's translation, about how welcome the familiar sight of combining was, and with a smile she replied that when my parents were there in the early spring of 1993, Dad had expressed more interest in the farm machinery and the land than anything else. He wanted to know what they planted. He wanted to talk about yield and the challenges of farming in southern Moravia. He even wanted to see the tractors they used, and she showed me a picture she had of him in front of a tractor, his arm resting on the back wheel as he leaned on the machine like it was an old friend.

Silvia had mapped out for that weekend an intricate schedule of people to meet, and as we went from house to house, sometimes having to drive several miles to another village, Little Silvie briefed me on which cousin or second cousin I was visiting next and alerted me to how much time we had before we had to be off to the next destination. The one constant of these visits was that everywhere I went, I was expected to eat and drink. Plates of pastries and often little shot glasses filled with various brandies were set before me at each stop. At one house my second cousin Karel, along with his wife, their grown children, and their assorted boyfriends and girlfriends, sang a traditional toasting song that builds up to a rousing chorus where they repeated the invocation "Živio!"—"To life!"

Afterward we returned to Silvia's house, where we were joined by Zdenka and Jarda and a dozen relatives I hadn't met yet. As Silvia laid a plate of cream-filled pastries before us, I joked that I'd already met more than two-dozen relatives and eaten nearly as many pastries. "To je nic," Silvia waved off, laughing. I didn't know whether her "That is nothing" meant I could expect more food or more relatives. I soon found out she meant both. At six she announced we were all going on a walk through the village, and all the cousins in the house gathered in the yard. We strolled en masse down the middle of the narrow road, but we had it to ourselves on this quiet Saturday afternoon. I don't think I heard a car anywhere in the village. Half a block from Silvia's we came to the roundabout at the center of the village. At the town square she pointed out the post office where she had worked for years until her retirement just the spring before. The architecture of this building and the other Višňové buildings, huddled together with their beige stuccoed walls and red tile roofs, reminded me of the old Spanish missions in the American Southwest, and I fully understood for the first time why my mother had always been so in love with photos and paintings of the old California missions. Little Silvie pointed off to the left down the road to a large, white, two-story structure surrounded by huge trees, which she indicated was the house of the local nobleman. The house had figured prominently in my mother's stories about home. For her it had been a dramatic symbol of class distinctions in the years before the Nazis declared the Czech Lands a protectorate of Germany. Now, Silvie said, it was some kind of public rehabilitation house for teens.

We headed down a spur road off the main square toward the west. The two Silvias walked with me, while Zdenka and her oldest sister, another Anna, were involved in an animated conversation ahead of us. Beyond that a group of second cousins and their children laughed. Still others lagged behind us. I wasn't sure where we were going, and it didn't matter. It was enough to be a part of this crowd of family, to be in this place where everyone in the village seemed to be related to me.

Zdenka and Anna and the rest had paused in front of a small house, and as we caught up with them, Silvia indicated to Little Silvie that she should tell me this was the original site of our grandparents' home and where our parents had been raised. Nothing remained of the actual house where Josef and Karolina raised ten children, but one of the cousins had recently taken over the property. He and his wife had just finished building on the narrow footprint of the original structure the modest, two-story house that everyone now called the "villa." Its newness was a bit of an anomaly among the village's old Czech architecture, but it looked comfortable and well built. All told, it couldn't have been more than a thousand square feet in size. The small house huddled so close to the street that you could almost touch its walls from the middle of the dirt road where my cousins stood looking at it with a collective pride.

My cousin Václav and his wife emerged from the side gate. They hugged Zdenka and greeted the others before coming up to be introduced to me. Václav shyly reached out to shake my hand, but his smile was genuine. He shepherded Silvia, Zdenka, Little Silvie, Jarda, and Milan into the side yard, as some of the younger cousins drifted on somewhere down the road, where we were to meet them later. Within the sheltered side garden the small yard looked charming. Flowering vines climbed the fence, and two small chairs sat on a small brick patio. Václav guided us to the dark opening of a cellar door, situated along the back of the courtyard, and he said something to me in Czech that I couldn't make out. "Babička a Dědiček" or "Grandmother and Grandfather" was all I understood. Little Silvie translated. "He's showing you the cellar, which is still the building from your grandparents' time. It's all that remains."

Václav's wife stepped up and handed me a small card, about the size of a business card. On it was the picture of a young haloed child who was knocking at a door. Worn to a clothlike softness, the card was obviously old, and the picture was slightly faded, the colors muted, the edges just a bit tattered. It appeared to be a church devotional card. Václav gestured that I should turn it over. On the back I saw a signature in blue pencil, written carefully, as if the writer had been very young, but the angular letters of my mother's signature were nevertheless very familiar: Antonie Kratochvílová. I'd have recognized that handwriting anywhere: the European *t* that had once puzzled my father, the *a* that doubled back on itself with a loop, the sharp accent that seemed decisive, even in this adolescent writing. Václav had found the card in the cellar, Little Silvie translated. They were cleaning things out before they started building the villa, and they came across it in the corner of the cellar under some old barrels.

Václav said he wanted me to have the card and nodded insistently that I should understand him. I swallowed hard, thinking that if I ever believed in ghosts, I certainly perceived one now in the signature that slanted across the back of the card. I could imagine little Toni crawling through the cramped space to the back of the cellar where her father's prized apples were buried in the hay. She probably feared a scolding for taking the fruit without permission, so she didn't notice when the little card slipped out of the pocket of her dress. Later, when she complained that the card was lost, her mother probably shrugged and said again, "You're too careless."

Silvie said the card probably dated to Toni's confirmation year, and quickly calculating, I realized it had probably been in that cellar since 1938, the year Hitler began making serious threats against Czechoslovakia and set into motion a series of historical events that would force my mother to eventually leave this home. The card, then, represented a key moment in her life. Like the angelic child pictured on the front of the card, her life in 1938 had been at a threshold, but rather than joining the family of God, as the card invited her to do, she had lost practically everything— family, home, country, and faith. She couldn't have fathomed what a turn her life would take when she so innocently took up that pencil on the event of her confirmation. That Václav should have recognized the little card's talismanic significance and then given it to me moved me deeply. I felt as if I had circled back to my mother's point of beginning. Not only had I come to the site of her birth, but I felt I had been handed a single, significant moment of her life's story. Even though the gift represented the turning point of innocence lost, that didn't seem to matter quite as much when I looked into the faces of my cousins.

But I didn't begin to know how to express any of this. Uncomfortable with my obvious emotion, Václav said something brusquely to his wife, waving toward the back door of their house as they moved in that direction. Minutes later they emerged with a tray full of shot glasses filled with a dark liquid. "Ořechovka," Silvia said, and Little Silvie explained that this homemade drink was a special liqueur, a Moravian favorite made from green walnuts. Václav made a toast in my honor, and we all drank. Unlike *slivovice*, the fiery plum brandy that is the Czech national drink, the *ořechovka* was pleasantly sweet and fragrant with spices. It warmed rather than burned my throat. Pointing to the walnut tree behind me and then the cellar behind him, Václav emphasized that he had made the liqueur himself, right there in our grandparents' cellar.

Václav and his wife showed me a picture of my grandparents I hadn't seen before, one taken in the very courtyard where we were standing. At that time Josef and Karolina only had four children. Zdenka pointed to her mother in the picture, who was about three years old in the scene. Neither my mother nor Silvia's mother had been born yet. We were a future unrealized.

I asked what Josef had done for a living, but the answer my cousins gave was rather vague. He didn't have a trade, one of them indicated. "He farmed," Silvia said with a shrug. "To je vescheno." That is all. But, someone insisted, he was not a *sedlac*. Unlike English, where the one word *farmer* is broadly used for anyone who cultivates a crop, no matter the size of their land holdings, the Czech language makes finer distinctions that capture the class differences of traditional village life. The sedlacs were an independent class of farmers who owned and farmed significant plots of land, equivalent to a hundred acres or more. They kept horses or draft animals and might hire help during harvest. More important, they sold their crop in the marketplace. Josef was not a sedlac, my cousins insisted. Instead they identified him as a *malorolník*, or "cottager"—a status just above a landless peasant whose life was taken up by producing the food his family would eat from the dozen or fewer acres of land he owned. Rarely did a cottager have any surplus to sell in the market. My maternal grandparents, therefore, had measured their success by "enough" ("Do we have enough to eat this winter?") rather than by my father's "how much" ("How much yield will I get? How much will I get for the crop?"). For the Kratochvil family the food you grew went into the mouths of your children, or they had none.

I had been culturally trained to consider farming an occupation based on a business model that connected the farmer to the marketplace; if he was to be a success, he must sell his harvest and at a profit that would allow him to further participate in the marketplace as a consumer. He sold crops so he could buy goods. But the cottager class of my mother's family was removed from that. That was true agricultural autonomy—with all its inherent uncertainties. In this model simple survival was success. There was none of my father's "next year" dreams because for a cottager like my grandfather Josef the here and now was the key.

"What about Josef and Karolina's parents?" I asked my cousins. "Were they from Višňové too? Were they cottagers?" I realized I hadn't seen the graves of my great-grandparents earlier that afternoon when Little Silvie and I briefly stopped at the village cemetery. Now the reply was shrugs all around. No one knew.

Even Milan, the only one of the family to express much interest in family history, shook his head. "I don't even know their
names," he admitted. "Research into village records isn't easy.
Records are kept in individual villages, so they aren't easily ac-
cessible. Mostly, no one bothers to look. Generally, Czechs are
amused by the American need to 'trace your roots.'"

As if embarrassed by this genealogical dead end, Silvia moved
to the gate, saying goodbye to Václav and his wife as she directed
us all back out onto the little street. Headed west again, we walked
toward the edge of the village, where I was told the family was
gathering for a picnic at the home of yet another cousin. Trees
that threw shade across the road framed our view of the ripe fields
of grain that glowed in the late afternoon sun, and I could see the
slight undulation of the hills go on for quite a distance. I knew
that the nature of agricultural life in Eastern Europe still was village centered. People lived within the village and walked each
morning to their work in the fields on the outskirts of the community. I said to Silvia that this was "krásna vlast," a beautiful landscape, and I asked her to point out the family plot of land, that
piece of ground that the restitution policies of the early 1990s
had restored to the family. Yes, she indicated, it was off in that
direction to the west of the village. Vaguely she pointed toward
the field of grain we were looking at. But, she added, the lot they
now farmed wasn't the original land the family had owned. The
government had kept the other land for itself. The family's original land had been much better—richer soil, she said with bitter-
ness. It was the only time that weekend I heard my even-tempered
cousin speak with anything but kindness. I noticed she didn't indicate where the family ground had been originally. Cheated once
again, I thought. Lasting claims to land always seemed to elude
my family.

I looked toward the fields where the combines hadn't yet cut the grain. I suddenly realized that while I had been in southern Moravia for most of the day, and a good part of that time had been spent driving through miles of this agricultural region, I hadn't seen any fences. The fields stretched toward the horizon without demarcation. It wasn't as if I expected to see barbed wire—that cliché of the American West—here in southern Moravia. However, unlike American agriculture, where farmhouses sit like sentinels at the edge of the fields and fence lines and "No Trespassing" signs warn you not to cross the boundary between mine and yours, here those distinctions lacked relevance. Separate plots of land were indicated only by the intrusion of a narrow road or by the subtle differences between the combed line of grain in this field or that; it was as if one crop ended and another took up without pause, verification of the common Czech saying, "Do not protect yourself with a fence but rather by your friends."

I don't mean to overromanticize Czech agriculture as a model of communal living without the taint of competitive, American agribusiness. To do that would be to ignore the country's recent history. As compelling as this vision of a land without fences was, it had come at a cost, having been shaped by the Communist legacy of the collective farm, which revealed that without individual ownership it was difficult to inspire personal investment in a place. Even more than a decade after the Velvet Revolution and the restitution policies that followed, collective farming was still taking a toll on the health of the land and farmers. The heavy machinery of the collective farms had damaged topsoil. Incompetent management and a lack of motivation among farmers in the collective had led to lower production rates, which in turn led to efforts to boost production with herbicides and pesticides. Those chemicals still lingered, contaminating the soil and ground water. In a classic case of "you reap what you sow," cancer rates had been steadily climbing, as I was to learn over the next few days. Several of my own relatives suffered serious health problems. Silvia's husband traveled regularly to a hospital in Brno to be treated for a form of leukemia, and Silvia herself had a variety of health problems that had led to her retirement. Although my cousin Anna was cheerful and upbeat that weekend, I knew she was worried about her son-in-law, still in his early thirties, who had been admitted to the hospital that week, possibly with a malignant brain tumor. Another cousin, Jenda, had died of cancer that spring and left his family shrouded in grief. And the only living relative from my mother's generation was cousin Václav's mother, Aunt Blažena, who had been the wife of my mother's youngest brother, Josef. She too was very ill with breast cancer. There was no telling how many others in the family were affected.

After another pause at the windmill where my mother had drawn water for the pigs during her chores, Silvia indicated we should turn into the courtyard of a yellow stucco house at the edge of the village. Red geraniums spilled from window boxes, and tables and chairs had been placed in the courtyard, where relatives, some that I'd met that afternoon and many that I had not, were already gathering for another feast, a picnic of sandwiches and beer. As it had been all day, food was plentiful. With regularity someone would shove into my hands a drink or a new plate heaped with sandwiches or kolaches. "Almost as good as my mother's kolaches!" I teased.

Several paused to tell me stories about our grandparents or about my mother. One of the three Josefs of my generation looked at me closely, examining my face, and then pronounced that, yes, I was family. He waved over cousin Jiřina, who worked as a teacher in the local elementary school, and he asked Milan to confirm that his theory was true, that the two of us looked like we could be sisters—and indeed, Milan said, we could be.

As the cousins came up one by one to introduce themselves to me, Little Silvie and I documented what they knew about the family tree, particularly the names and the birth and death dates of their parents. Often balancing a filled plate on one hand, they would identify their parent in the 1935 family picture we had of Josef, Karolina, and most of their children. They told me stories of their parent or of one of the others in the picture, like the daughter Josefa, who had never married, or Frantisek, who had been a soldier. One cousin told me about her father, Karel—ironically missing from this early picture—who had been killed in 1949 by the Communists, who had made his hanging look like a suicide. When I asked why he had been killed, Karel's daughter shook her head, as if accepting that we would never know. Then someone else stepped up to ask if we had listed her children yet. My cousins studied the expanding family tree of Josef and Karolina's children and grandchildren, making sure we listed everyone and in the right order. Once satisfied, they moved off to another conversation.

During the evening we counted twenty-nine first cousins in our generation, the grandchildren of Josef and Karolina. Among Jake's generation of great-grandchildren we estimated somewhere near a hundred offspring. These numbers were an idle curiosity to my cousins, who remarked casually in Czech, "Hmmm . . . that many, eh?" As for me, however, the final tally was dumbfounding. Until that moment I had spent my whole life thinking of myself as an only child, as the only grandchild on my father's side, and as the mother of Frank and Annie's only great-grandchild. On my father's side of the family, which had loomed so large in my thinking, the numbers were very small. Here in Moravia, however, I was just one of a crowd. For my relatives the rush of our big and boisterous family was a given, and documenting how we were all related to this "American cousin" was little more than one evening's diversion.

In fact my cousins were much more interested in telling me stories of my mother, who, they told me, was remembered locally as a beauty. I had always thought that in pictures of my mother with Mrs. Pejskar, Frances was the pretty one, while my mother's hair was always a little too curly and her face a little too broad. But no. "Like a movie star!" one of my cousins insisted. She'd been nicknamed "Zita," I was told, after a famous Czech actress of the 1930s and 1940s who was the Czech equivalent of Greta Garbo. Everyone called her by that nickname, they said. This explained the US citizenship papers I'd found where my mother had signed her name with "Zita" as one of her two middle names.

I was to learn that weekend that my mother had gained a degree of fame in Višňové for more than just her beauty. Her work in the Resistance movement against the Communists and her subsequent escape were generally known and regarded as significant details within the village history. Here the impact of the war and the Communist occupation that followed was still immediate and consequential, and the players in those events were still the subjects of discussion.

With the aid of Milan's translation my cousin Ludmilla told me she was among the last to see my mother before she escaped. My mother had come to talk privately with Ludmilla's father, her oldest brother, Václav. That meeting was the first and only time my mother was to say anything to anyone in the family about her work in the Resistance. But she had come for Václav's advice. My mother had learned that she was about to be arrested, and she had a chance for escape, but was uncertain about whether or not she should leave because she was heartbroken at the thought of leaving her lover.

"A lover?" I repeated to Milan with surprise.

"Yes," Milan said. "A lover." This was not a matter of a sloppy translation—with words like *beau*, *boyfriend*, and *lover* used synonymously by someone unsure of English nuances. Milan, of all people, knew exactly what the term implied: not only a sexual relationship but, more important, a level of commitment I'd been unaware of. Ludmilla nodded. Apparently, everyone was aware of this relationship but me. I had thought all Mother's serious relationships prior to my father occurred in Germany in the years after her escape, and until now I had never wondered why I hadn't heard of any men in her home village. It made sense, however, since mother was twenty-five when she escaped.

According to Ludmilla's story Toni had been willing to risk certain personal danger—very likely death, like her brother Karel—because, as she told Václav, she deeply loved this man. Her oldest brother, however, was adamant: staying was suicide. It wasn't even a choice. She had to go.

"My father," Ludmilla emphasized proudly, "was the only one to know anything—about the escape or about her work."

"Did her lover know . . . about the Resistance, I mean?" I asked, finding it as awkward to use the word *lover* as it was to picture the man.

Milan turned to ask Ludmilla, who looked at me and shrugged. She didn't know.

"Does she know who he was? Or whether he was from here or Znojmo?" I asked Milan. Another shrug. If Ludmilla did know his identity, she obviously wasn't going to say. After all, Višňové remained a tiny village where, undoubtedly, gossip could still taint lives—even gossip about what dead lovers might, or might not, have known.

His identity aside, the real point was that more than blood had bound Toni to this place. This new detail suggested that at some point she had imagined a future there in Moravia, and, had she been allowed to stay without fear of torture and death, her daughter—some other form of me—wouldn't have been the center of the celebration. She would have been just another one of these many cousins gathered that dusk in a village courtyard.

Redirecting the story, Ludmilla instructed Milan to tell me about how the family had been treated after Toni's escape. Although our grandfather Josef was dead by the time of Toni's escape, her mother and siblings—including Václav—were questioned, watched, and harassed by Communist officials for a long time. With the exception of Václav, who didn't tell his family about what my mother had revealed in that last conversation until years later, they could all honestly deny prior knowledge of her escape plan. Until one of Pejskar's former associates translated a coded message on Radio Free Europe many months later, they assumed that Ántonia was dead. Beyond this message they would know nothing else about Toni's fate for years.

I was struck by how none of the cousins ever implied any trace of resentment in the family for the way Toni's political involvement had caused family members hardship. The best way to survive Communist rule was to be so inconspicuous as to stay off their radar, and undoubtedly that had been impossible for them after her escape, especially given her connection to Pejskar. No one ever went into detail about exactly how their families were harassed by officials—though certainly I've read horrific stories about such cases. But none of that clouded their feeling of pride in my mother. In fact my cousin Silvia noted with satisfaction that the last public event in the village Toni attended was her own baptism, held just days before Toni disappeared. My mother fulfilled that family duty and then quietly slipped away.

That night I slept in Little Silvie's room, my pillow below an oval-framed picture of Mary and child. The next morning both Silvias and I were to attend early mass in the church where my mother had worshipped as a child. The war had made my mother, like many refugees, unable to trust in a benevolent God, and she had become a lapsed Catholic, taking me to attend mass only a handful of times in my life. I had not attended a Catholic mass since I was nine years old, and I couldn't help but feel a bit nervous—as unsure of what was expected of me as I had been two days before when I was leaving Znojmo, and Milan's five-year-old, pigtailed daughter solemnly reached up to bless me by marking an invisible cross on my forehead with her thumb.

As the bells tolled, Little Silvie and I joined the two-dozen people already in the sanctuary. The white stucco walls made the chapel lighter than I had expected, and the narrow stained-glass windows let in morning light. Dark beams characterized the Gothic buttresses of the nave at the front, which had been the original part of the building constructed in the twelfth century, but the attached sanctuary, Silvie told me, was a later addition that dated to the early sixteenth century. I was moved by the thought that the room where I now sat predated the founding of the nation where I claimed citizenship. Although I am not religious, the fact that this building had stood so long in my mother's village inspired a feeling of spiritual comfort, an illusion of permanence and stability that felt like grace.

Little Silvie, who was then completing a master's degree in music theory, sang the hymns with a strong and expressive soprano voice. As we seated ourselves after one song, I noticed that next to her on the wall lining our side of the sanctuary was one of a series of four stone tablets that, according to the engravings, dated back to the mid-sixteenth and early seventeenth centuries. Carved in relief to depict a man, a nun, and two children, these large tablets—just under four feet tall—were positioned in such a way that the serene faces were at eye level when you were seated in the pew. The effect of these high-relief sculptures, with their soft rounded faces and distinct details of the stitching and the folds of their clothes, was to make it seem as if the figures were emerging from the walls, ready and willing to join us in morning mass. The figure of the nun, with her arms folded across her robes, was inches away from Silvie's elbow, and although she had her eyes closed, as if in prayer, the figure of the man next to her stared straight ahead at the occupants of the pew behind us. Just ahead of us were the two children, a boy who looked to be three and a girl who looked to be about five years old.

Silvie saw me eyeing the tablets, and when I gave her a questioning look, she whispered, "Very old. They are gravestones." She pointed to the figure of the nun next to her and added casually, "Those are the people buried behind the walls."

I tried not to look startled as I turned my attention to the priest at the front, but I remained aware of the presences the carvings depicted and the bones that had been laid just inches from where I sat. Throughout the mass I studied the reliefs with sidelong glances. The nun seemed dignified if a little bit haughty. But the man, who was shorter than the nun and had a chip off the end of his nose, had deep, kind eyes, yet an intensity in his gaze too. I didn't think he was a clergyman because he held in front of him a shield that was decorated with what looked like a family crest. Related to the village nobleman, I thought.

Who the two children were and why they had merited interment behind the church walls, however, seemed more mysterious, and I couldn't begin to make sense of the Czech words carved along the edges of their stones. The little girl, I noticed, had a broad face and forehead that reminded me of the pictures I had seen the day before of my mother when she was that age. What had my mother thought of this stone child or the others who had stood vigil, eye to eye, at the side of these pews for more than four hundred years?

At the site of my parents' graves in Idaho I might be able to touch the ground and be within a few feet of my mother's and father's bones, but I was always aware that grass, soil, impervious steel, polished mahogany, and then the tufted silk interior of their coffins were barriers that kept me from them. Here, though, even stone was barely a curtain between those bones and me. And yet their presences didn't unnerve me. It wasn't macabre. Their burial behind the walls seemed like an assertion of remembering. They represented continuity.

After the service, as people filed out, the petite, elderly woman who had been sitting in the row where the stone children stared turned to look at me. She studied my face and then, without taking her eyes off me, said something in Czech to Silvie. She smiled at me and extended her hand as Silvie translated: "She asked if you are Tonička's daughter? She said you look like her." I realized that while I had been busy taking in all the details of my mother's childhood church, the villagers attending mass had been eyeing me, fully aware of who I was. "She remembers your mother well," Silvie continued. "They were schoolmates." The woman smiled and nodded as if to confirm Silvie's translation—although I'm sure she couldn't speak a word of English—and then without elaboration she loosened her grip on my hand, turned to the aisle, and walked out the door.

I suppose it's an American characteristic to assume we are anonymous in unfamiliar places. But in such a small village, far from the usual tourist traps, I'd been naïve in thinking that only my relatives had been expecting my arrival. Truth was, I might have been an unfamiliar face as I seated myself in the pew, but I knew now I wasn't a stranger either.

On Monday morning, after saying goodbye to cousins who made me promise to return and to bring Jake next time, Silvia and Little Silvie drove Zdenka, Jarda, and me back to the Znojmo bus station. We drove through the countryside, where combines had taken up their harvest again after Sunday's rest, and on the way we passed one of the many wayside shrines I'd seen already that weekend. These markers consistently dot the edges of the Moravian fields and are locally known as *boží mukou*. Ordinarily translated as "the stations of the cross," the literal translation, however, would be "God's suffering" or "divine suffering." Later I discovered that nearly two thousand of them have been cataloged in Bohemia and Moravia, and a thousand others exist all over Eastern Europe. Many of them date back to the seventeenth century, although most were installed during the National Revival period of the late nineteenth and early twentieth centuries. Often as tall as eight feet, these monuments look like tombs or miniature houses, with their columns, white stucco, and red-tiled roofs. Typically they have alcoves or niches that are enclosed by filigreed ironwork, and the enclosures shelter carvings of Christ on the cross, statues of Mary, or paintings of the holy family or local monks. Often decorated with fresh flowers, the shrines obviously still hold significance to the local people.

In the flat lands of southern Moravia they seem to rise up out of the land itself, and Silvie was quite bemused by my exclamations of "Oh, there's one!" as we drove the countryside. For her they were so familiar, she hardly noticed them. I could discern no rhyme or reason to their placement—some were close to villages or crossroads, but many were not. Occasionally I would see one located right in the middle of a rye or barley field, surrounded by planted flowers so that the spot created an island that farmers had to steer around with their tractors.

Polish writer Tadeusz Seweryn has called the shrines "prayers, scattered in the . . . countryside." According to art historian Milda Baksys Richardson the "interplay of their symbolic values with the environment dramatically influences the landscape, making it conspicuously and intensely sacred." As a "totem" they offer the fields divine powers of protection and represent the religious and social solidarity of the community, and, insists Richardson, they are "never placed in the landscape for purely aesthetic reason." The shrines were a reminder to me that, in spite of the Communist disruptions, agriculture in my mother's village remained a spiritual act, and farming continued to be a main livelihood for my mother's family.

What the weekend in Višňové had proven to me, I was surprised to realize, was that my true ancestral roots in agriculture came from my mother's lineage, not from my father's side of the family, where most of Frank's stories about homesteading in the West— which I had once been so willing to believe—had faded under scrutiny, like so much disappearing ink. And yet, ironically, my trip to the Czech Republic had returned me more intensely, more sufficiently, to the Idaho farm, to realizing that land is transformed into home as much by the stories we create there as by the crops we cultivate. The Emmett farmland had been central to my life, the touchstone for so much of my experience, the belonging that I was obliged to remember, but now I realized that it connected me also to a landscape in southern Moravia and to a church outside of Prague. My family of exiles had taught me that I could have roots in one place and grow in another.

There is nothing inherently special about my family's farm in Idaho. Until now it has been written about only in legal documents, like the description listed on all those deeds that reads, "That portion of the NW¼ of the NW¼ of Section 36, Township 7 North, Range 2 W, Boise Meridian, Gem County, Idaho, lying East of the Garmon Ditch." But that jumble of numbers and letters is meaningless to me. The surveyor's exacting description of that property, which goes on for more than a page, is equally incomprehensible with its talk of "commencing" at an iron pin in the ground and moving x and y "feet thence" by turns and calculated degrees to an end that the document calls "the TRUE POINT OF BEGINNING." Apparently we must go out into the unknown to recognize the true point of beginning. Although symbolically evocative, that capitalized phrase, however, is still an abstraction, so if you care to locate that farm in other ways, the post office has kindly assigned it a mailing address: 1817 West Black Canyon Highway, which you can use to see that land for yourself by simply logging on to Google Maps and selecting a street view of the landscape. There you can virtually drive back and forth along the highway, as I recently did, and see a burly stranger whip by you on a Harley during a hot, autumn day when the corn is drying in the fields and the sky is a watercolor blue with wispy clouds. You can see the huge poplars and what remains of the little orchard that my grandfather planted, as well as my mother's profuse rose bushes, the white-barked paper birch that she loved, and the elm that she hated because it constantly dropped sticks onto the lawn. You can see the faded paint of the ranch-style house my parents built in the 1970s, although you can't see the "little house" where we lived before that because it's hidden in the grove of pine and poplar trees at the south end of the lane. To the east of the house you can see the split rail fence the Alaskan couple erected in late 2001, as my father was dying. To the west you'll see the silver gated pipe lying where I used to "swim" in the Garmon ditch. Horses perpetually graze in the pasture on the west side where Dad used to raise corn, though for some reason the Google picture makes the pasture look level, instead of the sloping field I know it still to be. You can turn to see the house where Jo and Eddie used to live across the highway, and you can take note of how the entrance to the drive is flanked by an old, two-row planter on one side and a repainted, four-row planter on the other, both of which, as I recall, were bought at the 2002 auction of Dad's machinery. You can go down the Black Canyon Highway in one direction to see Vi and James Frank's old place or back in the other direction to see the blue of Squaw Butte and the Little Butte next to it, though again they seemed flattened, as if this virtual view cannot accommodate highs and lows. You can see our old mailbox, still propped up by a post set in an old milk can weighed down with sand. Ironically, however, Google Maps has the address all wrong, and the location of the homeplace is listed as 1628 West, rather than 1817. "Address is approximate," the pop-up window cautions. The colors are muted, the dimensions are flattened, and the location is only an approximation, but as cultural geographer Yi-Fu Tuan says, this landscape is still "personal and tribal history made visible." Setting out from abstraction, I have circled round to the true point of beginning. The human experience of all landscape, writes Tuan, requires this kind of psychic transformation in which "abstract space, lacking significance other than strangeness, becomes concrete place, filled with meaning."

For so long I had thought of my family history as something centered on Idaho. I had lamented the transformation and loss of that place, grieved the ideals of a culture that perhaps never was. However, a lament isn't just unrestrained sorrow or a wild wailing. At some point acceptance and understanding germinate in grief.

If I were able to ask my mother about exile from a homeland, she would have a different story to tell from my own, as would my grandparents Frank and Annie. As much as I was interested in their need to settle into their adopted Idaho home, the pattern I identified was one in which they reconciled themselves to living in some form of exile—from place or dreams. I used to think that no matter where I went or how I changed, the farm offered a permanence that I could count on. According to the mailing address the deed that still lists the last 2.5 acres in my name, and these virtual drive-bys, it *is* still there. But the farm I knew no longer exists, except here on these pages as another abstraction. And finally that is sufficient.

Land or no, my relationship with family continues to be a living, evolving thing. Research still brings discoveries about my parents, grandparents, and ancestors. Recently Little Silvie began showing more interest in the family history, and she offered to translate a letter from Josef Pejskar that I had hastily packed before the auction at my parents' farm. Dated 1966 from Munich, the letter talks about people he and Toni knew during their work for Radio Free Europe, his affection for his second wife, his belief that the mission of his life was the editorial work he was doing at the *České Slovo* (the newspaper for Czech exiles that he founded); finally, after asking about my mother's work on the farm, he closes with, "Please give Mr. Frank Funda our best regards. Recently I have read his article from *Hlasatel*, and so I have learned that he had stayed in Portland at his daughter's for some time." Here, from an outside, objective source, I had new evidence that Frank had indeed published *something* in the *Hlasatel*. Maybe Frank wasn't a liar after all. I still haven't found his stories, but once again I have circled back to believe they might be out there, that there might be a story about a horse and a bakery in Buhl. And then as I was tying up the last details of the book, I stumbled across another still-life photograph by Clarence Bisbee. Entitled *Idaho Industry* and dated 1913, the photo of a chicken pulling a wagon with a rabbit at the reins made it clear Frank had directly used Bisbee's image as an inspiration for the 1960s Easter painting he'd done for me. The image hadn't been something entirely of Frank's imagination, as I'd always thought. Leave it to Frank, I thought, to offer new twists in the story just when I thought I had a resolution. But resolutions are a fiction—and that is a miracle for which I am grateful.

ACKNOWLEDGMENTS

This is my version of these stories, and I'm sure others have their own versions, just as sincerely and deeply felt. What I've written here is true, as far as I know it; however, in some cases I've changed people's names, either to protect their privacy or to avoid confusion.

In the decade it has taken to write this book, I've been fortunate to have the support of many individuals and agencies. I received research assistance from the staff of the Idaho State Historical Society, the Twin Falls Public Library (especially staff connected with the Idaho Special Collections Room), and Utah State University's (usu's) Merrill Cazier Library (especially the staff of the Special Collections Room and the Interlibrary Loan office). When the book still felt tentative to me, I was lucky to be partially funded by the John Woods Scholarship Fund to attend the Gribner Manuscript Workshop, which is administered by the Prague Summer Program, and I thank program director Richard Katrovas, as well as those who were the first to see these separate essays pieced together as a whole, including workshop directors Ron Grant and Sue Ribner and my fellow "Gribnerites" from Ron's group, Shanna Mahin, Shelley Seale, Susan Dawson-Cook, and Lydia Okutoro.

Several chapters of this book were published, in earlier form, in literary journals. An essay entitled "Belongings," published in Linda Hasselstrom's collection *Crazy Woman Creek*, was the first place where I toyed with some of these ideas, and bits of that essay have found their way into this book. The chapter "Wild Oats" was first published in the journal *Under the Sun;* "Dodder" (under the title "Weeds: A Farm Daughter's Lament") was published in ISLE: *Interdisciplinary Studies in Literature and Enviroment,* vol 13, no. 2 (Summer 2006), 233–45, used here by permission of Oxford University Press; and "Loosetrife" was published in the *Prairie Schooner.* My special thanks to the *Prairie Schooner*'s editor, Hilda Raz, for her encouragement about the project as a whole.

I also received various university and state agency grants and financial assistance along the way that helped me write this book. As a department head Jeff Smitten was dependable and creative in finding ways to help fund a research trip or a course release so that I could write, and as a friend he never failed to cheer me on or to offer a scotch when I couldn't be cheered. For their financial and moral support I thank members of USU's College of Humanities, Arts, and Social Science, especially my former dean the late Gary Kiger; the now-emeritus associate dean Christine Hult; and the current dean of the College of Humanities and Social Sciences, John Allen. I also appreciate research grants and travel grants I received from the Utah Humanities Council (Albert J. Colton Research Fellowship for Work of National or International Significance), Brigham Young University's Charles Redd Center for Western Studies (John Topham and Susan Redd Butler Research Endowment, Charles Redd Center for Western Studies), and USU's Women and Gender Research Institute.

Among colleagues from around the country I want to thank my dear friend Becky Faber, from Lincoln, Nebraska, who lived her own version of the farm daughter story on a little acreage in Iowa and thus helped me stay true to our farm-girl values. I also thank emeritus professor Jim Maguire, who was the first to suggest I could embrace my rural heritage instead of run away from it.

Ladette Randolph, former humanities editor at the University of Nebraska Press, was quick to say this story was worth publishing in book form, and when she left the press, Kristen Elias-Rowley graciously assumed the responsibility of guiding it through to publication. I admired the work of Mary Clearman Blew and Kim Barnes, even before I profited from their encouragement as friends, and they, and far-flung colleagues Susanne Bloomfield and Judy Nolte Temple, have been willing listeners, all. Several of my former students—including Susan Borklund Andersen, Bonnie Moore, Brandon Schrand, Maure Smith, Liz Stephens, and Rosa Thornley—have now become fellow writers and educators, and their friendships deserve to be noted.

While this is mainly a story about exile from Idaho, I learned to value my friends in Utah all the more during the writing. I want to single out the encouragement of Paige Smitten (who wisely reminded me I had a life beyond the book), Melody Graulich (who was among the first I trusted to read the manuscript as a whole and who has been unfailing in her encouragement), Sabine Barcatta (who generously helped me with editing, providing German translations and sharing her personal photos of some of the same sites my mother had visited), and Thorana Nelson (who took on the no-small-task of teaching me to trust myself). I also want to recognize the encouragement and assistance of current department head Jeannie Thomas and USU colleagues Chris Cokinos (now at the University of Arizona), Marina Hall, Norm Jones, Joyce Kinkead, Jan Roush, and Steve Shively. Thanks, too, to friend Luba Otrusnik, who helped me translate some of the Czech documents.

Friends of my parents, Leonard Bowers, Bob and Irene Canfield, and Alena Sehnal, were also generous with their stories and should be acknowledged here, although I am sad to say that Leonard and Bob didn't live long enough to see the project in print.

Among family members I would like to recognize my ex-husband, Mark Peplinski, who was along for so much of the ride, as well as my aunt Gladys Hewitt, who believes as passionately as I do in family. I include in this portion of the list Eddie and JoLynn Wilkerson. They became like family, mine as well as Toni and Lumir's, and I'm grateful for the part they played in our lives. I want to offer a special thanks to my relatives in the Czech Republic, who were generous beyond measure to a cousin they barely knew. There are too many to name (or remember!), but I want to single out the Silvies (my dear cousin Silvia Adamová and her daughter "Little Silvie"), cousins Anna Šobová and her son Milan Šoba (one of my able translators), Marie Krautová, Marie Peterková, Václav Kratochvil, Josef Lahodný, and finally Zdenka Bulinová and her husband, Jarda, who were my personal guides for some of my Czech travels.

Lastly, eternal love and thanks to my son, Jake Peplinski, for acting as my personal computer geek, for being such a good sport on the road, and for being like your grandfather in so many of the best ways. When all is said and done, this book is for you.

NOTES

Preface

The Michael Pollan quote comes from *The Botany of Desire: A Plant's Eye View of the World* (Random House, 2002). The quotes from Jefferson are from *Notes on the State of Virginia* (1781) and private letters found in *Thomas Jefferson: Writings: Autobiography/ Notes on the State of Virginia/Public and Private Papers/Addresses/ Letters* (Library of America, 1984). The reference to "SOLE" food comes from *homegrown.org*: see "Everyday SOLE Food: (Sustainable, Organic, Local, Ethical," http://www.homegrown.org/profiles/blogs/ everyday-sole-food (accessed July 30, 2011). Jennifer Meta Robinson and J. A. Hartenfeld's book is entitled *The Farmers' Market Book: Growing Food, Cultivating Community* (University of Indiana Press, 2007). Information about the changing face of farm population statistics can be found in numerous places, including "Historical Timeline—Farmers and the Land" and "Growing a Nation: The Story of American Agriculture," http://www.agclassroom.org/gan/ timeline/farmers_land.htm and http://www.agclassroom.org/gan/ timeline/index.htm (both accessed Sept. 30, 2011). Wendell Berry talks about how farmers became "statistically insignificant" as of the 1993 census in his essay "Conserving Communities," which was published in his 1995 collection *Another Turn of the Crank* (Counter-point, 2011). The story about Přemyslid comes from Alois Jirásek's *Staré pověsti české* (or *Old Bohemian Legends*, 1894), translated by Edna Pargeter (Paul Hamlyn, 1963).

1. Dodder

The history of Freezeout Hill and of Emmett's founding comes from Ruth B. Lyon's *The Village That Grew: Emmettsville, Martinsville, Emmett* (Lithocraft, 1979). Also consulted were "Freezeout Hill Monument," http://www.idahoheritage.org/assets/popups/sw/sw_freezeout.html (accessed July 1, 2010); "Boise to Payette River," http://www.idahogenealogy.com/goodale/boise_payette.htm (accessed July 1, 2010); and "Freezeout Hill Area: Goodale's Cutoff and Ridge Trail," *Trail Dust*, Feb. 2007 http://www.idahoocta.org/TD_February_2007.pdf (accessed July 6, 2010). Mark Fiege's book *Irrigated Eden: The Making of an Agricultural Landscape in the American West* (University of Washington Press, 2002) is an excellent history of irrigation projects in Idaho. Figures about the valley's agricultural production, as well as the quotes from the 1910 promotional pamphlet, come from Cort Conley's *Idaho for the Curious: A Guide* (Backeddy Books, 1982). Information also comes from Tim Woodward's "After Hard Times, Idaho Town of Emmett Reinvents Itself," *Idaho Statesman*, Oct. 13, 2009; and "Water Questions and Answers," http://ga.water.usgs.gov/edu/qa-usage-stateirr.html (accessed Sept. 3, 2011).

The Department of Agriculture bulletin I refer to is entitled "Dodder and Its Control" and was written by William O. Lee and F. Timmons in 1958. The botanical information on dodder comes from David Attenborough, *The Private Lives of Plants: A Natural History of Plant Behavior* (Princeton University Press, 1995); William H. Amos, *The Life of the Pond* (McGraw-Hill, 1967); and Justin B. Runyon, et al., "Volatile Chemical Cues Guide Host Location and Host Selection by Parasitic Plants," *Science*, Sept. 29, 2006, 1964–67. David Malakoff's "Devious Dodder Vine Sniffs Out Its Victims," where Colin Purrington is cited, was broadcast on NPR's *All Things Considered*, Sept. 26, 2006. For the discussion of historical methods for controlling weeds, I referred to Ada E. Georgia's 1914 *A Manual*

NOTES

of Weeds, With Descriptions of All the Most Pernicious and Trouble-some Plants in the United States and Canada, Their Habits of Growth and Distribution, With Methods of Control (reprint, MacMillian, 1919).

The discussion of the Ceres and Demeter myth was informed by Barbette Stanley Spaeth's *The Roman Goddess Ceres* (University of Texas Press, 1996); Christine Downing's *The Long Journey Home: Re-Visioning the Myth of Demeter and Persephone for Our Time* (Shambhala, 1994); and—the work I quote from—Kathie Carlson's *Life's Daughter/Death's Bride: Inner Transformations through the Goddess Demeter/Persephone* (Shambhala, 1997). Information on women's roles on the farm comes from Deborah Fink's *Agrarian Women: Wives and Mothers in Rural Nebraska, 1880–1940* (University of North Carolina Press, 1992); and Mary Neth's *Preserving the Family Farm: Women, Community, and the Foundations of Agribusiness in the Midwest, 1900–1940* (Johns Hopkins University Press, 1995).

For my discussion of hybridization I quote from Paul Raeburn's *The Last Harvest: The Genetic Gamble That Threatens to Destroy American Agriculture* (Simon and Schuster, 1995). I also consulted Denis Murphy's *Plant Breeding and Biotechnology: Societal Context and the Future of Agriculture* (Cambridge University Press, 2007); and Malcolm Wilkin's *Plantwatching: How Plants Remember, Tell Time, Form Relationships, and More* (Facts on File, 1988). Information on herbicide-tolerant crops comes from S. Z. Knezevic and K. G. Cassman's 2003 essay "Use of Herbicide-Tolerant Crops as a Component of an Integrated Weed Management Program," http://www.plantmanagementnetwork.org/pub/cm/management/2003/htc/ (accessed Sept. 26, 2006).

The quotes from Jefferson are from *Notes on the State of Virginia* (1781) and private letters, especially those to John Jay, found in *Thomas Jefferson: Writings: Autobiography/Notes*. Joseph A. Cocannouer's *Weeds: Guardians of the Soil* was published in 1964 by

Devin-Adair Company. For background on the European use of dyer's woad I consulted Tom Gard's essay "Gascony's Dyeing Tradition," *Everything France* 22 (Mar. 2004), as well as "All about Woad," http://www.woad.org.uk/index.html, and "Bleu de Pastel de Lectoure," http://www.bleu-de-lectoure.com/ (both accessed Sept. 28, 2007). Information on the bounty system and attitudes toward dyer's woad in the West comes from "Bag o Woad," http://www .cachecounty.org/weeds/bagowoad.php (accessed Sept. 28, 2007), and a pamphlet entitled "Bag o' Woad: I'm a Woad Warrior!" published by the Utah-Idaho Weed Management Cooperative. Alan Burdick's book, which contains information on kudzu's ecological history, is *Out of Eden: An Odyssey of Ecological Invasion* (Farrar, Straus and Giroux, 2006).

2. Loosestrife

The USDA publication that I mention is *Farmers in a Changing World: Yearbook of Agriculture, 1940* and was published by the USDA in the fall of 1940. The discussion of "exurban sprawl" is informed by the work of Yale Agrarian Studies fellow (Kirsten) Valentine Cadieux, and the quotes in that section come from her essay "Beyond the Rural Idyll: Agrarian Problems and Promises in Exurban Sprawl," http:// www.yale.edu/agrarianstudies/colloqpapers/18conspicuousproducti on.pdf, Feb. 2007. Cadieux has also recently coedited with Laura Taylor a related book entitled *Landscape and the Ideology of Nature in Exurbia: Green Sprawl* (Routledge, 2012). The quote about Pandora's hope comes from Mark P. O. Morford and Robert J. Lenardon's *Classic Mythology*, 6th ed. (Oxford University Press, 1999).

The history of Emmett is by Ruth B. Lyon and is entitled *The Village That Grew, Emmettsville, Martinsville, Emmett* (Lithocraft, 1979). In the discussion of the unearthed Indian bones I am referring to Leonard Arrington's *History of Idaho* (University of Idaho Press, 1994); and to *Idaho, A Guide in Word and Picture*, which is the WPA

project guide written in large part by Idaho writer Vardis Fisher in
1937.

For ecological succession see William H. Amos's *The Life of the
Pond* (McGraw-Hill, 1967); and "Disturbance and Succession,"
Brooklyn Botanical Gardens, Jan. 23, 2010, http://www.bbg.org/
gar2/topics/ecology/eco_disturbance.html. Information about Idaho's
farming population and the history of the state seal and motto come
from the following online resources: "State Fact Sheets: Idaho,"
http://www.ers.usda.gov/data-products/state-fact-sheets/state-data
.aspx?StateFIPS=16&StateName=Idaho (accessed May 1, 2009);
"Occupation, Industry, and Class of Worker of Employed Civilians
16 Years and Over: 2000," http://factfinder2.census.gov/faces/
tableservices/jsf/pages/productview.xhtml?pid=DEC_00_110S_
GCTP13.ST04&prodType=table (accessed Dec. 26, 2012); "The
Great Seal of Idaho," http://www.netstate.com/states/symb/seals/
id_seal.htm (accessed May 1, 2009); and "Selected Operation and
Operator Characteristics: 2007 and 2002," http://www.agcensus
.usda.gov/Publications/2007/Full_Report/Volume_1,_Chapter_2_
US_State_Level/st99_2_046_046.pdf (accessed May 1, 2009).

Gem County's legacy as a "downwind" county is discussed in
Lynn Rosellini's essay "Fallout," *Reader's Digest*, May 2005, which
tells the story of the crusade for compensation from the government
led by cancer victim Sherri Garmon, whose cancer-stricken father,
Don Garmon, was my father's neighbor and among his closest friends.

3. Wild Oats

The discussion of the International Refugee Organization (IRO) draws
heavily upon a 1948 pamphlet entitled "The Facts about Refugees,"
published in Geneva by the IRO. Information about the refugee
application process is gleaned from Carl J. Bon Tempo's *Americans at
the Gate: The United States and Refugees during the Cold War*
(Princeton University Press, 2008); see esp. pp. 11–59. For more
information about the "death strip" along the Czech border and other

Iron Curtain countries, see Colin Woodard's "Iron Curtain: Mine-field to Greenbelt," *Christian Science Monitor*, Apr. 28, 2005, http://www.csmonitor.com/2005/0428/p14s01-sten.htm.

The quote from Josef Pejskar's letter comes from a biography of Pejskar by Václav Kraus, first published in the *Prague Trade Union Daily* in 1967 and subsequently digitized and made available online by the Open Society Archives (osa) at the Central European University in Budapest. The osa collection specializes in research resources for the study of human rights issues in conjunction with Communism and the Cold War, particularly in Central and Eastern Europe. See http://files.osa.ceu.hu/holdings/300/8/3/text/17-5-63.shtml. Information about the activities of the Posednik group, the dissident group Pejskar led in Moravia, is also available in the osa collection at http://files.osa.ceu.hu/holdings/300/8/3/text/17-5-23.shtml (accessed Jan.–Feb. 2009). It should be noted, however, that both these documents published in Czechoslovakia in the 1960s have a decidedly Communist slant on Pejskar, whom the authors tend to portray as a fool in their efforts to discredit him. After Pejskar left Czechoslovakia, he published several books in Czech, particularly about the tribulations of Czech exiles, and in 1995, along with Milos Forman, Arnošt Lustig, and Milan Kundera, he was granted the Medal of Merit, First Grade, by President Václav Havel. Pejskar died in California in 1999.

The newspaper account of Lumir and Toni's marriage, "Lumir Funda Takes European Bride in Winnemucca Ceremony," was originally published in the Emmett newspaper, the *Messenger Index*, in 1957. The other documents I refer to, such as the letter about Toni and Frances's escape, written by Alena Sehnal (Pejskar's niece), and photographs and legal documents from Toni's time in Germany, remain in my personal collection. The quote by Arnošt Lustig comes from the award-winning 2000 film *Fighter*.

For information on land restitution policies in post–Velvet Revolution Czechoslovakia, I consulted Dirk J. Bezemer's "De-Collectivization in Czech and Slovak Agriculture: An Institutional Explanation," *Journal of Economic Issues* 36, no. 3 (Sept. 2002): 723–45; and Nigel Swain's "Agricultural Restitution and Co-operative Transformation in the Czech Republic, Hungary and Slovakia," *Europe-Asia Studies* 51, no. 7 (1999): 1199–219.

4. Sage

The translation of the passage from Tyl's play *Lesní panna aneb cesta do Ameriky* (The Forest Maiden: A Journey to America) comes from Stepanka Korytova-Magstadat's study *To Reap a Bountiful Harvest: Czech Immigration Beyond the Mississippi, 1850–1900* (Rudi Publishers, 1993). Immigration facts about Bohemians come from Tomáš Čapek's *Cechs in America* (Houghton Mifflin, 1920).

Regarding the history of Idaho irrigation and culture in the Snake River valley, I used Mark Fiege's excellent book *Irrigated Eden: The Making of an Agricultural Landscape in the American West* (University of Washington Press, 2000). I also consulted several essays by Hugh T. Lovin, including (my favorite) "Sage, Jacks, and Snake Plain Pioneers," *Idaho Yesterdays* 22, no. 4 (Winter 1979): 13–24; "Dreamers, Schemers, and Doers of Idaho Irrigation," *Agricultural History* 76, no. 2 (2002): 232–43; and "Water, Arid Land, and Visions of Advancement on the Snake River Plain," *Idaho Yesterdays* 35, no. 1 (Spring 1991): 3–18. Leonard J. Arrington's "Irrigation in the Snake River Valley: An Historical Overview," *Idaho Yesterdays* 30 (Spring 1986): 3–11, was also very useful. The quote from Charles Dana Wilber's "rain follows the plow" comes from *The Great Valleys and Prairies of Nebraska and the Northwest* (Daily Republican Print, 1881). The quotes about the Snake River area being called a "dead country" in the nineteenth century are from Bernard DeVoto's *The Year of Decision, 1846* (Little Brown and Company, 1943). Emphasis on the Snake River Valley's development of electricity can be seen in the *Twin Falls Times*, which often ran a special section entitled the "Electricity Page," where stories about the remarkable variety of ways electricity was being put to use locally demonstrated the motto of the times: "Electricity is my servant"; see esp. July 15, 1913.

Annie Pike Greenwood's 1934 *We Sagebrush Folks* is a remarkable memoir of life in southern Idaho in those early days of the twentieth century (University of Idaho Press, 1988). I've also drawn upon James R. Gentry's "Czechoslovakian Culture in the Buhl-Castleford Area," *Idaho Yesterdays* 29–30 (Winter 1987): 2–14, which was written from interviews conducted with several Czech immigrants whose parents Frank undoubtedly knew. Gentry also gives a lively portrayal of Czech lodge culture in the area, which I found useful, and he is the source for the mention of Anton Suchan's sagebrush art.

C. J. Blanchard's essay "The Spirit of the West: Wonderful Development since Dawn of Irrigation" was first published in *National Geographic* 21, no. 4 (1910): 333–60, and then reprinted in the *Buhl Herald* on Aug. 25, 1910. Additional information on the Carey Act comes from an Idaho State Historical Society publication entitled "The Carey Act in Idaho," http://www.idahohistory.net/ Carey_Act.pdf (accessed Sept. 23, 2007). The booster quotes are from the Commercial Club pamphlets for Buhl (1910 and 1914) and Boise (1908), and the striking cover paintings I mention are by William Bittle Wells, on the Gooding, Richfield, Pocatello, and American Falls brochures. All these pamphlets, developed in conjunction with the Oregon Short Line Railroad, are available at the Idaho State Historical Society among the Idaho Travel and Tourism Collection; however, several of the Wells paintings can be found reprinted in Fiege's book.

The Wilson Hunt Price expedition of 1811 was immortalized in Washington Irving's account *Astoria; or, Anecdotes of an Enterprise Beyond the Rocky Mountains* (Carey, Lea, and Blanchard, 1836). The history of the Hendricks grubber can be found in the *Twin Falls Times* (Feb. 27, 1912, Apr. 9, 1915), and the US patent office lists at least two other sage-grubbing machine patents (by William O. White in 1903 and Alonzo L. Dunavan in 1905); these can be found online at http://patft.uspto.gov/ (accessed Sept. 24, 2007).

Even though the *Ladies Home Journal* never published stories about the rabbit drives, the rabbits' "suicide" quote actually comes from a mainstream Eastern magazine, the *Saturday Evening Post*, and was part of a series of essays about western agricultural states written by Maude Radford Warren; this essay in the series was titled "A Woman Pioneer: In the Irrigated Country" and appeared on May 20, 1911.

Discussion of the reality of farming in sagebrush country was found in "The Twin Falls Project of Southern Idaho," which originally appeared in *Wallace's Farmer*, Oct. 1, 1909, and was later collected in *Henry A. Wallace's Irrigation Frontier, On the Trail of the Corn Belt Farmer* (reprint, University of Oklahoma Press, 1991).

Philip L. Fradkin's book is entitled *Sagebrush Country: Land and the American West* (Random House, 1991). I also consulted Stephen Trimble's *The Sagebrush Ocean: A Natural History of the Great Basin* (University of Nevada Press, 1999); and Bruce L. Welch's 2005 Department of Agriculture publication entitled *Big Sagebrush: A Sea Fragmented into Lakes, Ponds and Puddles*. Although I do not quote from these two sources, I found Trimble's and Welch's works useful for my understanding of the natural history of sagebrush deserts.

A transcript of the Western Literature Association's biography panel I refer to, featuring Susanne Bloomfield George, Mary Clearman Blew, Judy Nolte Temple, and Melody Graulich, can be found in "Writing Women's Biographies: Processes, Challenges, Rewards," *Western American Literature* 43, no. 1 (Summer 2008): 179–203.

The undated photo *Early Settlers* was found in the Bisbee Collection of photographs at the Twin Falls Public Library (catalog no. BIS TF 544).

Sources consulted for the discussion of crop circles are Hillary Mayell's "Crop Circles: Artworks or Alien Signs?" *National Geographic*, Aug. 2, 2002, http://NationalGeographic.com/news; stories in Utah's newspaper *Deseret News* (Aug. 28, 1996, July 12, 1997, July 24, 1998, Aug. 2, 1998); short, untitled essays by circle makers Rod Dickinson and Jim Schnabel that are available on the website

www.circlemakers.org (accessed Oct. 9, 2007); and Rob Irving and
John Lundberg's book *The Field Guide: The Art, History, and
Philosophy of Crop Circle Making* (Strange Attractor Press, 2006).
Lundberg's discussion of ostension can be found at http://www
.ostension.org (accessed Oct. 9, 2007).

The statistics on Bohemian religious affiliation come from Bruce
M. Garver's essay "Czech-American Protestants: A Minority within
a Minority," in *The Czech-American Experience*, a special issue of the
journal *Nebraska History* edited by Bruce Garver (Fall–Winter
1993): 150–67.

5. Cheatgrass

The opening section on cheatgrass draws upon the following sources:
"Cheatgrass: Drooping brome-grass)," http://www.dcnr.state.pa.us/
Forestry/invasivetutorial/cheatgrass.htm (accessed Nov. 30, 2011); P.
Dee Boersma, Sarah H. Reichard, and Amy N. Van Buren's *Invasive
Species in the Pacific Northwest* (University of Washington Press,
2006); and Aldo Leopold's *A Sand County Almanac* (Oxford
University Press, 1949). I've also consulted several online sources for
this section, including Bettina Boxall, "Beige Plague," *Los Angeles
Times*, Aug. 2, 2008, http://www.latimes.com/news/local/la-me
-wildfires2-2008aug02,0,2295107,full.story; Bill Gilbert, "Air
Tanker Crashes in Colorado," *Wild Fire Today*, Aug 28, 2008, http://
wildfiretoday.com/2008/08/page/2/; Eve Rickert, "Seeds of
Change: Post-Fire Reclamation Can Affect Western Rangelands for
Centuries," *High Country News*, Oct. 15, 2007, http://www.hcn
.org/issues/356/17279; and Patrick O'Driscoll, "Invasive Weed a
Fuel for West's Wildfires," *USA Today*, Aug. 31, 2007, http://www
.usatoday.com/news/nation/environment/2007-08-29-cheatgrass_N
.htm. The quote about cheatgrass from Utah senator Steve Urquhart
comes from Linda Rundell, "Alien Invader Enters New Mexico,"
Bureau of Land Management, Jan. 13, 2011, http://www.blm.gov/
nm/st/en/prog/restore_new_mexico/cheatgrass_op_ed.html.

My discussion of Frank's stories of the Catholic Church, Jan Hus, and the defeat at Bílá Hora are informed by Derek Sayer's excellent book *The Coasts of Bohemia: A Czech History* (Princeton University Press, 1998) and by the following account of Hus's burning at the stake: Peter from Mladonivic, "Eyewitness Report from the Event Site, How Was Executed Jan Hus," Sept. 2, 1415, reprinted by *New Yorkské Listy*, available on the Columbia University website, http://www.columbia.edu/~js322/misc/hus-eng.html (accessed Nov. 30, 2011).

Discussion of Bohemian Brethren and the Freethinker movement is informed by Dr. C. Matthew McMahon, "Some Brief Notes on Jan Amos Comenius," http://www.apuritansmind.com/the-christian -walk/jan-amos-comenius-by-dr-c-matthew-mcmahon (accessed Dec. 15, 2011); and *The Great Didactic of John Amos Comenius*, translated from the Latin by Maurice Walter Keatinge (Adam and Charles Black 1896). The discussion of Czechs' rate of agnosticism and atheism comes from Kenneth D. Miller's *The Czecho-slovaks in America* (George H. Doran Company, 1922).

All quotes from family letters or legal documents come from material in the author's personal collection.

My discussion of Lidice and Hitler's vow to wipe Czechoslovakia off the map is informed by many sources, including "The Liquidation of Lidice," The History Place, 1997, http://www.historyplace.com/ worldwar2/holocaust/h-lidice.htm; David Vaughan, "Josef Horak, a Twentieth Century Czech Hero," Radio Prague, July 24, 2002, http://www.radio.cz/en/article/30570; Camen T. Ilichmann, "Lidice: Remembering the Women and Children," *University of Wisconsin-La Crosse's Journal of Undergraduate Research* 8 (2005): http://www.uwlax.edu/urc/JUR-online/PDF/2005/illichman.pdf; and Branik Ceslav and Carmelo Lisciotto, "The Massacre at Lidice," Holocaust Education and Archive Research Team, 2008, http:// www.holocaustresearchproject.org/nazioccupation/lidice.html. Especially helpful were John Fortinbras's history "The Truth about

Lidice," *War Illustrated* 10, no. 242 (Sept. 27, 1946): 355–56, and John Bradley's *Lidice: Sacrificial Village* (Ballantine, 1972). I would also recommend Edna St. Vincent Millay's "dramatic verse-narrative" *The Murder of Lidice*, which was commissioned by the Writer's War Board and published by Harper and Brothers in 1942. Although not completely historically accurate, the poem, which was dramatized on NBC radio in the fall of 1942, is a moving portrayal of the tragedy. So too is the book *A Little Village Called Lidice, Story of the Return of the Women and Children of Lidice*, by Zdena Trinka (International Book Publishers, 1947); although some of her figures differ significantly from other sources, Trinka aims to portray the events of Lidice through the eyes of Marie, one of the women taken off to Ravensbruck. Newspaper accounts I refer to include Henry Kram, "A Victim, First of Nazi Anger, Now of Time," *New York Times*, Nov. 8, 1987; Clyde H. Fansworth, "To the 446 Inhabitants of Lidice, Dubcek and Svoboda Are Heroes," *New York Times*, Sept. 5, 1968; Henry Kamm, "Lidice, 25 Years Later, Lives Quietly with Memory of Horror," *New York Times*, Jan. 18, 1967; Edward D. Ball, "Blood Red Poppies in Wheat Field Cover Site of Exterminated Lidice," *New York Times*, June 2, 1945; "The Last Man of Lidice," *New York Times*, Sept. 25, 1943; "Nazis Blot Out Czech Village; Kill All Men, Disperse Others," *New York Times*, June 11, 1942; Joseph Wechsberg, "Communism's Child Hostages," *Saturday Evening Post*, Apr. 1, 1950; and "Lidice the Immortal," *New York Times*, June 12, 1942. *Lidice*, an excellent documentary series by *World News, Inc.* (Oct, 3, 2009), is narrated in English and can be found at http://wn.com/lidice.

Information about Reinhard Heydrich comes from Michal Burian, Aleš Knížek, Jiří Rajlich, and Eduard Stehlik'a *Assassination, Operation Anthropoid, 1941–1942*, published in Prague (Defense Ministry of the Czech Republic, 2002); František Kostlán's "70th Anniversary of Reichsprotektor Heydrich's Rule over Bohemia and Moravia," Czech Press Agency, Sept. 27, 2011, http://www.romea

.cz/english/index.php?id=detail&detail=2007_2849; and "J. R."'s
"Czechoslovakia during the War II—Bohemia and Moravia," *Bulletin
of International News* 21, no. 23 (Nov. 11, 1944): 943–50.

6. "The True Point of Beginning"

In the introduction to this chapter I refer to the title of Helen
Papanikolas's *An Amulet of Greek Earth: Generations of Immigrant
Folk Culture* (Ohio University Press, 2002). Richard Kratrovas's
discussion of the Prague Summer Program theme comes from
promotional, online materials he wrote in 2006 for the 2007 program; Katrovas's discussion of that year's theme is no longer posted on
the Prague Summer Program website (http://www.praguesummer
.com); however, Katrovas's remarks are still available as "Prague
Summer Program," Mar. 3, 2006, http://groups.yahoo.com/group/
study-czech/message/727. My discussion was also informed by Peter
Bilek, literature professor at Charles University in Prague, who
lectured at the 2007 Prague Summer Program; Bilek's lecture was
based on an essay he wrote entitled "Comparing Longings for a Sense
of Belonging: German *Heimat*, Czech *Domov*, Russian *Rodina*,"
*Germano-Slavica: A Canadian Journal of Germanic and Slavic
Comparative and Interdisciplinary Studies* 11 (1999): 39–46.
"Students Ring Keys as 'Final Bell' to the Communists," a short video
of the happenings in Wenscelas Square on Nov. 25, 1989, copyrighted 2006, can be seen under "The Velvet Revolution" in the online
Václav Havel Collection at http://havel.columbia.edu/the_velvet_
revolution.html.

Additional information about Kutná Hora can be found at Online
Travel Solutions, "Kutna Hora," http://www.kutna-hora.net/en/
silver-path.php, and a second page under the same name at http://
www.kutna-hora.net/en/silver-mine.php (both copyrighted 2007).
The Bone Church at Sedlec can be seen at a number of websites,
most notably on the TripSource website that published Helen Paris
Reimer's essay "The Skeletons of Sedlec: Bone Gallery of the Czech

Republic," http://www.tripsource.com/stories/Helen/SkeletonsOf Sedlec.htm (accessed Oct. 17, 2008). See also the panoramic views of the ossuary available at "Sedlec Ossurary, Kutna Hora, The Bone Church," taken on Aug. 28, 2007, just a few weeks after I visited the site: http://www.36ocities.net/image/sedlec-ossuary-kutna-hora-the -bone-church. Also useful was Margot Patterson's essay "Showcase of Death: Thousands of Medieval Skeletons Make Czech 'Bone Church' a Macabre Experience, Destinations: All Saints Church, Kutná Hora," *National Catholic Reporter*, Apr. 12, 2002.

Štěpánka Korytová-Magstadat's study *To Reap a Bountiful Harvest: Czech Immigration Beyond the Mississippi, 1850–1900* (Rupi Publishers, 1993) was useful in understanding the class differences among farmers in Bohemia and Moravia. In my discussion of the wayside shrines I consulted the "Fotogalerie Kaplicek a Bozich Muk" (Photo gallery of chapels and wayside shrines), where Milos Uhrmann catalogs thousands of photographs of the shrines in the Czech Republic: http://www.kaplicky.com (accessed Aug. 12, 2007). I found the quote from writer and ethnographer Tadeusz Seweryn at "Chapels in Bialystok, Poland," hosted on the University of Washington Bothell Chapels website: http://ettc.uwb.edu.pl/ strony/bialystok/kapliczki/index.html (accessed Aug. 12 2007). Milda Baksys Richardson's "Reverence and Resistence in Lithuanian Wayside Shrines," *Perspectives in Vernacular Architectures* 10 (2005): 249–67, was the best work I found to discuss the cultural significance of these shrines in Europe. Other resources I've consulted include David Kuchta, "Wayside Saints and Shrines," *Slovak Heritage Live* 8, no. 4 (Winter 2000): 361–65; H. W. Howes, "Some Functional Aspects of European Folklore," *Folklore* 41, no. 3 (1930): 249–65; Gregor Monger, "Modern Wayside Shrines," *Folklore* 108 (1997): 113–14; and Robert James Smith, "Roadside Memorials: Some Australian Examples," *Folklore* 110 (1999): 103–5.

The Google Maps scene I describe dates to Sept. 2007 and is available at https://maps.google.com/maps?client=safari&oe=UTF

-8&q=1817+West+Black+Canyon+Emmett+Idaho&ie=UTF-8&hq=
&hnear=0x54af0a637fa38025:0x9957679784442a39,1817+W+Bl
ack+Canyon+Hwy,+Emmett,+ID+83617&gl=us&ei=Xp_bULSLH
-7yiQLYtYD4Bw&ved=0CDIQ8gEwAA (accessed May 30, 2009). I
quote from Yi-Fu Tuan's *Space and Place: The Perspective of Experience* (University of Minnesota Press, 1977). The 1966 letter to Toni
Funda from Josef Pejskar is in possession of the author. The Bisbee
photo entitled *Idaho Industry* can be seen in the Flicker album posted
by the Twin Falls Public Library at http://www.flickr.com/photos/
twinfallspubliclibrary/6899867240/in/set-72157629741390129
(accessed June 30, 2012).

To order or obtain more information on these or other University of Nebraska Press titles, visit www.nebraskapress.unl.edu.